# STUDENT DIVERSITY, CHOICE, AND SCHOOL IMPROVEMENT

# STUDENT DIVERSITY, CHOICE, AND SCHOOL IMPROVEMENT

Charles V. Willie, Ralph Edwards,
and Michael J. Alves

**BERGIN & GARVEY**
Westport, Connecticut • London

**Library of Congress Cataloging-in-Publication Data**

Willie, Charles Vert, 1927–
    Student diversity, choice, and school improvement/Charles V. Willie, Ralph Edwards, and Michael J. Alves.
        p.   cm.
    Includes bibliographical references (p.) and index.
    ISBN 0–89789–847–8 (alk. paper)—ISBN 0–89789–848–6 (pbk. : alk. paper)
    1. Multicultural education—United States.   2. School improvement programs—United States.   I. Edwards, Ralph, 1930—   II. Alves, Michael J., 1956—   III. Title.
LC1099.3.W53   2002
370.117′0973—dc21      2001037669

British Library Cataloguing in Publication Data is available.

Library of Congress Catalog Card Number: 2001037669
ISBN: 0–89789–847–8
      0–89789–848–6 (pbk.)

First published in 2002

Bergin & Garvey, 88 Post Road West, Westport, CT 06881
An imprint of Greenwood Publishing Group, Inc.

www.greenwood.com

Printed in the United States of America

The paper used in this book complies with the
Permanent Paper Standard issued by the National
Information Standards Organization (Z39.48-1984).

10  9  8  7  6  5  4  3  2  1

# CONTENTS

# PREFACE

This book is about student diversity and school improvement—not one or the other but both. Likewise, this book is about excellence and equity—not one or the other but both. These phrases and concepts are complementary. The components of each set should always be considered together. Accordingly, the main thrust of this book is to provide examples of Controlled Choice student assignment plans that reflect our commitment to these principles. As is discussed later, Controlled Choice uses parents' wishes in determining public school assignments for students.

Excellence focuses on the individual—his or her aspirations, motivation, and personal performance. Personal performance, of course, requires group support. This is the significance of the recently popularized old African proverb: It takes a village to raise a child. Effective performance of each student is, in part, a function of the support offered by one's parents and peers, of the policies promulgated by local and state educational agencies, and of practices pertaining to teaching and learning implemented by school staff. Understanding excellence requires an examination of personal adaptations.

Understanding equity, however, requires exploration of relationships between the group or aggregate and its individual members. Thus, equity has to do with collectivities—how their resources are cultivated and distributed to members and whether each member has fair access to all opportunities.

The linkage between student diversity and school improvement as well as excellence and equity are analyzed in this book. Careful attention is given to the interrelationship of activities to fulfill the goals of these concepts mandated by state and federal educational reform that promote school choice and achievement for all students, especially students of low-income families.

Florida's 1991 School Improvement and Accountability Act, for example, set high standards for students and held schools accountable for expected results through annual performance grades for students and schools. Public Law 228.057, known as the Public School Parental Choice Law, allowed the state's school districts, through a Controlled Choice plan, "to make ... assignments [for students] using parents' indicated ... school choice as a significant factor," and urged school districts to develop "procedures to maintain socioeconomic, demographic, and racial balance."

It is fair to characterize the Florida School Improvement and Accountability Act as legislation designed to achieve excellence, and the Public School Parental Choice Law as legislation designed to achieve equity.

Our conclusions and recommendations will indicate ways to achieve student diversity and school improvement as well as excellence and equity. The Controlled Choice plans presented in this book are intended to facilitate the effective implementation of public law, court orders, and school board policies pertaining to effective education.

We believe that "whole school improvement" and "system-wide support" are the most promising ways to achieve durable reform. The components of such reform are thoroughly discussed here.

Part I includes an introduction that reviews past practices and contemporary strategies in designing student attendance zones. It also indicates the principles and assumptions on which Controlled Choice student assignment plans are based. It continues with an in-depth study of Cambridge, Massachusetts; Lee County, Florida; and other stories of successful school choice plans. Part I, "Public School Choice and Educational Outcomes," concludes with a discussion of the development and operation of Parent Information Centers.

Acknowledging the linkage between "School Reform Strategies and Student Improvement," Part II examines important school improvement principles with illustrations from Boston, Massachusetts; Santa Rosa and Hillsborough counties in Florida; and from other localities. Principles derived from "More Effective Schools" and "Unusually Effective Schools" models are emphasized. An analysis is presented on the association between race, socioeconomic status, and academic achievement using Florida data available on the Internet and Cambridge, Massachusetts, data.

The book concludes with Part III, which summarizes the components of an effective student assignment plan and ways of achieving school improvement and systemic enhancement. This section presents information on what should and should not be done in effective planning. Three important memoranda may be found in the Appendixes: a memorandum from Janet Pulliam on legal issues, directed particularly to the issue of whether or not implementation of a Controlled Choice plan would interfere with the achievement of unitary status by a school district; a memorandum from Michael Turza that offers reflections on transportation, based on his experience in Wisconsin; and a memorandum by the authors regarding ways of creating an effective controlled choice plan.

Thus, we share with you an analysis and discussion pertaining to school reform that deals with theory and practice. We look at what models of "school change" should be used, why these models should be used, and how they should be implemented. The findings in this book are based on research and acceptable planning principles; however, they are presented in manual forms that indicate what should be done and demonstrate how to do it. Thus, there is a fair amount of repetition in the text that is deliberate.

The views expressed here are those of the authors and do not necessarily reflect endorsement by any local education agency, private or public organization, or the institutions with which the authors are affiliated. The authors acknowledge with appreciation Dr. Jose Alicea, who assisted with the statistical analysis of Charleston County school data, and Dr. Erica Walker, who assisted with the statistical analysis of Florida state school data. We also appreciate the fine work of Kathleen George, administrative assistant and project secretary.

# PART I

## PUBLIC SCHOOL CHOICE AND EDUCATIONAL OUTCOMES

# 1

# INTRODUCTION

Three major trends affecting public school education today are diversity, school improvement, and choice. This book examines data about these trends in several communities where one or another of the authors has worked as a consultant. Our goal is to determine the association, if any, between these trends and student achievement.

A major finding of studies reported in this book is that schools with diversified student bodies—socioeconomically, racially, or both—are more effective learning communities than schools that are poverty-concentrated and racially homogenous. Our second major finding is that public school choice implemented by way of the Controlled Choice method of student assignment, with enrollment fairness guidelines for schools in student attendance zones consisting of pluralistic populations and several school sites equitably available to all zone residents, is the most appropriate way to achieve diversified student bodies. Our third major finding is that whole school change with a focused curriculum for all enrolled students is a more effective learning environment than magnet school attractor programs within schools that are available to some but not all members of the student body.

We have worked with local school districts in several states—Massachusetts, California, Arkansas, Florida, Illinois, New York, Washington, and elsewhere. Our research in some of these settings (which will be discussed in detail later in this book) reveals that choice, indeed, is associated with student performance. The average student achievement score for public schools in Boston tended to be higher in those schools that were the first choice schools for almost all students enrolled (Willie, Alves, and Haggerty, 1996).

Peter Cookson, Jr., writes in his book titled *School Choice* (1994) that "in Cambridge, Fall River and White Plains, we have seen that choice leads to school improvement because it compels parents to become involved in the lives of the schools to which they send their children" (Cookson, 1994: 90). While Cookson's conclusion is uncertain regarding whether there is a continuous effect of school choice on student achievement, it does make sense, he said, "to think of choice as a way of creating community" (Cookson, 1994: 98).

An effective community, of course, is based on confidence, trust, and respect among its members. Thus, "if choice does create more social trust," then Cookson believes "it is an experiment worth pursuing, within the context of improving and transforming public education" (Cookson, 1994: 98). Please note that choice discussed in our book focuses on public schools only.

We found in Boston that student assignment by way of a public school choice plan stimulated schools to make themselves more attractive, since they had to compete for public school students. Attractiveness was achieved in several ways. Some schools became attractive by introducing new programs designed to enhance student learning. Other schools became attractive by introducing creative after-school programs for their students. Still others were attractive because of their unique school culture.

Evidence of the diminishing significance of neighborhood schools as primary attractors for students is the increased proportion of school-age children transported to and from school in the United States. During the middle years of the twentieth century, up to 1954 when the Supreme Court of the United States ruled that segregated education was illegal, one-third or less of public school pupils were transported at public expense to and from school. Today, this proportion has almost doubled. And the per pupil cost for transportation in 1998 constant dollars more than doubled from an average of $220 per pupil transported in 1954 to an average of $471 in 1998 (U.S. Department of Education, 2000a: 64).

Back in 1954, this nation transported 8.4 million students (or 33 percent) to and from school; today, we transport 24.3 million students (or 50 percent) to and from school (U.S. Department of Education, 2000a: 64). The National Center for Education Statistics reported that "by 1996, 69 percent of the public favored allowing parents to choose which schools in the community students attend" (U.S. Department of Education, 2000b: 61). And schools chosen usually were not neighborhood schools.

Some but not all of this transportation was for the purpose of facilitating school desegregation and school improvement. Marshall Smith, former undersecretary of education in the U.S. Department of Education, has written that "desegregation had powerful effects on the racial and social class composition of schools, improving conditions that are ... positively related to student achievement for blacks and whites, though more so for low-income students" (Smith, 2000: 258). Thus, enhanced educational opportunities increased along with increased transportation of students to and from school.

After several years of experiencing desegregated education in Boston with a Controlled Choice student assignment plan that promoted student diversity in all schools, 44 percent of the parents participating in a study by Bain and Company, which inquired about the reason why some schools were frequently mentioned as first-choice schools, indicated that the quality of education was the primary reason for choosing a school. Only 20 percent of the parents chose a school for their children because of its location (Willie and Alves, 1996: 100).

The diversity observed in public schools is increasing in other educational institutions. Harvard University, for example, became increasingly diversified over the years. Twenty percent of its students in all of its colleges are foreign or international (*Chronicle of Higher Education*, August 31, 2001: 24), and 35 percent of its students are Black, Asian, Native American, and Hispanic (Office of News and Public Affairs, 2000: 72). The university explains that "diversity is an essential source of vitality and strength" and asserts that "it is often our differences—our varying perspectives—that can enhance our learning and work experiences, enriching everything we endeavor to achieve" (*Fortune*, June 21, 1999: S14).

We mention Harvard University not only because the three coauthors of this book (who are affiliated with a variety of racial and ethnic groups) have earned or honorary degrees from this institution, but also because it has achieved educational eminence while deliberately seeking to diversify itself. Harvard, founded as a school for New England gentlemen, now has a student body that is approximately half male and half female. Also represented in the college's student body are students from all fifty states in the United States and more than 130 nation-states. This diversity is notable because, between the years of 1737 and 1790, Harvard was so provincial that "not a single New Yorker entered the college" (Amory, 1947: 294). A school that was founded to accommodate the educational needs of the sons of proper Bostonians now enrolls undergraduate students, 70 percent of whom receive some kind of financial aid and 45 percent of whom receive substantial scholarship assistance (Office of News and Public Affairs, 2000: 61–62).

Because of the controversies associated with affirmative action during the 1990s, former Harvard President Neil Rudenstein thought it necessary to remind us in his *President's Report, 1993–1995* that "student diversity has for more than a century been valued for its capacity to contribute powerfully to the process of learning and to the creation of an effective educational environment" (Rudenstein, 1996: 1).

We contend that the educational eminence of Harvard is, in part, a function of standards and diversity—not one or the other, but both. If one identifies standards as an aspect of excellence, and diversity as an aspect of equity, then excellence and equity complement each other. It is this complex of characteristics that results in educational eminence. Neither excellence alone with its excluding tendency, nor equity alone with its including tendency, is sufficient for the attainment of educational eminence. Indeed, equity without a commitment to excellence could result in mediocrity. Since excellence and equity complement each other to their mutual benefit, one wonders how they ever were thought to be contradictory or in opposition.

Our guess is that the error in linking these two as contradictory tendencies has resulted from faulty conceptualization. Excellence is a quality, a deed, some would even say a virtue. As such, it is a property of an individual. Equity is a method or technique of distributing limited resources, opportunities, and services among many individuals in a way that is fair. As such, equity is a property of groups, organizations, associations, and institutions. Characteristics of individuals and of groups can easily be joined to the benefit of both. One of the purposes of education, for example, is to enhance individuals and, at the same time, advance the group or community. This twofold goal, when it is achieved, fits into our conception of a double victory.

When excellence is erroneously conceptualized as a property of the group, the possibility of abuse is present. A group or institution that strives for excellence may arbitrarily slough off detracting individuals. The well-being and freedom of some individuals are at risk in an excellence-oriented institution because that kind of institution tends to be arbitrary in the individuals it rejects. Also, an institution that sloughs off individuals for the good of the group behaves in a way that is contrary to a nurturing social order. In physical and organic systems, the parts are the foundation of the whole; their reason for being is to sustain the whole. But in the human social system, the whole is the foundation of the parts; its reason for being is to support and sustain each individual. Sloughing off individuals is inappropriate when it requires sacrificing the parts of a human social system for the good of the whole.

No one, including a school or any other institution, has the right to sacrifice another or to demand self-sacrifice. To sacrifice or not to sacrifice is a decision that each individual should make for herself or himself. For this reason, aspiration for excellence is and must remain personal, and should not be conceptualized as a social requirement and treated as a property of an institution. Anyone who aspires to be excellent must be prepared to make necessary sacrifices. This is why excellence is conceptualized as a property of an individual rather than a group. We do not oppose excellence in education. It is commendable for one to aspire to be excellent and to work diligently for its achievement. But we insist that the decision to sacrifice for its attainment is a personal decision and is harmful if imposed upon an individual by a group.

An important outcome of equity is diversity. The increased diversity we are experiencing on school campuses today is likely to continue for many years. William P. O'Hare of the Annie E. Casey Foundation tells us that minority children under eighteen years of age increased 43 percent between 1900 and 2000. While White children continue to be a majority of school-age children in this nation, their proportion dropped to 61 percent in 2000. The reciprocal proportion—39 percent—consisted largely of Black, Hispanic, Asian, and Native American children (O'Hare, 2001: 13). Thus, equity that embraces multicultural populations contributes to fairness in educational and other institutional practices.

An observation by the National Center for Educational Statistics is a fitting conclusion to this discussion on student body diversity. This governmental agency reports that "although variety in student backgrounds can enhance the learning environment, it can also create new or increased challenges for schools to accommodate the needs of a wide variety of students. Knowledge of these shifts in the racial-ethnic distribution of public school students in grades 1–12 may help schools plan for this change" (U.S. Department of Education, 2000b: 9).

## CREATING COMMON STUDENT ATTENDANCE ZONES FOR SEVERAL SCHOOLS

Our experience in effective ways of creating equitable student assignment plans is derived from working with school districts in all regions of the United States—North, South, East, and West. This experience reveals that permitting students to rank-order their choices of schools and assigning students to their schools of choice is both efficient and effective, if the new student attendance zone encompasses a heterogeneous student population and several schools available to all area residents in an equitable way. Such an assignment process facilitates the achievement of both excellence and equity.

The choice process is an annual referendum on the attractiveness of individual schools. Least chosen schools should become targets for immediate upgrading efforts by educational administrators and policy makers. The enrollment fairness guidelines that initially reserve space in each school for the various student groups residing in relatively large student attendance zones also guarantee diversity and prevent experiences of racial and socioeconomic isolation in most schools. Research evidence presented here will demonstrate the value of maintaining diversity in learning environments.

## REVIEW OF PAST ZONING PRACTICES DESIGNED TO ACHIEVE EQUITY

Larry Hughes, William Gordon, and Larry Hillman, proteges of Gordon Foster, formerly of the Southeastern Equity Center in Florida, prepared a handbook for the development of desegregation plans (*Desegregating America's Schools*, 1980). They reviewed and illustrated the techniques most frequently used to eliminate duality in a school system that is largely due to school-specific student attendance zones that are racially or socioeconomically homogeneous.

As reported by Hughes, Gordon, and Hillman (1980: 55), the remedy frequently proposed for schools with student bodies that are racially, ethnically, or socio-economically isolated was to redraw attendance zones so that a nearby student population different from the one served would have to attend the formerly segregated school. This desegregation remedy, known as redistricting, tended to generate controversy and much consternation because it was arbitrary and capricious. Moreover, it seldom had a permanent effect because the people in the annexed zone could move elsewhere if they were sufficiently unhappy with their new school assignment, leaving the new multiracial or multicultural school again with a relatively homogeneous student body. Repeated reconfiguration of the student attendance zone for a single school has been a troubling and troublesome experience throughout the nation and has diverted the attention of policy makers from other, probably more important, educational matters. It therefore is not recommended as a remedy.

A case study prepared by one of the authors in a 1973 publication titled *Race Mixing in the Public Schools* (Willie 1973: 12–14) indicates how long this nation has struggled with the student assignment issue.

In the spring of 1962, the principal of Spring Street Elementary School (pseudonym) requested the Research Department of the Centralia School District (pseudonym) in upstate New York to develop a plan to alleviate overcrowding at the Spring Street Elementary School. The school district was committed to the neighborhood school concept. The research department usually met such requests by adjusting boundaries between two or more neighborhood schools.

The research department recommended that the students who live near the southern boundary of the Spring Street Elementary School student assignment zone should enroll in the Simpson Elementary School (pseudonym). Unlike similar recommendations in the past that were routinely approved by the school board as submitted by the superintendent, this one was tabled and eventually rejected.

The reason for rejecting the proposal was the controversy that followed about racial balance in Centralia Public Schools. Spring Street Elementary School was located on the periphery of the black ghetto; several black families had moved from the ghetto into this school district, seeking an integrated education for their children. The Spring Street Elementary School was 30 percent black. The Mothers' Club and several community associations protested because all of the children to be transferred out of Spring Street were white and that further reduction of the number of white children in this school could contribute to racial imbalance in the student body. The proposal of the research department would reduce the total number of children and overcome crowding in the Spring Street Elementary School. However, it would also increase the proportion of black children enrolled in the school. Community groups insisted that they liked the racial composition of the school as it was and wanted to keep it that way.

Although the school board did not approve the research department's recommendation, it would not formally acknowledge race as a legitimate factor in defining school boundaries. Reacting to the school board's failure to acknowledge race as a legitimate factor in reconfiguring the boundaries of school attendance zones, the Congress of Racial Equality (CORE) broadened the issue to a citywide attack on de facto segregated schools. In general, the school board took the position that it should be "colorblind" in dealing with children. CORE interpreted the school board's position not as a commitment to racial justice but as a method of evading any responsibility for the existence of racially segregated schools.

Thus, CORE and several other community groups picketed the headquarters of the Centralia School District and staged a boycott on the first day of school at an elementary school whose student population was 90 percent black. Eight out of every ten students honored the boycott and stayed at home. This was the first effective boycott ever carried out against the Centralia School District. The school board's reaction was a mixture of surprise and outrage (Willie 1973: 12–14).

This case study indicates the conventional way school authorities tended to react to demonstrations against racially and socioeconomically segregated schools in years gone by. Today, we should realize that reactions of surprise and outrage toward pressure to diversify student bodies in public schools are insufficient and inappropriate, especially because new and better ways like controlled choice are available to accomplish this goal.

## THE CONTROLLED CHOICE SOLUTION

Controlled Choice is comprehensive and prevents resegregation even when school districts experience substantial demographic changes. It can be implemented effectively with or without a court order. It is in no way incompatible with a declaration of unitary status by the court for a school district. Indeed, some districts that are mentioned below have been declared unitary because of their Controlled Choice student assignment plan. Other districts have adopted a Controlled Choice plan with court approval or without court protest after achieving unitary status.

John Correiro, a former superintendent of schools in Fall River, Massachusetts, which has a Controlled Choice plan, and currently a staff member of the Education Alliance at Brown University, stated that the plan "presents a theory of desegregation that is rooted in experience and offer[s] a model ... which guarantees fairness and quality of education for all." Moreover, he said, "Controlled Choice is a model that when properly applied, simply works" (Correiro, 1996: v). A number of school districts in all regions of the United States have implemented comprehensive Controlled Choice student assignment plans.

The St. Lucie County School District in Florida, with approximately 29,000 students in 1999, has had a comprehensive Controlled Choice student assignment plan for nearly a decade. Each of its schools provides a unique combination of opportunities and services for students. The county is divided into three zones, as shown in Figure 1.1. With hindsight, the number of zones should have been limited to two for a public school district of this size—15,000 to 30,000 students—because each of the two zones could have offered more diversity of choice in students and in schools than a three-zone model. Also, larger zones are more likely to reflect the population of the total school district. In the current three-zone model, each zone contains several elementary schools, one to three middle schools, and one or two high schools.

St. Lucie parents apply during one of the four "choice application periods" for the school that presumably best meets the needs of their child. All applications received during a choice application period are processed at the end of that period. Assignment is by zone, seat availability, proximity to school, and sibling preference. According to a school district bulletin, "Finding the Perfect Fit," from which the information presented above was taken, "The St. Lucie County School District ranked in the top one-third of school districts in the state based on Florida's school report card" and "has 19 schools that are distinguished Five Star Schools" (St. Lucie County Public Schools, no date). It is also interesting to note that, since inauguration of its Controlled Choice plan, the St. Lucie School District has been declared unitary by the district court.

Lee County launched a comprehensive Controlled Choice plan in 1998. The public school population in the school district in 1999 was approximately 56,000. The student assignment plan is designed to give parents the opportunity to make selections from a wide range of school offerings. The plan is phased in through kindergarten in elementary school, grade 6 in middle school, and grade 9 in high school.

The Lee County School District is organized into three large geographic choice zones: West Lee County, South Lee County, and East Lee County. Each zone contains several elementary schools, two to four middle schools, and two to three high

**Figure 1.1** Zone Map, St. Lucie County

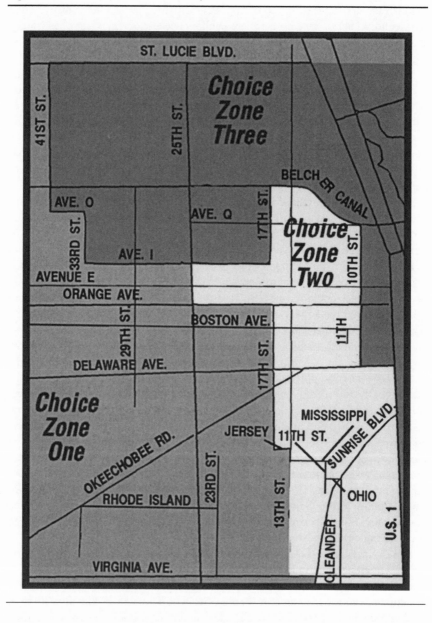

schools, as seen in Figure 1.2. Parents and students list their preferences, in rank-order, for schools within their choice zone and for district-wide magnet schools. Students are assigned to schools where space exists and according to racial and

**Figure 1.2** The School District of Lee County, Florida

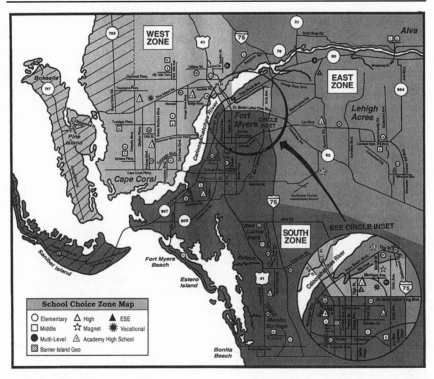

ethnic diversity guidelines. Sibling and proximity preferences are honored. Any student who does not receive his or her first-choice school is placed in the eligibility pool for future assignment to that school if an opening materializes. Socioeconomic, racial, ethnic, and language characteristics of students are considered in the process of developing zone boundaries. Each zone is more or less a mirror of the total school district in its proportions of minority, gifted, special education, bilingual, and low-income students.

The school board is committed to maintaining equivalency of facilities and adequate student capacity in all zones. Lee County is developing a school improvement process that promotes the replication of popular and effective thematic schools and programs while also encouraging differentiation among schools within zones. This process is assisted by the Countywide School Improvement Committee. Transportation is provided for all students assigned to zone schools.

To ensure that student assignments are tamperproof, authority to assign students to their schools of choice resides in a director of student assignment, who coordinates the process. Principals and other school system personnel may not enroll students in schools.

Due largely to implementation of a genuine and comprehensive Controlled Choice student assignment plan and other changes, Lee County has been declared a unitary public school system and has been released from direct and continuous supervision by the U.S. District Court.

Controlled Choice, used in several school districts throughout the nation for nearly two decades, has never been declared illegal in any court of law. Indeed, some school superintendents and judges, including the late Judge W. Arthur Garrity, Jr., of the U.S. District Court in Boston, have observed that Controlled Choice has served well the parents and pupils in public schools and has withstood constant criticism. Specifically, Judge Garrity said, "The basic concepts of Controlled Choice have worked in many ... communities and will survive."

## THE BOSTON CONTROLLED CHOICE EXPERIENCE
## AND URBAN SOCIAL ORGANIZATION

In Boston, a Controlled Choice student assignment plan initiated in 1989 achieved excellent outcomes in some schools and enabled this city to retain its status as a unitary school system. The plan had a threefold goal of providing student choice, guaranteeing school diversity, and promoting school improvement. Three relatively large student attendance zones embracing heterogeneous racial and socioeconomic populations, as seen in Figure 1.3, were delineated. The student population in each zone was more or less similar to the demographic characteristics of the total school district, and the student body in each school was more or less similar to the zonewide student population. Both schools and zones could vary from the ideal population proportions by not more than 10 percentage points. Students and their parents chose schools they wished to attend and rank-ordered their choices. The analysis of choice data, in effect, is used as a referendum on the attractiveness of schools. Some schools in each zone were overchosen; that is, students in every racial group opted for a school in numbers that exceeded seats allotted for each group. And some schools in each zone were underchosen; none of the underchosen schools was picked by enough students in any racial group to come close to the number of seats allotted for them, according to the racial fairness guidelines. Our message to the school authorities was that they should replicate the overchosen schools and take remedial action to upgrade the underchosen schools. This is the way that Controlled Choice contributes to demographic diversity and school improvement simultaneously. Moreover, Controlled Choice helps ensure both excellence and equity by requiring that each zone should have a similar quantity, quality, and range of educational services and opportunities.

The overchosen schools in each of the three zones in Boston had lower dropout and suspension rates than other schools. Children attending these schools tended to have higher reading scores than students in other schools. Nine out of every ten students in overchosen schools were in a first-choice school. And approximately seven out of every ten students in an overchosen school elected a school that required a bus ride; students in other schools were about equally divided between

**Figure 1.3** Proposed Student Assignment Plan for Boston Public Schools, December 1988

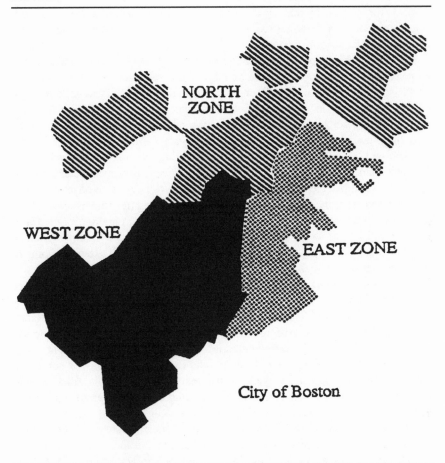

walkers and bus riders (Willie, Alves, and Hagerty, 1996: 6–10). These facts suggest that students in overchosen schools are more concerned with the quality of education they receive than with the nearness of a school to their homes and will endure the inconvenience of a bus ride to access the education of their choice.

After experimenting with several different methods of assigning students to schools, we conclude that the organization of a school district into zones that allow students who reside in these zones to choose their school of attendance is the most effective way. This approach neutralizes variations in the racial and socioeconomic characteristics of neighborhoods surrounding individual schools that tend to contribute to demographic imbalance when students are assigned to their neighborhood school. This approach eliminates the overcrowding or underutilization of facilities associated with some single-school attendance zones. It also does away with the continual pain and problem of redrawing boundaries of single-school attendance zones from time to time. And it enhances education because schools must compete for students by making themselves attractive, rather than having a guaranteed student body mandatorily assigned whether or not students wished to attend a particular school.

The history of residential segregation by race and socioeconomic status in the United States is an important reason for eliminating mandatory assignments of students to neighborhood schools. Economist Herman Miller, who was affiliated with the U.S. Bureau of the Census in the 1970s, said, "The constantly growing concentration of [black people] in the central cities of metropolitan areas is one of the most important population trends in the United States" (Miller 1971: 62). This was an important trend then and continues today. During the same time, psychologist Kenneth Clark gave clear and concise advice: "If we really mean to stabilize our cities, our suburbs, and our society as a whole, plans have to be developed with the clear goal of reducing present ghettos and preventing the establishment of future ones" (Clark, 1968: 135). Geographer Harold Rose, in his *Black Suburbanization* published while the United States was celebrating its 200th birthday, stated that "the most active suburban growth communities are spatial extensions of central city ghettos for racial minorities" (Rose, 1976: 263).

The kind of planning suggested directly and indirectly by the findings of Clark and Rose was never implemented to avoid the continuation of racial and socioeconomic ghettoization. Thus, in 1992, demographers Douglas Massey and Nancy Denton declared that "racial segregation is the principal structural feature of American society responsible for the perpetuation of urban poverty and represents a primary cause of racial inequality" (Massey and Denton, 1993: viii). In summary, they said, "Most Americans vaguely realize that urban America is still a residentially segregated society ... maintained by on-going institutional arrangements and contemporary individual actions" (Massey and Denton, 1993: 1).

Institutional planning also is necessary to shift concern about the consequences of ghettoization from a Black/White issue only to concern about this phenomenon for other minorities and poor people. When any group grows to a critical mass that exceeds 20 percent of the student population, the unique needs of that group must be recognized and planned for in a student assignment plan. In most school districts in the United States, specific planning should recognize White, Black, Hispanic, and other students. When any group in another category reaches 20 percent, it too should be named and planned for as a separate population group.

## CAMBRIDGE AND BROCKTON, MASSACHUSETTS

Many school districts in this nation are small. Attention will be given to how small school districts have handled student assignments. Cambridge, Massachusetts, in 1995–96, had only 6,019 students in its kindergarten through grade 8 schools. These students were educated in fifteen schools.

Up until 1981, each school had a neighborhood student attendance zone. However, in 1981, the Cambridge School Committee approved a Controlled Choice student assignment plan that has been in effect for two decades. School authorities describe the implementation of Controlled Choice in Cambridge as a process developed at the grass-roots level by parents and teachers. This process eliminated neighborhood schools and made all schools available to all students in the district.

The plan has been modified since 1981 but remains essentially the same. Listed below are major features of the one-zone plan as first adopted by the Cambridge community.

1. Students new to the Cambridge Public Schools, students who request a transfer, and students subject to mandatory assignment, such as former students in bilingual education who are mainstreaming, are assigned to a school they chose or to a school nearest to their home if space is available.

2. During the registration period, students (and their parents) may indicate three or more schools that they prefer. Preferred schools may be rank-ordered.

3. Parents with two or more school-age children may request that all of their children attend the same school. Such requests, if made during the registration period, are given priority in the assignment process.

4. During registration, students (and their parents) may request to be assigned to the regular education program of a school, to a magnet school, or to a magnet program within a school. Requests for assignment to magnet programs within a school, or to its regular education program, require separate choices or listings. Acceptance in the regular education program of a school does not automatically permit enrollment in that school's magnet program or programs.

5. During registration period, students (and their parents) may request that they be assigned to a school that is one-quarter of a mile or less from their home. Assignment priority is given to this request.

6. Any student who requires a bilingual program will be assigned to such a program, regardless of other provisions of the student assignment policy. And, any student who requires a special education will be assigned according to the Core Evaluation process, regardless of other provisions of the student assignment policy.

7. The Cambridge school system has adopted a "living" definition of racial balance. The goal is to achieve minority/non-minority percentages in each school, program, and grade that vary not more than plus or minus five percentage points from the average of the school system as a whole. According to school committee policies adopted in 1981, the minority category is a combination of Asians, Blacks, Hispanics, and Native Americans. The non-minority category consists of Whites only.

8. Efforts are made to ensure that all potential students (and their parents) know about kindergarten registration and its procedures. The Parent Information Center conducts information meetings for all parents and their children in locations

throughout the city. The center encourages students and parents to visit schools prior to registration so that informed choices may be made.

9. When there are more applicants than available seats, a lottery is conducted to fill the available spaces.

10. A student not assigned to a school or program of his or her first choice may have his or her name placed on a waiting list. Students on waiting lists receive priority assignments over other newly registered students.

11. Students dissatisfied with their school of choice may request a transfer and will be accommodated in another school if space is available, in accordance with the racial fairness guidelines.

Cambridge, Massachusetts, still has a Controlled Choice student assignment plan two decades after it was initiated in 1981. The implementation of it today is presided over by Superintendent Bobbie D'Alessandro, former superintendent of the Lee County School District in Florida and currently includes socioeconomic status as an enrollment fairness guideline.

Brockton, with a 12,000-student population in kindergarten through grade 8 in 1997, adopted a plan that divided its schools into two zones, as seen in Figure 1.4. The details of the plan are presented in a summary prepared by the Brockton Desegregation Planning team in a draft report dated February 1995:

- Two zones equivalent in quality and range of educational offerings consist of seven elementary and two junior high schools available for any student to choose

- A renovated or new super-K–8 magnet school in downtown Brockton is available to all students in the city

- Methods are planned for achieving school improvement and magnetizing least-chosen schools

- Opportunities are available for students currently enrolled in a specific school to remain in that school, if they choose, until they graduate

- Priority of assignment, according to flexible racial fairness guidelines, is given to siblings and students who choose a school within walking distance of their home

- Experimentation with extended-day kindergarten in selected schools is planned

- New construction and renovation of several inner-city schools will occur

- Modification of walking distances to schools of different levels will be made, if fiscally feasible

- A faculty and staff diversity plan will be developed

- Establishment of a Parent Information Center is planned

- A "user-friendly" and workable implementation time line is included in the plan.

With this plan, according to the report, "Brockton is well positioned to enter a new educational era in full conformity with public laws and in full pursuit of excellence without compromising equity."

**Figure 1.4** Two-Zone Attendance Model

| NORTH ZONE | CITYWIDE | SOUTH ZONE |
|---|---|---|
| *Brookfield Kindergarten* | *Arnone* | *Davis Kindergarten* |
| *Ashfield* | | *Davis* |
| *Brookfield* | | *Downey* |
| *Franklin* | | *Gilmore* |
| *Hancock* | | *Goddard* |
| *Raymond* | | *Huntington* |
| *Whitman* | | *Kennedy* |
| *Winthrop* | | *Paine* |
| *North JHS* | | *East JHS* |
| *West JHS* | | *South JHS* |

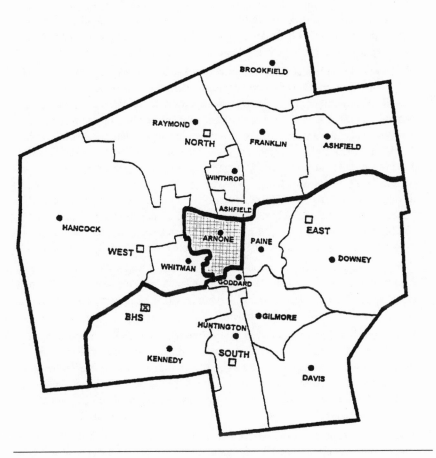

*Source*: Brockton Public Schools, Voluntary Desegregation and Educational Equity Plan, February 7, 1995.

## CONTRAINDICATED PROCEDURES
## IN CONSTRUCTION OF ZONES

1. Selected neighborhoods in a school district should not be exempted from participating in a Controlled Choice student assignment plan. Elimination of exemptions
   should apply to all neighborhoods, including neighborhoods that are "naturally
   integrated." The fairness principle requires equal treatment for all individuals,
   groups, and neighborhoods within a school district. District student assignment
   plans that exempt some neighborhoods tend to generate hostility and bitterness
   among students and their families in other neighborhoods who are required to
   participate. Also, students and families exempted from participation in a district-
   wide student assignment plan may look upon their exemption as an entitlement.
   This attitude may contribute to further estrangement in the community. Such feelings tend to interfere with the development of a sense of community that is essential in the achievement of both excellence and equity in a public school system.

2. Neighborhood student attendance zones associated with specific schools should
   be eliminated. In the construction of student attendance zones, several features
   should be considered: (1) single zones are appropriate for districts with a student
   body of 15,000 or less; (2) one or two zones are appropriate for districts with
   15,000–30,000 students; (3) two to four zones are appropriate for districts with
   30,000–100,000 students; (4) four to eight zones are appropriate for districts with
   100,000–200,000 students; (5) eight to twelve zones are appropriate for districts
   with 200,000–300,000 students; (6) twelve to sixteen zones are appropriate for
   districts with 300,000–400,000 students; (7) contiguous neighborhoods should be
   linked together to create zones, thereby avoiding suspicion of gerrymandering;
   and (8) zones consisting of multiple, noncontiguous neighborhoods should be
   avoided. Each zone should consist of several schools of similar grade levels.

3. Relatively large and heterogeneous student attendance zones should never accommodate the coexistence of single-school attendance areas or smaller student attendance areas within the larger zone. All schools within large student attendance
   zones should be available to all students.

4. Large student attendance zones may vary from the demographic proportions of
   the school district but may not be so imbalanced that they vary more than 5 to 10
   percentage points. In deciding on the size of variation permitted, the delineators
   of zone boundaries should be careful not to reduce the pool of students in any
   group with a critical mass of 20 percent or more of the total district's student
   population to a proportion within a zone that is less than one-fifth.

5. Magnet schools, pilot schools, charter schools, and other public schools should not
   have enrollment periods that differ from the enrollment periods for general or regular
   public schools. To offer separate enrollment periods for magnet schools and other
   schools is to differentiate the school system into more important and less important
   schools. Symbolically, the school that is chosen first is believed to be better than
   other schools. Also, in a Controlled Choice plan, existing magnet schools may re-

main city-wide schools, but consideration should be given to locating new magnet schools within zones as a way of enriching educational offerings in each zone and as a way of reducing transportation costs connected with citywide enrollments.

6. When Controlled Choice is introduced as a new way of assigning students to schools, students already enrolled in specific schools should not be displaced. All students enrolled in a school at the beginning of Controlled Choice should be permitted to remain in their school of enrollment until they finish the top grade of that school. Also, it is better to introduce Controlled Choice for the entering kindergarten or grade 1 of elementary school, for grade 6 of middle school, and for grade 9 of high school. If there are enrollment fairness guidelines associated with these grades, the diversity they generate will eventually work its way throughout the school from year to succeeding year. Thus, Controlled Choice has it greatest effect on entering grades.

7. Controlled Choice should not be introduced to and implemented in a school system without enrollment fairness guidelines for student assignments. As indicated in the professional literature, freedom-of-choice plans have not been successful in attaining diversity, equity, and fairness in the distribution of educational resources by schools among students with a variety of group affiliations. Enrollment fairness guidelines guarantee that all students have equal access to all educational opportunities available in a school system. Since race, social class, and gender have served as barriers that prevent equal participation in the educational opportunity system, it is meet and right to provide racial, socioeconomic, or gender fairness guidelines (any or all of these) for student assignments so that dominant people of power in these aggregations do not get in line first and take all of the "goodies" before subdominant people of power have a chance to obtain their fair share.

In this introduction, we have indicated some things that ought to be done and some things that ought not to be done in achieving the goals outlined above. The remainder of this book will discuss the issues of school reform (including school diversity and school improvement) in greater detail.

## REFERENCES

*Chronicle of Higher Education.* 2001. Almanac Issue (August 31): 24.

Clark, Kenneth B. 1968. "The Negro and the Urban Crisis." In Kermit Gordon (ed.), *Agenda for the Nation.* Washington, DC: The Brookings Institution.

Cookson, Peter, Jr. 1994. *School Choice.* New Haven, CT: Yale University Press.

Correiro, John. 1996. "Preface." In Charles V. Willie and Michael J. Alves (eds.), *Controlled Choice, a New Approach to Desegregated Education and School Improvement.* Providence, RI: Educational Alliance Press at Brown University.

*Fortune.* (special advertising section.) 1999. "Harvard University: Building on Past Achievement" (June 21), pp. S14–S15.

Massey, Douglas, and Nancy Denton. 1993. *American Apartheid.* Cambridge, MA: Harvard University Press.

Miller, Herman. 1971. *Rich Man, Poor Man*. New York: Thomas Crowell.

Office of News and Public Affairs. 2000. *The Harvard Guide*. Cambridge, MA: Harvard University.

O'Hare, William P. 2001. *The Child Population: First Data from the 2000 Census*. Baltimore, MD: Anne E. Casey Foundation.

Rose, Harold. 1976. *Black Suburbanization*. Cambridge, MA: Ballinger.

Rudenstein, Neil L. 1996. *The President's Report, 1993–1995*. Cambridge, MA: Harvard University.

Smith, Marshall S. 2000. "Assessment Trends in a Contemporary Policy Context." In David W. Grissmer and J. Michael Ross (eds.), *Analytic Issues in the Assessment of Student Achievement*. Washington, DC: U.S. Department of Education, National Center for Education Statistics, pp. 249–278.

U.S. Department of Education. 2000a. *Digest of Education Statistics*. Washington, DC: U.S. Government Printing Office.

U.S. Department of Education, National Center for Education Statistics. 2000b. *The Condition of Education 2000*. Washington DC: U.S. Government Printing Office.

Willie, Charles. 1999. "Excellence, Equity and Diversity in Education." *Prospectus* 29, no. 4 (December): 493.

Willie, Charles V., and Michael J. Alves. 1996. *Controlled Choice*. Providence, RI: Education Alliance Press at Brown University.

Willie, Charles V., Michael Alves, and George Hagerty. 1996. "Multicultural, Attractive City Schools: Controlled Choice in Boston." *Equity and Excellence in Education* 29, no. 2 (September): 5–19.

Willie, Charles V., with Jerome Beker. 1973. *Race Mixing in the Public Schools*. Westport, CT: Praeger.

# 2

# PRINCIPLES AND ASSUMPTIONS OF CONTROLLED CHOICE

Controlled Choice differs from other methods of achieving school desegregation because it is comprehensive and immediate, not piecemeal and incremental. John Dewey's idea—"what the best and wisest parent wants for his own child, that must the community want for all its children" (Dewey, 1900)—is an appropriate goal of Controlled Choice. This is but another way of saying that education as a means of individual enhancement and education as a means of community advancement must go hand in hand.

## BASIC ASSUMPTIONS OF CONTROLLED CHOICE

A basic assumption of the Controlled Choice method of student assignment is that every child and every child's group should have access to all educational opportunities that a community offers, and that no child and no child's group should be educationally disadvantaged because of personal or situational circumstances. If a community maintains any educational services and experiences that are harmful to children, these should not be restricted to any particular population group. Risks for good public school experiences and against bad public school experiences should be shared in an equitable way among all children in a community.

Controlled Choice introduces the concept of population group that many in the United States have difficulty accepting as relevant. This society has attempted to offer opportunities to individuals without realizing that people live, move, and have their being within the context of groups. According to the wisdom of sociology, effective individuals, in part, derive their effectiveness from the groups with which they affiliate and in which they participate. Likewise, effective groups derive their effectiveness, in part, from the skills and performance of their members. All of this is to say that individuals operate within the context of social organization.

Without it, human beings could not survive. Thus, Controlled Choice provides educational opportunities for individuals and for groups.

Controlled Choice provides educational opportunities for individuals by permitting each student to choose a number of schools that he or she would like to attend and to rank-order these by personal preference. Regardless of residential neighborhood, race, ethnicity, socioeconomic status, gender, aptitude, or other attributes, each student may choose any school in the city or any school in a large zone of the city.

The comprehensive city-wide or zonewide educational offerings of Controlled Choice sever the hostage relationship between real estate market forces and personal educational opportunities. With Controlled Choice, an individual's schooling opportunities are no longer constrained or facilitated by the capacity to rent or purchase housing near to or distant from a preferred school. Controlled Choice operates on the premise that schools are public and should be available to everyone, while housing is private and its use is, therefore, limited to an individual or a family of individuals. Thus, the Controlled Choice method assumes that schooling opportunities should not be dependent upon anyone's financial capacity to rent or purchase various housing accommodations. Indeed, Controlled Choice prevents these experiences from being linked by ensuring that all schools are available to all students.

Controlled Choice provides comprehensive educational opportunities to population groups by insisting that groups with which individuals choose to identify, and that are recognized by the school system, should receive proportional access to all public educational opportunities provided. If school assignments were made in a random way, this would occur automatically. Since individuals are granted the freedom of choosing schools, this individual freedom must be constrained by reserving seats for groups. This method is fair to individuals and to groups. Moreover, by reserving a proportion of school seats for members of various population groups, Controlled Choice ensures the presence of a critical mass of students unlike the prevailing group and thereby guarantees diversity in all schools.

## FREEDOM AND CONSTRAINT

Freedom and constraint are two important and essential functions in social organization. They complement each other and control excesses of groups and individuals. The allocation of seats within all schools by groups is a way of constraining some individuals from grabbing all of the goodies (educational opportunities) before others are able to access them. Permitting individuals to choose the schools they will attend is a way of freeing them from their group constraints. Group constraints come in many forms such as race, ethnicity, gender, socioeconomic status, residential location, and so on.

As stated earlier, the essential components of Controlled Choice are student body diversity, personal choice, and school improvement. These components of educational reform are not new. What is new is the requirement in Controlled Choice that these three components should be implemented simultaneously and not incrementally.

## INCREMENTAL, SIMULTANEOUS, AND COMPREHENSIVE PLANNING

Jennifer Hochschild provides a thorough and insightful discussion on the liability of incremental policies in school desegregation (Hochschild, 1984). She states that incrementalism's proponents tout its ability to proceed through a sequence of approximations as if this is the most appropriate way to introduce social change. By way of sequential change, incremental efforts can have a constant reaction to action (Hochschild, 1984: 51–52). This, the incrementalists believe, is a virtue. With reference to school desegregation, Hochschild declares that this virtue is a fault (1984: 52). The trick, according to Hochschild, is to "ensure that ... improvements are brought into play simultaneously" (1984: 53).

Robin Williams and Margaret Ryan, in their book *Schools in Transition* published in 1954 (the year of the *Brown* decision), provided strategic evidence against incrementalism. They found that in some communities "time ... gives opportunity for opposition to crystallize and for community cleavages to develop" (1954: 239). In general, they found that "a clear-cut policy, administrated with understanding but also with resolution, seems to have been most effective in accomplishing desegregation with a minimum of difficulty" (1954: 242). Actually, "long drawn-out efforts and fluctuating policies appear to have maximized confusion and resistance" (Williams and Ryan, 1954: 242).

The findings of Williams and Ryan rule out the piecemeal approach so often advocated by incrementalists. They discovered that "partial desegregation that affects only ... a few schools in a community opens the door to charges that 'we are being asked to do this, but the others aren't'" (Williams and Ryan, 1954: 243). The consequences are usually negative when a partial and incremental approach to school desegregation is used rather than a comprehensive approach such as Controlled Choice.

Controlled Choice does precisely what Hochschild has suggested: It guarantees desegregation, provides for choice of school of attendance by individuals, and promotes school improvement simultaneously. Simultaneity is one of the lynchpins of this method because it permits individual choice as long as choice does not violate enrollment fairness guidelines which are group-derived. Controlled Choice uses the choice data as a referendum on the attractiveness of schools. Moreover, school authorities are obligated by Controlled Choice to use their limited resources to upgrade and make more attractive least-chosen schools. This way, a school system may enhance itself by pushing up or magnetizing its bottom schools annually. To use a metaphor, "a rising tide raises all ships." This method of school improvement helps the whole system. Controlled Choice rules out arbitrary and capricious action such as offering additional resources to principals who have "pull" with central administrators or to schools in neighborhoods where parents have "clout." Because the results of a Controlled Choice process reveal schools that are least attractive and in need of assistance, none can declare that the evaluation is influenced by prejudicial attitudes of administrators, that someone is picking on a particular school because of its location or because of its leadership.

## IMPROVING LEAST-CHOSEN SCHOOLS

The school improvement component of Controlled Choice is a puzzlement to many who like its other components. They are so wedded to the economic ideology of survival of the fittest that they fail to understand the focus of Controlled Choice on pushing up the bottom by improving least-attractive schools. This puzzlement is a direct outcome of projecting principles and practices appropriate for one institutional system, like economics, upon another, like education. In a capitalistic economy, value is enhanced by scarcity; thus, less is better than more, according to the wisdom of the market. But in democratic education, value is enhanced by abundance and plurality; the more the better. Consequently, state governments in the United States require compulsory education for all young people.

Thomas Jefferson, one of the founders of this country, promoted free public education as a way of preventing tyranny. He believed that public education would equip the people with virtue and wisdom, as well as prepare them for public trust leadership roles. Thus, education was a way of enabling people to manage their common concerns in a democratic way (Jefferson, 1813: 116). Although Jefferson did not call for universal education at secondary and college levels, he nevertheless ran into opposition from the dominant people of power during his time for his notion of free elementary school education. Jefferson was sent away to France as ambassador and missed the Constitutional Convention. While we cannot claim a cause-and-effect relationship between Jefferson's absence and the final version of the Constitution of the United States, we note that the federal government is not given any responsibility for education. When this country was founded, education was identified as a privilege and not a right. Consequently, only a privileged few were educated. In Jefferson's Virginia, for example, most poor Whites as well as black and brown people were uneducated.

With this national heritage as a context, it is difficult to get citizens toward the close of the twentieth century and the beginning of the twenty-first century to understand the school improvement component of Controlled Choice that focuses on least-chosen schools. It seemed to the public that our plan was designed to reward failure.

We finally broke through public misunderstanding in Boston of why Controlled Choice focuses on less-effective schools by way of an analogy. When one of the plan's designers was invited in 1989 to discuss the Controlled Choice plan on a radio station that broadcasted the Boston Celtics professional basketball games, he stated that Controlled Choice was like professional athletics and the National Basketball Association. The lowest-ranked team during one season gets first chance at the best talent in the new pool of players for the next season. By following this procedure, all teams remain relatively balanced in the professional athletic skills of their players. And a league or association of teams all more or less balanced in talent offers genuine competition in the games that they play.

With reference to education, when schools at the bottom are pushed up and enhanced each year, the whole system (like the professional athletic league or association) is helped. When all schools are adequate and more than adequate, students have a broader range of acceptable schools from which to choose. As a result of this broader range of choice, 90 percent of the students in Boston who are assigned by its Controlled Choice plan get a first-choice or second-choice school. Less than 10 percent of Boston's students are mandatorily assigned to a school that they did not choose.

## CONTROLLED CHOICE AND MAGNET SCHOOLS

Controlled Choice embraces the concept of magnet schools. However, instead of magnetizing the best schools in the community, Controlled Choice magnetizes the worst schools in the community. Instead of using limited community resources to make good schools better and better schools best, Controlled Choice recommends that limited community resources should be used to make bad schools good and better. If the worst schools in the community are continuously improved, eventually a school system will not have any bad schools.

While Controlled Choice requires that immediate attention should be given to least chosen schools, it, as a student assignment method, embraces magnet schools that are designed to enrich the whole public school system. Such schools may be added to broaden curriculum offerings in the system as well as to upgrade particular schools. When magnet schools are included in a Controlled Choice plan, they should be available for city-wide enrollment or they should be duplicated in each zone to fulfill the fairness requirement.

Our Controlled Choice plan was not implemented in Milwaukee during the late 1980s because some parents wanted to treat magnet schools as sanctuaries of privilege and opposed the proposal to replicate them by zones. The opponents in Milwaukee, of course, violated the fairness principle, which prevents all students from experiencing educationally disadvantaged circumstances because of their residence and which requires equity in the range and kinds of educational services available in each zone.

The above discussion indicates that the school improvement component of Controlled Choice is a complex of actions based on theoretical premises that differ from those of social Darwinism and other nineteenth-century ideas and ideologies that are inappropriate foundations for the organization of education during the twenty-first century. The theoretical foundation on which Controlled Choice is based urges us to pay attention to the meek and the weak and to schools that are least attractive. These practices are based on a theoretical observation made by a famous sociologist years ago. Robert Merton wrote approximately a half century ago that "it is not infrequently the case that the nonconforming minority in a society represents the interests and ultimate values of the group more effectively than the conforming majority" (Merton, 1949: 367). Controlled Choice caters to the nonconforming minority as well as the conforming majority. By so doing, Controlled Choice is fair to all.

When student assignments are made according to the enrollment fairness guidelines of Controlled Choice no one can claim that a least-chosen or most-chosen school is due to the racial composition of the student body, since all schools more or less have similar student bodies. Also, no one can claim schools that receive resources to assist in their improvement receive such resources because of the kinds of students enrolled, when all students are granted proportional access to all schools.

The Controlled Choice approach not only identifies schools in need of assistance, it recognizes schools that are most attractive to all groups. Since seats are reserved for all racial and ethnic groups and/or all socioeconomic groups according to their proportions in the system-wide school-going student body, the schools which are chosen as first choice or second choice in numbers that exceed the seats reserved for each group are labeled "overchosen" schools. The annual choices are a referendum that indicates which schools are doing something right, since students in all racial, ethnic, or socioeconomic groups prefer these schools. Schools so selected by students apparently indicate the educational programs that are attractive in a local community. These programs probably should be replicated. This, therefore, is another benefit of Controlled Choice. It can identify both more- and less-attractive schools in a system; these schools, then, can be used as negative and positive models to be avoided or emulated.

Controlled Choice overcomes the problem inherent in phasing in educational programs sequentially and incrementally. Initially, school systems tried desegregation alone. While minority and majority students were integrated, the quality of education did not always improve. So planners decided to give less attention to ways of desegregating all schools and, sequentially, turned toward a new experiment—magnet schools. Magnet schools did improve education. But they were expensive and few in number. Magnet schools never accommodated more than 30 percent of the students in a school system and frequently accommodated a smaller proportion. While they were beneficial for the few who could enroll in them, magnet schools were unfair to most students in the system who could not attend them. Thus, in a trial-and-error way, educational planners finally fixated on choice. While interdistrict choice benefited schools in the suburbs, it did not help the schools or the school system left behind. In interdistrict choice arrangements, actually a new phenomenon, the reverse of the Robin Hood story, was created. Since state pupil financial allowances were transferred to suburban school districts that some central city students chose, the city district, which usually was poorer than suburban districts, was left with even fewer resources. These interdistrict choice plans actually took from the poor and gave to the rich.

What we see in this brief summary is the negative outcome of remedies that were applied singly or sequentially. We used these same remedies in Controlled Choice but introduced them simultaneously so that one activity influenced each of the other activities. By using the simultaneous approach, school desegregation influences school choice; school choice influences school improvement; and school improvement influences school desegregation.

Thus, Controlled Choice rejects the notion of assigning students to schools that have distinct curricular identities based on student achievement scores or aptitude indicators. Schools that have been magnetized should be equally available to poor and affluent children and to racial and ethnic majority and minority children. The child's interest in participating in a school whose curriculum has been magnetized should be the basic criterion for admission, in addition to racial and socioeconomic fairness guidelines that guarantee group equity in admission. Moreover, Controlled Choice requires schools with specific educational missions like two-way bilingual education, inclusive education (the integration of regular and special-needs students), or advanced learning to be racially and socioeconomically integrated.

By making all kinds of schools available to all kinds of students in all kinds of neighborhoods and by mandating the availability of resources for the enhancement of least-chosen schools, Controlled Choice eliminates race, ethnicity, socioeconomic status, residential location, and a host of other restraints upon the availability of educational opportunities. Controlled Choice truly makes educational services and opportunities available to all students in a way that is fair.

## CONTROLLED CHOICE AND TRANSPORTATION

In urban and suburban school districts where transportation is a requirement for many students, Controlled Choice equalizes the burden of using transportation or the opportunity of walking to and from school by eliminating neighborhood student assignment zones. Moreover, students who use transportation to go to and from school in a Controlled Choice plan do so because they choose to do so. Mandatory assignments are minimal under Controlled Choice; hence, no population group is required to use more or less transportation than another to go to and from school. This is another way in which Controlled Choice is fair.

Beyond being fair, we discovered that it made sense conceptually to eliminate neighborhoods as the basis for assigning students to school. According to Herbert Richardson, there must be asymmetry between the form in which evil manifests itself and the form of our opposition to it (Richardson, 1968: 202). Martin Luther King, Jr., stated the proposition this way: "Darkness cannot drive out darkness; only light can do that" (King, 1964: 45). Light, of course, is asymmetrical to darkness. Using a neighborhood-based plan to overcome *de facto* or *de jure* segregation is not very helpful, since most neighborhoods in the United States are segregated. This approach is not asymmetrical to the evil of segregated housing it seeks to correct. Controlled Choice, however, is asymmetrical to student assignments by neighborhoods.

## LIMITATIONS OF NEIGHBORHOOD-BASED DESEGREGATION PLANS

We review briefly some of the more conventional ways of achieving school desegregation in the past that rely on neighborhood student attendance zones. Among the approaches most frequently recommended in the literature are expanding or contracting a neighborhood student attendance zone, pairing two contiguous neighborhoods, clustering several neighborhoods, and closing a neighborhood school building for the purpose of redistributing a homogeneous population among other schools to achieve increased desegregation. We summarize below the traditional diversification methods and indicate value added by controlled choice.

After the *Brown* decision, school boards manipulated the racial composition of public schools by *moving the boundary line of a school zone one, two, or three blocks.* If the resident population in a block differed from the prevailing population in a student body, the racially different block might be taken from one school attendance zone and added to another. The same arbitrary procedure was followed in changing the student attendance zone of a segregated school. Blocks of students whose population was similar to the other students in a segregated school were cut off. It is difficult to achieve racial desegregation by moving the boundary lines of zones one or two blocks, because city neighborhoods are usually too small to encompass a mixed racial population. Moreover, the racial composition of neighborhood blocks changes from time to time. The block by block method of changing the racial composition of a school attendance zone is not likely to yield permanent results and tends to create feelings of anger that the block in which one lives is being assigned to or withdrawn from a school attendance zone in an arbitrary way.

Another neighborhood-based approach is the *pairing* of two contiguous neighborhoods that have racially identifiable populations that are different from each other. Under such an arrangement, the schools in the two attendance zones are linked so that one school houses elementary school grades 1, 2, and 3, and the other school grades 4, 5, and 6. All students in the two zones attend the first school together for the lower-division elementary grades and the second school for the upper-division elementary grades. Thus, "by combining two contiguous attendance zones and changing the grade configuration of two schools, both schools are desegregated and reflect the combined racial composition of the two zones" (Hughes, Gordon, and Hillman, 1980: 56). While the pairing approach achieves some desegregation, it does this by violating an important principle of education, the principle of continuity in elementary education in the same building for young people.

Still another neighborhood-based arrangement is to pair student bodies in attendance zones that are distant from each other and do not share a common boundary. Again, this approach achieves some desegregation; but the interruption of a continuous experience in the same learning environment is a limitation of this approach, too.

Finally, *clustering* of several neighborhoods has been used to desegregate racially identifiable schools. The clustering arrangement permits students to remain in segregated neighborhood schools until they reach, for example, the top grades of elementary school. Then, they must attend a desegregated middle or junior high school in the cluster. Obviously, this is part-time desegregation only and does not fully redress the grievances of minority plaintiffs about segregated education. Some clustering arrangements may involve three schools at the same level. This approach is similar to the pairing arrangement between two schools, mentioned earlier; all students may have a desegregated education in one school of the cluster in grades 1 and 2, and in another school of the cluster for grades 3 and 4, and in a third school of the cluster for grades 5 and 6 (Hughes et al., 1990s: 59–61). The limitation of this approach is the same as that discussed in pairing, and contributes to even greater disruption in educational continuity.

More radical than clustering or pairing to achieve desegregation is the *closing of a school building*, especially in a segregated neighborhood, and dispersing its homogeneous student body into other schools where the racial characteristics of the new students contribute to desegregation. School closings have been used most frequently in inner-city, Black neighborhoods. The selective use of this method is not fair. Under this arrangement, neighborhood schools for black and brown populations have been eliminated while those for Whites have been retained.

Population shifts in racially segregated neighborhood housing patterns have defeated many neighborhood-based school desegregation plans, even those that appeared to be successful when first implemented. Unless neighborhood-based student attendance zones are readjusted in response to changing population patterns, Robert Dentler and Marvin Scott declare that a school desegregation plan of geocodes or residential neighborhoods eventually will be defeated.

All of this suggests that neighborhood-based school desegregation plans represent only a short-term victory and do not eliminate segregated education root and branch. Even when they work, they achieve the goal of mixing children of different racial groups but do not necessarily guarantee an enhanced education.

Other approaches to school desegregation that differ from the neighborhood-based approach are freedom-of-choice plans and majority-to-minority transfers. However, these plans have not been effective in achieving school desegregation. Indeed, when these are the only plans in use, they tend to result in increased segregation since they provide no educational improvement incentive for students to make cross-racial school choices.

Voluntary plans (which is the name sometimes given to freedom-of-choice plans) may not achieve desegregation but may enhance the quality of education of a specific student. The quality-enhancement factor is beneficial for an individual if it also contributes to community advancement, a duality that freedom-of-choice plans seldom acccomplish. This is another reason why we prefer Controlled Choice: It achieves multiple goals simultaneously.

Unlike neighborhood-based student assignment methods, the efficacy of Controlled Choice is not dependent upon the immutability of neighborhood housing patterns and the stability of neighborhood populations. Nor does the policy limit choice to a relatively few magnet or specialized schools and programs. In Controlled Choice, the access of minority and majority students to effective schools is not determined by the racial or socioeconomic characteristics of neighborhoods. Controlled Choice requires all schools to educate children in all population groups and to maintain schools that are attractive to all.

The fairness phenomenon which permeates all aspects of Controlled Choice is essential in constructing relatively large, heterogeneous student attendance zones. Most school districts can be divided into not more than two, three, or maybe four large student attendance zones. Zones are best constructed by aggregating contiguous neighborhoods of different population groups. It is important that each zone include adjacent rather than discontinuous neighbors. This method of designing student attendance zones guards against the appearance of "gerrymandering." If citizens suspect gerrymandering, public confidence in the planning process could be undermined.

Zones should be large enough to encompass heterogeneous population groups but small enough to limit student transportation time to and from school within the zone to not more than thirty, thirty-five, or forty minutes.

Zones should encompass an equivalent range of educational programs and services. The achievement of equivalency is one of the first responsibilities of zonewide school authorities and zone advisory groups. The racial composition of the students residing in each zone should reflect the district-wide student body, although modest variations from it are permitted as long as the minority population that may consist of a combination of groups is not less than one-fifth of the zonewide public school student body. To be effective in negotiating with the population at large in a zone, subdominant people of power should have a minimum critical mass. At or above the critical mass level of one-fifth, minorities have a better chance of negotiating a fair solution to the various issues that may arise.

## SUMMARY OF CONTROLLED CHOICE BENEFITS

A comprehensive desegregation plan, Controlled Choice governs all student assignment decisions, including: new admissions, intra- and interdistrict transfers, the mainstreaming of bilingual and special-needs students into regular or standard education classes, and the reassignments of students resulting from school closings, school consolidations, and new school construction. The policy also serves as an innovative planning tool that can readily expedite the creation of more effective magnet or specialized schools while also stimulating the development of improved instructional practices and enhanced educational opportunities in existing schools. Moreover, Controlled Choice allows local school officials to implement a truly "living" plan that will accommodate changes in legal, political, and educational requirements and in the demographic characteristics of a district.

If Controlled Choice is implemented correctly, it provides local officials with a final student assignment policy that maximizes family and student choice and effective desegregation outcomes on a district-wide basis, provides stability in student assignments and continuity in educational experiences, frees the public schools from their hostage status to real estate and other regressive neighborhood interests, and makes all schools and programs available to students of diverse racial, ethnic, and socioeconomic backgrounds in an equitable way. And since Controlled Choice is grounded in parent empowerment and uses the reputational method of evaluating schools, the policy gives local school officials a clear mandate to ensure that all desegregating schools provide distinctive or enhanced educational opportunities.

To recapitulate, Controlled Choice eliminates individual school attendance boundaries in favor of large heterogeneous zones or a city-wide attendance zone, adopts a definition of desegregation that guarantees minority and majority group students genuine proportional access to all schools and programs, allows students to choose schools they prefer to attend and to rank-order their preferences without guarantee that any student will receive his or her first choice (although most students will), and ensures complete honesty and integrity in the disposition of all assignment decisions.

## PARENT INFORMATION CENTERS

To "level the playing field" so that parents in varying racial, ethnic, and socioeconomic groups have equal access to the choice process and are able to make informed decisions in a timely fashion, Parent Information Centers are needed. These Centers, staffed by parents, are an outreach service provided by the school system for the community at large. The Parent Information Center should serve as an advocate for all parents. The Harvard Seminar on Choice has documented the absence of universal information among racial and ethnic groups about extraordinary educational offerings. In Montgomery County, Maryland, where nineteen magnet schools were established by 1987, "72% of white parents [had] heard the term whereas just 39% of Hispanic parents [could] recall hearing the term "magnet school" (Fuller, 1995: 5). Parent Information Centers in our Controlled Choice plan help overcome this problem.

## DIFFERENCE BETWEEN CONTROLLED CHOICE
## AND OTHER CHOICE PLANS

Finally, we discuss how Controlled Choice differs from other choice plans. Choice has been advocated as one approach to educational reform. It is something of value. But choice is of limited value if used alone, as a single, simplistic approach. Human society and its institutions must be understood as complexes of characteristics that defy simplistic solutions.

Choice, we suspect, has captured the attention of educational planners and reformers because it is compatible with the increasing belief in individualism that Robert Bellah has observed in American society. He tells us that "self-reliance is an old American value" (Bellah, 1985: 48), that meeting the utilitarian and expressive needs of individuals is an important societal goal (Bellah, 1985: 50), and that we often attempt to fulfill utilitarian individualism in the public institutions of our society (Bellah, 1985: 46), such as education and religion. This function of institutions has led some to believe that "the individual is the only firm reality." Bellah tells us that "separation and individualism have reached a kind of culmination," but then he states, "their triumph is far from complete" (Bellah, 1985: 276).

Individuation has been unable to triumph completely because it is a human characteristic of social organizations that is of limited value without the human characteristic of participation or commitment (Bellah, 1985: 277). In the human community, fulfillment of the individual and commitment to participate in groups and institutions are complementary. One action without the other is insufficient. If education performs a complex function of enhancing individuals at the same time that it advances the community, then we understand how any monistic approach to educational reform such as choice is too limited and, therefore, inappropriate.

This is the conceptual orientation with which we should approach the issue of choice. However, this orientation is often ignored in educational reform programs. Choice as an educational reform method has been severely tainted with the idea of privilege and even exclusiveness. The problem with advocating *choice* as "the key" to educational reform, as claimed by some of its proponents is their failure to embrace the principle of complementarity that recognizes the need for an opposing concept like *control* which also contributes to educational reform. Opposites inform and correct each other when held together in creative tension. When choice and control coexist in an educational system, such a system has a better chance of fulfilling the needs of all. An educational system that experiences the creativity of freedom and the discipline of conformity is better positioned to meet the twofold goal of education: individual enhancement and community advancement. Both aspects of this goal are important. Thus, the celebration of choice, and choice alone, as the operative concept which will usher in educational reform is wrong.

It is hard for any idea about the limitations of choice to get a fair hearing because of the important role that choice supporters play in the molding of public opinion. State Governor Rudy Perpich said, unequivocally, "Choice is the key to improvement in education" (Perpich, 1989: 1). John Chubb of the Brookings Institute in Washington, D.C., asked himself this question: "What accounts for effective organizations?" His answer: "Autonomy!" He believes that autonomy is more important than anything else. If we want schools to be organized more effectively and to teach more successfully, Chubb states that we must give them autonomy. In his opinion, "the surest way to get autonomy and accountability into the public school system is not through regulation ... but through a mechanism of choice," such as "vouchers, open enrollment, magnet schools," and other approaches (Chubb, 1989: 5–10).

The *New York Times* reported that a forum held in June 1990 at the Brookings Institution in connection with the publication of Chubb's book, coauthored with Terry Moe of Stanford University and titled *Politics, Markets and American Schools*, "seemed to verge on becoming a celebration of the choice concept instead of an examination of ... the study" (Wycliff, 1990).

The study included an analysis of detailed data on 500 schools and the students who attend these schools as well as their teachers and principals. The study obtained information on the performance of students on mathematics, science, reading, writing, and vocabulary tests and combined the results obtained during students' sophomore year and again at graduation into a comprehensive measure of student achievement (Chubb, 1989: 6).

Chubb and his colleague committed the error of oversimplification in their discussion of causes of effective schooling. They attributed effective schooling more or less to a single characteristic—autonomy. Another error of oversimplification is to attribute the source of autonomy and accountability in school more or less to another single mechanism—choice. Actually, autonomy and participation are complementary functions and so are choice and control. Autonomy or choice alone is insufficient to solve the problems of schooling unless linked with its opposite.

Another problem with choice plans other than Controlled Choice is their tendency to be modeled in the image of the economic system. For example, Chubb and Moe speak of the beneficial effects of schools controlled by markets and schools competing for students in the open market. Analogies are helpful up to a point, but they have grave explanatory limitations.

The rules that govern the economic system concerned with producing and distributing goods and services are different from those that govern the educational system concerned with developing and disseminating knowledge and information. In the economic system, there may be unworthy buyers who are unwilling to pay the asking price. But in education, there are no unworthy seekers of knowledge. In business dealings, when a product is given away, it depresses the market. But in educational transactions, knowledge increases as it is shared and given to others. Thus, a market orientation is inappropriate for operating an educational system.

For these reasons, we advocate Controlled Choice which enhances education through student choice, student body diversity, and school improvement. Controlled Choice is more than permitting students "who have not succeeded in one public school to enroll in another district's school," an approach permitted in Minnesota (Perpich, 1989: 2). School reform should promote human diversity, require that all schools be brought up to an adequate and acceptable level, distribute common educational resources equitably to all population groups in accordance with their unique needs, and provide opportunities for students to indicate schools of preference. These and other functions of schooling as an institution are responsibilities too great to be fulfilled by autonomy or choice that operates according to market forces.

The leaders of the Harvard Seminar on Choice evaluated selected programs of choice in a few communities and concluded that "school choice will do little to diversify enrollment" if public school authorities fail to capitalize on appealing features such as smaller enrollments, enthusiastic and experienced teachers, and distinct curricular identities. (Fuller, 1995: 6). Unfortunately, the Seminar did not examine, in depth, Controlled Choice, which differs from other choice plans. Boston, which has operated under a Revised Controlled Choice Student Assignment Plan since 1992, has desegregated and diversified all elementary and middle schools in an equitable way, largely because Controlled Choice required it to implement choice, school improvement, and student body diversity *simultaneously*. Urging schools to develop distinctive curricula is something of value. However, we have no evidence that size of enrollment, as mentioned in the report of the Harvard Seminar, is an essential feature in the achievement of diversity or school improvement. We do know that choice, desegregation, and school improvement must be implemented at the same time and not singly as San Antonio, Milwaukee, and Montgomery County attempted to do. (These were the school districts primarily featured in the policy brief issued by leaders of the Harvard Seminar.)

## CONCLUSIONS

Actually, we concur with the conclusion of the Harvard Seminar's policy brief that choice alone will not diversify schools. Also, we concur with the conclusion of Larry Hughes, William Gordon, and Larry Hillman that magnet programs have had only "minimal impact on the overall racial balances of [school systems in Dallas, Houston, Indianapolis, Minneapolis, and Philadelphia]" and that "there are no instances where a major school system has noticeably desegregated its public schools by using a voluntary magnet program" (Hughes, Gordon, and Hillman 1980: 20). We also have seen in our Boston studies that desegregation alone will not improve education. All of this is to say that the principle of simultaneity must be continuously evoked, that choice, school improvement, and student body diversity must go hand in hand. This is the complexity of the matter which should not be distorted by oversimplification.

We conclude that regulation as well as autonomy, and choice as well as control, are essential in school reform. These two, like love and justice or excellence and equity, ought to always be kept together, held in creative tension. They should not be permitted to separate.

Another conclusion that may be drawn from this discussion is that school reform plans, including those that emphasize choice or Controlled Choice, should be tailored to accommodate all sorts and conditions of students and should not be skewed to deal primarily with the needs of White students or middle-class students at the expense of others. To cater to one student group at the expense of other student groups is unfair.

In all that we do, we must be fair. Without fairness, our public policies and plans will be of limited value. Controlled Choice aims to be fair and to provide a permanent experience of desegregation and school improvement.

## NOTE

This chapter was originally published by The Education Alliance at Brown University in *Controlled Choice, A New Approach to School Desegregation and School Improvement* by Charles V. Willie and Michael J. Alves in 1996. Reproduced with permission.

## REFERENCES

Bellah, Robert. 1985. *Habits of the Heart*. New York: Harper & Row.

Chubb, John. 1989. "Making Schools Better: Choice and Educational Improvement." *Equity and Choice* 5 (May): 5–10.

Dentler, Robert, and Marvin Scott. 1981. *Schools on Trial*. Cambridge, MA: Abt Books.

Dewey, John. 1900. *The School and Society*. New York: McClure, Phillips and Company.

Fuller, Bruce, 1995: "Who Gains, Who Loses from School Choice: A Research Summary." *A Policy Brief from the National Conference of State Legislatures*: National Conference of State Legislatures.

Hochschild, Jennifer. 1984. *The New American Dilemma*. New Haven, CT: Yale University Press.

Hughes, Larry, William Gordon, and Larry Hillman. 1980. *Desegregating America's Schools*. New York: Longman.

Jefferson, Thomas. 1813. "Letters from Thomas Jefferson to John Adams on Natural Aristocracy." In Stuart Gerry Brown (ed.), *We Hold These Truths*. New York: Harper, 1941, pp. 114–118.

Merton, Robert K. 1949. *Social Theory and Social Structure*. New York: The Free Press.

Perpich, Rudy. 1990. "Foreword." In Joe Nathan (ed.), *Public Schools by Choice*. St. Paul: Institute for Learning and Teaching, pp. 1–3.

Richardson, Herbert W. 1968. "Martin Luther King, Jr. Unsung Theologian." *Commonweal* (May 3).

Walberg, Herbert J. 1989. "Educational Productivity and Choice." In Joe Nathan (ed.), *Public Schools by Choice*. St. Paul: Institute for Learning and Teaching.

Williams, Robin M., and Margaret Ryan. 1954. *Schools in Transition*. Chapel Hill; University of North Carolina Press.

Wycliff, Don. 1990. "Right to Choose Gains in Debate Over Schools." *New York Times* (June 10).

# 3

# LEE COUNTY: A SUCCESS STORY IN CONTROLLED CHOICE

During the past twenty-five years, Lee County, Florida, has tripled in size. The school-going population has increased by an average of 1,500 students each year. To manage this growth, student assignments were disrupted annually by school boundary changes to relieve the overcrowding in some schools, fill empty seats in others and satisfy a 25-year-old court order to achieve racial and ethnic diversity.

Lee County has 56,104 public school students—two-thirds (67 percent) White and one-third (33 percent) minority. Among minorities in the school-going population, 16 percent are Black, 14 percent Hispanic, 1 percent Asian, and less than 1 percent Native American; also, about 1 percent of the student population may be characterized as multiracial. Together these racial and ethnic groups constitute one out of every three students in Lee County public schools. Forty-two percent of the Lee County student body for the entire school system is eligible for free/reduced-cost lunch.

To accommodate rapid growth in its student population, eliminate the annual disruptions due to school-boundary changes, and achieve unitary status and relief from continuous supervision by the U.S. District Court, the Lee County School Board adopted a school choice plan, commonly called "Controlled Choice," in 1997. The plan was initially implemented during the 1998–99 school year and completed its second year, 1999–2000, "with great success," according to the assessment of Elizabeth Russell, executive director of accountability and planning in Lee County when this study was conducted.

Three large geographic zones were created that included student populations similar to the school district's total public school population. The East Zone in Lee County included seven elementary schools, three middle schools, and two high schools. The South Zone included eleven elementary schools, four middle schools, and three high schools. The West Zone included ten elementary schools, five middle schools, and three high schools.

The choice program was deemed a great success by the school system because, during the first assignment period from January through February, 98 percent of the students in the East Zone, 94 percent of the students in the South Zone, and 94 percent of the students in the West Zone received their first-choice schools. Parents were encouraged to review information about the schools in their zones at the Parent Information Center and elsewhere and to file application forms in February with the rank-ordered schools they preferred for their children for the next school year. A large number of families were able to obtain the schools they preferred.

To guarantee equitable access to all educational offerings in a zone, the school district's goal was to have a minority component of the student body in each school that varied not more than plus or minus 15 percentage points above or below the district-wide proportion of minority students. For the 1999–2000 school year, about 33 percent of elementary school students, 30 percent of middle school students, and 27 percent of high school students were minorities in the district. These facts mean the minority population could vary as high as 48 percent and as low as 18 percent in attendance zone elementary schools, as high as 45 percent and as low as 15 percent in zone attendance middle schools, and as high as 42 percent and as low as 12 percent in zone attendance high schools. While a variation of 15 percentage points in the minority student population has been used in several communities with Controlled Choice plans, we prefer a variation of 5 to 10 percentage points in the district-wide or zonewide proportions so that the minority student population in a school could not fall below 20 percent. Our experience in schools and in other organizations has revealed that when minority groups are collectively less than one-fifth of the total body, their power base is too small to negotiate effectively with the majority population.

The distribution of students by race turned out to be very balanced in each of the three zones and in most schools in Lee County, even though a rather wide range of variation was permissible (see Table 3.1). Only three elementary schools—Orange River and Tice in the East Zone and Tanglewood in the South Zone—exceeded the upper limit of the district's goal for a balanced student body. In the West Zone, none of the schools exceeded the upper limit. Also, none of the schools in any of the three zones had less than the district-wide minimum of minority students in elementary schools. With the exception of Gulf Middle School in the West Zone, which was below the designated minimum limit of minority students, none of the other middle schools in any of the three zones varied above or below the district-wide permissible limits. All the high schools in all the zones were within acceptable limits. Although Lee County permitted a wide variance in minority students in each school, *it confined most of the actual variation to less than 10 percentage points above or below the minority student population for each school level in each zone* (which is probably a better way of deriving appropriate permissible limits of variation).

This analysis reveals that Lee County has done an excellent job in creating well-balanced student bodies of minority and majority students by use of the Controlled Choice method of assigning students. We call attention to this fact because our

**Table 3.1** 1999–2000 School Listing by Zones, Current Enrollment, and Available Student Seats

| EAST ZONE SCHOOLS | PreK Cycle 9 Enrollment | K-12th Cycle 9 Enrollment | Total Cycle 9 Enrollment[1] | K-12th Enrollment Minority Percentage[2] | Permanent Student Seats[3] | Relocatable Student Seats | Total Student Seats | Permanent Seats Available or Needed (-) | Free/ Reduced Lunch %[4] |
|---|---|---|---|---|---|---|---|---|---|
| Alva Elem. | 20 | 363 | 383 | 23.7% | 404 | 0 | 404 | 21 | 48% |
| Bayshore Elem. | 20 | 482 | 502 | 31.3% | 445 | 44 | 489 | -57 | 54% |
| Lehigh Elem. | 40 | 904 | 944 | 41.9% | 859 | 0 | 859 | -85 | 62% |
| Mirror Lakes Elem. | 42 | 802 | 844 | 36.7% | 741 | 11 | 752 | -103 | 57% |
| Orange River Elem. | 39 | 726 | 765 | 50.0% | 668 | 31 | 699 | -97 | 71% |
| Sunshine Elem. | 20 | 962 | 982 | 41.0% | 862 | 38 | 900 | -120 | 58% |
| Tice Elem. | 77 | 581 | 658 | 53.9% | 672 | 19 | 691 | 14 | 80% |
| Alva Middle | 0 | 640 | 640 | 22.8% | 614 | 132 | 746 | -26 | 47% |
| Lehigh Acres Middle | 0 | 1,298 | 1,298 | 40.4% | 1,004 | 187 | 1,191 | -294 | 61% |
| Lehigh Sr. High | 0 | 1,317 | 1,317 | 33.7% | 1,575 | 0 | 1,575 | 258 | 34% |
| Riverdale High | 7 | 1,197 | 1,204 | 32.9% | 1,700 | 0 | 1,700 | 318 | 27% |
| Riverdale Middle | 0 | 178 | 178 | | | | | | |
| Elem. Totals-East | 258 | 4,820 | 5,078 | 41.1% | 4,651 | 143 | 4,794 | -427 | 72% |
| Middle Totals-East | 0 | 2,116 | 2,116 | 33.8% | 1,618 | 319 | 1,937 | -320 | 36% |
| High Totals-East | 7 | 2,514 | 2,521 | 33.9% | 3,275 | 0 | 3,275 | 576 | 27% |
| Total East | 265 | 9,450 | 9,715 | 37.5% | | | | | 52% |

| SOUTH ZONE SCHOOLS | PreK Cycle 9 Enrollment | K-12th Cycle 9 Enrollment | Total Cycle 9 Enrollment[1] | K-12th Enrollment Minority Percentage[2] | Permanent Student Seats[3] | Relocatable Student Seats | Total Student Seats | Permanent Seats Available or Needed (-) | Free/ Reduced Lunch %[4] |
|---|---|---|---|---|---|---|---|---|---|
| Allen Park Elem. | 90 | 717 | 807 | 46.2% | 798 | 0 | 798 | -9 | 59% |
| Bonita Springs Elem. | 19 | 284 | 303 | 37.3% | 289 | 0 | 289 | -14 | 69% |
| Colonial Elem. | 31 | 706 | 737 | 48.9% | 886 | 0 | 886 | 149 | 62% |
| Heights Elem. | 0 | 753 | 753 | 45.2% | 820 | 0 | 820 | 67 | 56% |
| Orangewood Elem. | 85 | 721 | 806 | 43.8% | 740 | 8 | 748 | -66 | 55% |
| Pinewoods Elem. | 38 | 884 | 922 | 31.1% | 897 | 0 | 897 | -25 | 41% |
| San Carlos Park Elem. | 20 | 925 | 945 | 36.1% | 923 | 0 | 923 | -22 | 49% |
| Spring Creek Elem. | 42 | 871 | 913 | 45.1% | 901 | 25 | 926 | -12 | 56% |
| Three Oaks Elem. | 78 | 891 | 969 | 22.1% | 886 | 11 | 897 | -83 | 35% |
| Villas Elem. | 49 | 723 | 772 | 47.2% | 765 | 0 | 765 | -7 | 69% |
| Bonita Springs Middle | 0 | 1,053 | 1,053 | 40.1% | 1,101 | 0 | 1,101 | 48 | 48% |
| Cypress Lake Middle | 0 | 1,047 | 1,047 | 31.2% | 1,023 | 109 | 1,132 | -24 | 37% |
| P. L. Dunbar Middle | 0 | 900 | 900 | 43.0% | 1,101 | 0 | 1,101 | 201 | 48% |
| Three Oaks Middle | 0 | 1,022 | 1,022 | 21.6% | 1,090 | 0 | 1,090 | 68 | 25% |
| Cypress Lake High | 3 | 1,830 | 1,833 | 31.5% | 1,833 | 78 | 1,911 | 0 | 23% |
| Estero High | 0 | 1,682 | 1,682 | 21.8% | 1,790 | 321 | 2,111 | 108 | 20% |
| Fort Myers High | 0 | 1,845 | 1,845 | 28.0% | 1,769 | 52 | 1,821 | -76 | 16% |
| Tanglewood/Rs Elem. | 35 | 534 | 569 | 50.4% | 582 | 0 | 582 | 5 | 58% |
| Tanglewood/Rs Middle | 0 | 3 | 3 | | | | | | |
| Tanglewood/Rs High | 0 | 5 | 5 | | | | | | |
| Elem. Totals-South | 487 | 8,009 | 8,496 | 40.6% | 8,487 | 44 | 8,531 | -17 | 54% |
| Middle Totals-South | 0 | 4,025 | 4,025 | 33.7% | 4,315 | 109 | 4,424 | 293 | 39% |
| High Totals-South | 3 | 5,362 | 5,365 | 27.3% | 5,392 | 451 | 5,843 | 32 | 20% |
| Total South | 490 | 17,396 | 17,886 | 34.9% | | | | | 40% |

1. Cycle Report—Enrollment totals *include* ALL PreK students.

2. Minority percentages *exclude* ALL PreK students.

3. The student seats listed are based on plant survey dated April 1998, and DOE negotiated changes as of September 1999. Information provided by the Facilities Dept.

4. Free/Reduced Lunch percentages for period April 10 to May 12, 2000. Information provided by Dr. Carolyn Morrow, Food Services.

Minority percentage for district PreK is listed but is excluded from total average.

Table 3.1 (Continued)

| WEST ZONE SCHOOLS | PreK Cycle 9 Enrollment | K-12th Cycle 9 Enrollment | Total Cycle 9 Enrollment¹ | K-12th Enrollment Minority Percentage² | Permanent Student Seats³ | Relocatable Student Seats | Total Student Seats | Permanent Seats Available or Needed (-) | Free/ Reduced Lunch %⁴ |
|---|---|---|---|---|---|---|---|---|---|
| Caloosa Elem. | 70 | 876 | 946 | 28.3% | 0 | 807 | 807 | -946 | 46% |
| Cape Elem. | 0 | 952 | 952 | 22.0% | 885 | 0 | 885 | -67 | 35% |
| Diplomat Elem. | 20 | 932 | 952 | 20.7% | 885 | 56 | 941 | -67 | 46% |
| Gulf Elem. | 0 | 950 | 950 | 18.9% | 907 | 47 | 954 | -43 | 25% |
| Hancock Creek Elem. | 20 | 910 | 930 | 22.9% | 879 | 0 | 879 | -51 | 43% |
| J.C. English Elem. | 56 | 711 | 767 | 38.4% | 699 | 0 | 699 | -68 | 72% |
| Pelican Elem. | 0 | 966 | 966 | 20.4% | 894 | 82 | 976 | -72 | 35% |
| Skyline Elem. | 58 | 958 | 1,016 | 21.6% | 886 | 55 | 941 | -130 | 41% |
| Suncoast Elem. | 59 | 710 | 769 | 44.2% | 882 | 19 | 901 | 113 | 87% |
| Tropic Isles Elem. | 91 | 899 | 990 | 35.0% | 850 | 35 | 885 | -140 | 63% |
| Caloosa Middle | 0 | 914 | 914 | 25.8% | 0 | 0 | 0 | -914 | 40% |
| Diplomat Middle | 0 | 541 | 541 | 19.4% | 993 | 300 | 1,293 | 452 | |
| Gulf Middle | 0 | 1,182 | 1,182 | 17.4% | 1,086 | 67 | 1,153 | -96 | 28% |
| Suncoast Middle | 0 | 719 | 719 | 35.6% | 1,112 | 70 | 1,182 | 393 | 67% |
| Trafalgar Middle | 0 | 1,287 | 1,287 | 20.3% | 1,163 | 189 | 1,352 | -124 | 37% |
| Cape Coral High | 9 | 1,562 | 1,571 | 21.5% | 1,827 | 16 | 1,843 | 256 | 24% |
| Mariner High | 1 | 1,648 | 1,649 | 18.0% | 1,826 | 0 | 1,826 | 177 | 20% |
| North Fort Myers High | 1 | 1,609 | 1,610 | 27.7% | 1,838 | 0 | 1,838 | 228 | 24% |
| Elem. Totals-West | 374 | 8,864 | 9,238 | 26.4% | 7,767 | 1,101 | 8,868 | -1,471 | 48% |
| Middle Totals-West | 0 | 4,643 | 4,643 | 22.9% | 4,354 | 626 | 4,980 | -289 | 40% |
| High Totals-West | 11 | 4,819 | 4,830 | 22.3% | 5,491 | 16 | 5,507 | 661 | 23% |
| Total West | 385 | 18,326 | 18,711 | 24.5% | | | | | 40% |

| MAGNET SCHOOLS | PreK Cycle 9 Enrollment | K-12th Cycle 9 Enrollment | Total Cycle 9 Enrollment¹ | K-12th Enrollment Minority Percentage² | Permanent Student Seats³ | Relocatable Student Seats | Total Student Seats | Permanent Seats Available or Needed (-) | Free/ Reduced Lunch %⁴ |
|---|---|---|---|---|---|---|---|---|---|
| Edgewood Elem. Magnet | 49 | 770 | 819 | 46.1% | 836 | 0 | 836 | 17 | 61% |
| Edison Park Elem. Magnet | 0 | 512 | 512 | 33.2% | 501 | 0 | 501 | -11 | 36% |
| Franklin Park Elem. Magnet | 64 | 407 | 471 | 58.2% | 621 | 8 | 629 | 150 | 66% |
| Gateway Elem. Magnet | 0 | 935 | 935 | 34.9% | 911 | 0 | 911 | -24 | 30% |
| Littleton Elem. Magnet | 19 | 897 | 916 | 31.3% | 912 | 0 | 912 | -4 | 44% |
| Fort Myers Middle Magnet | 0 | 895 | 895 | 45.5% | 904 | 191 | 1,095 | 9 | 48% |
| Lee Middle Magnet | 0 | 990 | 990 | 43.1% | 1,034 | 130 | 1,164 | 44 | 53% |
| Michigan Elem.Magnet | 20 | 430 | 450 | 47.7% | 799 | 0 | 799 | 257 | 75% |
| Michigan Middle Magnet | 0 | 92 | 92 | | | | | | |
| Total Elem. Magnets | 152 | 3,951 | 4,103 | 40.0% | 4,580 | 8 | 4,588 | 385 | 51% |
| Total Middle Magnets | 0 | 1,977 | 1,977 | 44.1% | 1,938 | 321 | 2,259 | 53 | 48% |
| Total Magnets | 152 | 5,928 | 6,080 | 41.4% | | | | | 50% |

| BARRIER ISLAND SCHOOLS | PreK Cycle 9 Enrollment | K-12th Cycle 9 Enrollment | Total Cycle 9 Enrollment¹ | K-12th Enrollment Minority Percentage² | Permanent Student Seats³ | Relocatable Student Seats | Total Student Seats | Permanent Seats Available or Needed (-) | Free/ Reduced Lunch %⁴ |
|---|---|---|---|---|---|---|---|---|---|
| Fort Myers Beach Elem. | 0 | 198 | 198 | 8.6% | 197 | 0 | 197 | -1 | 30% |
| Pine Island Elem. | 19 | 411 | 430 | 12.7% | 449 | 0 | 449 | 19 | 52% |
| Sanibel Elem. | 0 | 303 | 303 | 9.3% | 244 | 114 | 358 | -112 | 11% |
| Sanibel Middle | 0 | 53 | 53 | | | | | | |
| Total Elem. B.I. | 19 | 912 | 931 | 10.5% | 890 | 114 | 1,004 | -94 | 35% |
| Total Middle B.I. | 0 | 53 | 53 | | | | | | |
| Total Barrier Islands | 19 | 965 | 984 | 10.6% | | | 114 | 1,004 | 33% |

**Table 3.1** *(Continued)*

| ELEMENTARY, MIDDLE HIGH, BARRIER ISLAND & MAGNET SCHOOLS | PreK Cycle 9 Enrollment | K-12th Cycle 9 Enrollment | Total Cycle 9 Enrollment[1] | K-12th Enrollment Minority Percentage[2] | Permanent Student Seats[3] | Relocatable Student Seats | Total Student Seats | Permanent Seats Available or Needed (-) | Free/ Reduced Lunch %[4] |
|---|---|---|---|---|---|---|---|---|---|
| Elem. Totals | 1,290 | 26,556 | 27,846 | 34.9% | 26,375 | 1,410 | 27,785 | -1,624 | 54% |
| Middle Totals | 0 | 12,814 | 12,814 | 31.3% | 12,225 | 1,375 | 13,600 | -263 | 40% |
| High Totals | 21 | 12,695 | 12,716 | 26.7% | 14,158 | 467 | 14,625 | 1,269 | 22% |
| Totals | 1,311 | 52,065 | 53,376 | 32.0% | | | | | 43% |

**1999-2000 ALTERNATIVE & ESE SCHOOLS, STATE RESIDENTIAL FACILITIES CURRENT ENROLLMENT AND AVAILABLE STUDENT SEATS**

| SPECIAL FACILITIES | PreK Cycle 9 Enrollment | K-12th Cycle 9 Enrollment | Total Cycle 9 Enrollment[1] | K-12th Enrollment Minority Percentage[2] | Permanent Student Seats[3] | Relocatable Student Seats | Total Student Seats | Permanent Seats Available or Needed (-) | Free/ Reduced Lunch %[4] |
|---|---|---|---|---|---|---|---|---|---|
| **ALTERNATIVE & E.S.E.** | | | | | | | | | |
| Buckingham | 17 | 68 | 85 | 45.6% | 88 | | 88 | 3 | 74% |
| Countywide ESE | 47 | 103 | 150 | 16.5% | | | | | |
| District PreK[5] | 251 | 0 | 251 | 80.1% | | | | | |
| Edison Lrn Ctr | 1 | 121 | 122 | 61.2% | 105 | | 105 | -17 | 74% |
| New Directions | | | | | 635 | | 635 | -274 | |
| ALC--High | 0 | 200 | 200 | 48.5% | | | | | 62% |
| ALC--Middle | 0 | 228 | 228 | 55.3% | | | | | |
| The Academy | 0 | 318 | 318 | 36.8% | | | | | 27% |
| LAMP | 91 | 72 | 163 | 84.7% | | | | | 71% |
| Royal Palm | 0 | 186 | 186 | 55.9% | 207 | | 207 | 21 | 83% |
| Vo-Tech Central | 0 | 48 | 48 | 20.8% | | 135 | | | |
| Vo-Tech North | 0 | 26 | 26 | 11.5% | | | | | |
| Alt. & ESE Totals | 407 | 1,370 | 1,777 | 46.7% | | | | | |
| | | | | | | | | | |
| **STATE RESIDENTIAL** | | | | | | | | | |
| Detention Center | 0 | 92 | 92 | 45.7% | | | | | |
| Marine Inst. | 0 | 32 | 32 | 56.3% | | | | | 79% |
| Price Halfway | 0 | 38 | 38 | 42.1% | | | | | |
| State Res. Totals | 0 | 162 | 162 | 46.9% | | | | | |
| Elem. Special Total-District | 406 | 124 | 530 | 50.0% | | | | | |
| Middle Special Total-District | 0 | 401 | 401 | 53.9% | | | | | |
| High Special Total-District | 1 | 1,007 | 1,008 | 43.5% | | | | | |
| Special Total District | 407 | 1,532 | 1,939 | 46.7% | | | | | |
| | | | | | | | | | |
| Elem. Grand Total-District | 1,696 | 26,680 | 28,376 | 34.9% | | | | | |
| Middle Grand Total-District | 0 | 13,215 | 13,215 | 32.0% | | | | | |
| High Grand Total-District | 22 | 13,702 | 13,724 | 28.0% | | | | | |
| Grand Total District | 1,718 | 53,597 | 55,315 | 32.4% | | | | | 44% |

*Source*: Student Welfare and Attendance, Cycle Enrollment/Attendance Report, 2000.

studies in Hillsborough County, Boston, and Cambridge revealed that schools with balanced, diversified student bodies of minority and majority pupils tended to have higher average achievement scores. All of the student assignments in Lee County were made according to majority/minority racial and ethnic enrollment fairness guidelines.

The second-year implementation of the Controlled Choice student assignment plan in Lee County revealed some very interesting findings regarding school improvement (see Tables 3.2 and 3.3). With more or less balanced student bodies of

**Table 3.2** School District of Lee County, Florida, School Accountability Report

| Elementary Schools | 1998-99 | 1999-00 |
|---|---|---|
| Allen Park | B | C |
| Alva | C | C |
| Bayshore | B | B |
| Bonita Springs | D | A |
| Caloosa | C | A |
| Cape | A | B |
| Colonial | C | C |
| Diplomat | C | A |
| Edgewood Magnet | C | A |
| Edison Park Magnet | A | A |
| Fort Myers Beach | B | B |
| Franklin Park Magnet | D | C |
| Gateway Magnet | C | A |
| Gulf | B | A |
| Hancock Creek | C | A |
| Heights | C | B |
| J.C. English | C | C |
| Lehigh | C | C |
| Littleton Magnet | B | A |
| Michigan Magnet | C | A |
| Mirror Lakes | C | B |
| Orange River | D | C |
| Orangewood | C | A |
| Pelican | A | A |
| Pine Island | A | A |
| Pinewoods | C | A |
| San Carlos Park | C | C |
| Sanibel | A | A |
| Skyline | C | A |
| Spring Creek | C | C |
| Suncoast | F | C |
| Sunshine | C | C |
| Tanglewood/Rs | D | C |
| Three Oaks | A | A |
| Tice | D | C |
| Tropic Isles | C | B |
| Villas | D | C |

**Table 3.2** *(Continued)*

| Middle School | 1998-99 | 1999-00 |
|---|---|---|
| Alva | C | C |
| Bonita Springs | C | C |
| Caloosa | C | C |
| Cypress Lake | A | C |
| Fort Myers Magnet | C | C |
| Gulf | A | C |
| Lee Magnet | C | B |
| Lehigh Acres | C | C |
| P. L. Dunbar | C | C |
| Suncoast | D | C |
| Three Oaks | C | A |
| Trafalgar | A | A |

## High School Performance Grades

| High School | 1998-99 | 1999-00 |
|---|---|---|
| Cape Coral | C | C |
| Cypress Lake | C | C |
| Estero | C | C |
| Fort Myers | C | B |
| Lehigh Sr. | C | C |
| Mariner | C | C |
| North Fort Myers | C | C |
| Riverdale | D | C |

minority and majority students in nearly all Lee County schools, the proportion of schools that received "A" grades during the 1999–2000 school year increased from 16 percent a year earlier to 32 percent. Nearly half of Lee County's schools performed at "A" and "B" levels during the school year 1999–2000 compared to only 25 percent a year earlier. In addition to an 86 percent increase in grade "A" and "B" schools in the 1999–2000 school year, Lee County also witnessed a 29 percent decrease in medium- to low-graded schools. In 1998–99 there were thirty-

**Table 3.3** State-Awarded Grades during First Year and Second Year of School Desegregation, Lee County, Florida, 1998–99, 1999–2000

| Schools by Grade | 1998 - 99 | | 1999 - 2000 | | Difference 1998 - 2000 | Percent of Change |
|---|---|---|---|---|---|---|
| | # | % | # | % | | |
| A | 9 | 16 | 18 | 32 | +9 | +100 |
| B | 5 | 9 | 8 | 14 | +3 | +60 |
| C | 33 | 59 | 30 | 54 | -3 | -9 |
| D | 8 | 14 | - | - | -8 | -100 |
| F | 1 | 1 | - | - | -1 | -100 |
| TOTAL | 56 | 100 | 56 | 100 | | |

three "C," eight "D," and one "F" schools in Lee County. But in 1999–2000, Lee County had reduced the number of "C" schools and eliminated all "D" and "F" schools.

Using a more conventional definition of racial balance, such as plus or minus 10 percentage points around the average percentage of minorities in elementary, middle, and high schools in each of the three zones, we identified an appropriate permissible range of balanced variation for East Zone elementary schools as 31 to 51 percentage points around a minority average of 41 percent; for East Zone middle schools as 24 to 44 percentage points around a minority average of 34 percent; and for East Zone high schools as 17 to 37 percentage points around a minority average of 27 percent. All but three of the eleven public schools in the East Zone were racially balanced within plus or minus 10 percentage points of the minority average. The three imbalanced schools were Alva Elementary (imbalanced in favor of Whites), Tice Elementary (imbalanced in favor of minorities), and Alva Middle School (imbalanced in favor of Whites). None of the East Zone schools was racially isolated.

We identified an appropriate permissible range of balanced variation for South Zone elementary schools as 31 to 51 percentage points around a minority average of 41 percent, for South Zone middle schools as 24 to 44 percentage points around a minority average of 34 percent, and for South Zone high schools as 17 to 37 percentage points around a minority average of 27 percent. Only one of the eighteen schools in the South Zone was racially imbalanced. Three Oaks Middle School, with a minority student population of 22 percent was slightly below the minimum permissible range—by 2 percentage points. South Zone had no racially isolated schools.

We identified an appropriate, permissible range of balanced variation for West Zone elementary schools as 16 to 36 percentage points around a minority average of 26 percent; for West Zone middle schools as 13 to 33 percentage points around a minority average of 23 percent; and for West Zone high schools as 12 to 32 percentage points around a minority average of 22 percent. Only three of eighteen schools in the West Zone were racially imbalanced: Sun Coast and J. C. English elementary schools and Suncoast middle school. No schools were racially isolated in the West Zone.

Of the forty-seven Lee County public schools studied,[1] only seven (or one-sixth) of the total number were slightly imbalanced, and no schools were racially isolated with student bodies in which 80 percent or more of the students were members of a single racial group. Even after employing a more narrow definition of racial balance, one must declare that Lee County, Florida, has done an extraordinary job of desegregating its public schools by using racial fairness guidelines and the Controlled Choice method of assigning students to schools. Eight-five percent of Lee County public schools are racially balanced. This is a remarkable achievement.

The large increase in the number and proportion of "A" and "B" schools and the substantial drop in the number and proportion of medium- to low-graded schools between 1998–99 and 1999–2000 are further evidence of a positive correlation between student body diversity and high achievement as indicated by state-awarded grades to schools. By achieving diversity in all of its schools and leaving none as a racially isolated remnant of the past, Lee County has enhanced the total school system and the quality of education it offers.

Because of the demonstrated association between diversity and achievement reported in this chapter and elsewhere, we conclude that enrollment fairness guidelines are necessary and essential ways of guaranteeing school diversity. We arrive at this conclusion because of evidence presented elsewhere that student assignment plans based on freedom of choice seldom desegregate school student bodies and that low average achievement scores for students are most frequently found in schools that are racially isolated in favor of minorities and poverty-concentrated. The Lee County experience demonstrated that such schools can be eliminated to the benefit of the total school system.

Because racial diversity and socioeconomic diversity seem to be associated with student average achievement scores in schools, enrollment fairness guidelines should consider both. We recommend consideration of both because the absence of socioeconomic diversity within a school that has a high concentration of low-income students will probably result in a lower average achievement score for its student body.

Both racial and socioeconomic diversity seem to be associated with achievement, but in different ways. Thus, both should be included in enrollment fairness guidelines. If, however, for legal or other reasons it is not possible to use both factors, either one will yield a beneficial effect that is better than using no enrollment fairness guidelines at all. We repeat, freedom-of-choice student assignment plans without enrollment fairness guidelines have not worked effectively in the past and are not likely to work effectively in the present or future. Thus, enrollment fairness guidelines for student assignments are necessary and essential.

The Lee County experience, which successfully desegregated public schools in an equitable way and promoted increased excellence in academic achievement, has important implications for other school districts in Florida and elsewhere that may wish to do likewise.

School enrollment fairness guidelines are necessary and essential, if educational policy makers, public administrators, teachers, parents, pupils, and other citizens are interested in equity and excellence in public education and in fulfilling the twofold goal of education—individual enhancement and community advancement. The Lee County student assignment plan demands that we deal simultaneously with equity as well as excellence and with a range of other educational issues, such as school improvement, choice, and diversity.

To achieve the beneficial outcomes that Lee County has experienced, an honest definition of the situation is needed. Lee County acknowledged that the school district had experienced rapid growth in recent years, and that the racial and ethnic mix of its student population had grown more diverse while the demographic composition of neighborhoods had remained more or less homogeneous. These circumstances challenged the district's ability to assure racial and ethnic diversity within all schools. While Lee County was under court order to desegregate its public schools, the district wanted to do more. It wanted to offer all students and staff experiences that would help them develop greater skills and increased sensitivity in working with people of differing backgrounds so that they could function well as members of a culturally diverse society. Lee County recognized that it could not accomplish these goals if it continued to contain students in racially isolated segregated school-specific student attendance zones.

To achieve these lofty educational goals that transcended the requirements of a court order, Lee County adopted a policy of making all new assignments to all of its schools in accordance with racial and ethnic diversity guidelines. In a grant application to the state for funds to continue Controlled Choice, Lee County emphasized that it was demonstrating a long-term commitment to an open enrollment student assignment plan and that it had made school choice *the* student assignment method for its entire inventory of regular educational facilities. This is the kind of commitment that other school districts must make if they wish to derive the beneficial outcome that Lee County has experienced thus far from its Controlled Choice student assignment plan.

It is difficult, if not impossible, for a school district to overcome the negative historic effects of race or socioeconomic status without considering either of these in the student assignment process. Lee County avoided this error by adopting racial and ethnic diversity guidelines for its new student assignment plan, and consequently created situations in which race and ethnicity had little, if any, negative effect on school student bodies and student achievement.

To give students access to a broader range of educational services outside of their segregated neighborhoods, Lee County accepted the obligation of providing

transportation for students assigned to their schools of choice. Appropriately, Lee
County, which has embarked on a new commitment to provide equitable and un-
restricted access to educational opportunities, has recognized that free transportation services are essential to fulfilling the promise. Lee County currently spends
more on transportation than other school districts of comparable size that do not
have comprehensive Controlled Choice plans and has already sent a signal to state
government that more assistance must be given to school districts that have adopted
comprehensive Controlled Choice Plans.

In 1999, Lee County requested slightly more than $500,000 from the state and
indicated that this amount covers only a small portion of the actual expenditure required to accommodate students and their transportation needs in the court sanctioned Controlled Choice program. Clearly, Lee County and others that wish to
adopt Controlled Choice for the academic benefits that flow therefrom by way of
increased diversity in student bodies deserve assistance for transportation costs.
Many years ago, Massachusetts developed an incentive plan similar to the sug-
gestion contained in this book. School districts that developed comprehensive, voluntary desegregation plans were given assistance with the costs of new building
structures that were part of the plan. Assistance with transportation costs would
also be a welcome incentive for other school districts like Lee County and would
encourage them to develop comprehensive school desegregation plans like Controlled Choice.

Since the academic benefits of diversified student bodies have been demonstrated
in this chapter, and in view of the fact that Controlled Choice student assignment
plans facilitate the attainment of more diversity in student bodies, state authorities
should consider requiring the development and implementation of a comprehensive Controlled Choice Plan as a condition for obtaining more assistance on a regular basis with transportation costs.

Meanwhile, Lee County has identified another financial constraint to implementing public school choice programs. It is the absence of effective and efficient
two-way communication enabling parents to make informed choices about where
their children should attend school, since they have multiple opportunities available through Controlled Choice. Thus Lee County has petitioned the state for assistance in launching and stabilizing parent communication by way of a Parent Information Center. This, too, is a necessary service for effectively implementing a
school choice program, and it could become a targeted opportunity for state support to local school districts that have developed, and are in the process of implementing, comprehensive Controlled Choice Plans.

In summary, then, Lee County has performed a distinct service for the nation by
clearly showing the advantages, potential problems, and hopeful possibilities of a
Controlled Choice student assignment process that other school districts may wish
to adopt. We reported that through using racial fairness guidelines as a central feature of its Controlled Choice plan, Lee County has achieved remarkable racial balance in its schools. Eighty-five percent of the county's schools are now racially
balanced, which means that the minority population in each school does not vary

more than plus or minus 15 percentage points above or below the district-wide proportion of minority students. Moreover, during its first assignment period (1998–99), 94 percent or more of the students in each of the district's three geographic zones received their first choice of schools, an outstanding rate of accommodation that thus far has been sustained.

In addition, we reported that racial diversity in Lee County and in other school districts with Controlled Choice correlates significantly with improved academic achievement. Lee County's proportion of "A" schools, for example, increased from 16 to 32 percent after the first year (1998–99) of Controlled Choice implementation, while the district eliminated all school grades of "D" and "F" during this same period. We consider the high correlation between racial balance and improved academic performance to be an extremely important finding and have expanded upon it elsewhere in this book.

We also noted that achieving racial balance, with both the educational and social benefits it consistently yields, requires enrollment fairness guidelines; it will not occur through unregulated, freedom-of-choice procedures. Ideally, we pointed out, such guidelines ought to address both the racial and socioeconomic demographics of a school district. Racial balance, we found, is significantly correlated with high student achievement, while concentrated lower socioeconomic student populations usually record low academic performance.

Finally, we discussed the indispensable role that transportation plays in successful Controlled Choice programs and the necessity of operating Parent Information Centers for promoting and implementing those programs. We further urged that states make the funding of both transportation and Parent Information Centers a top priority when allocating program resources. (See "Memorandum on Transportation" by Michael Turza in Appendix B.)

Again, Lee County is to be commended, not only for implementing an exemplary Controlled Choice program, but for achieving "unitary" status in the process. Lee County, therefore, has demonstrated that the Controlled Choice model is entirely compatible with the desegregation goals of the federal court as stated in Janet Pulliam's memorandum in Appendix A. This knowledge, in our opinion, should provide a powerful incentive for other counties to consider this model if they too are seeking or wish to maintain unitary status.

## NOTE

1. Three island schools (Ft. Meyers Beach, Pine Island, and Sanibel Island) and eight magnet schools were excluded from this analysis.

# 4

## CONTROLLED CHOICE IN CAMBRIDGE

Cambridge was a leader among public school systems when it adopted a Controlled Choice student assignment plan in 1981. This plan was designed to promote student choice, student body diversity, and school improvement.

Two decades later, this bold new plan has achieved some but not all of its goals. Student Choice, which in 1981 was supposed to be available to all students for all schools, was modified by a 1989 school committee policy that gave priority in school assignments to students according to neighborhoods in which they lived. Upgrading least-chosen schools is recognized as important, but no systematic program has been designed to do this annually. Over the years, student bodies in several Cambridge schools have drifted into racial and socioeconomic imbalance. These were the problems the school committee asked us to investigate in 1995 in order to restore some of the initial benefits of Controlled Choice.

Three years after Controlled Choice was implemented in Cambridge, more than 60 percent of students attended schools outside their old attendance zones (Alves, 1984: 10). More than four-fifths of all students received their first- or second-choice school (Alves and Willie 1987: 83), and less than 10 percent of all students were mandatorily assigned.

By 1986, after the institution of Controlled Choice, Cambridge realized "a significant increase in the proportion of school-age children attending public schools, including a 32 percent increase in new White students and a 13 percent increase in new minority students" (Alves and Willie, 1987: 50–52).

With the introduction of Controlled Choice, Cambridge also attained nearly perfect desegregation; any school in which the collective population of minority students did not vary more or less than 5 percentage points above or below the system-wide proportion was described as an effectively balanced school. Before Controlled Choice, nearly four-fifths of Cambridge's schools were racially imbalanced and half were racially isolated. In isolated schools, eight or more out of every ten students were of the same race. However, three years later, after the introduction of Controlled Choice, less than one-fifth of the city's schools were imbalanced and none was racially isolated (Alves and Willie, 1987: 85). Nearly a decade and a half later, Cambridge continued to have no racially isolated schools in which 80 percent or more of its students were of the same race, as seen in Table 4.1.

This analysis is limited in scope to the following actions that we promised to undertake. In our consultation with Cambridge, we promised to:

1. Review enrollment projections and assess their implications for facility and program needs for the future.

2. Review the location of programs in elementary schools to determine their impact on the demographic mix and multicultural characteristics of student bodies.

3. Review student assignment procedures and the racial and socioeconomic composition of student bodies in all elementary schools for the purpose of determining if there is equal access for all students to all educational opportunities in the school system.

4. Review the grade structure within schools to determine if there are justifiable reasons why the grade structures in some schools deviate from those in other schools and whether irregular grade structures facilitate or impede equal access.

5. Review the school system's policies for improving less-attractive schools, and for achieving diversity in schools that are tending toward racial and socioeconomic imbalance.

6. Determine whether schools are more or less attractive on the basis of geographic location, characteristics of their student bodies, and other factors.

After analyzing these matters, we promised to tell the school committee what was working well and what was not. Also, we promised to propose action initiatives to remedy the problems we discovered in our examination.

The recommendations proposed in this analysis are designed to (1) increase student choice so that all schools in Cambridge are available to all students on an equitable basis; (2) increase the number of seats available for developmental education which is popular among some patrons of the school system; (3) consolidate schools-within-a-school into a single school focus, in a single building, which most patrons of the Cambridge public schools seem to prefer; and (4) achieve better racial and socioeconomic balance in student bodies in all schools.

The recommendations are based on our understanding of what is good educational practice in the nation, on what is fair to all population groups in this city, and on the prevailing sentiment articulated in our various consultations with Cambridge citizens—that they wanted all of their schools to continue to be available to all students.

While we respectfully present our ideas on how to remedy the problems we discovered, we recognize others may discover in our findings interpretations of which we are unaware and, therefore, may propose additional remedies. The recommendations contained in this book do not preclude other models for organizing the public school system to achieve equity and excellence. Whatever models are recommended, however, should enhance individuals, schools, and the school system

**Table 4.1** Three-Year Distribution of Minority Student Enrollment by Schools That Are above, within, and below the District-wide Percentage of Minority Students, Cambridge, Massachusetts, 1995–96

|  | 1993-94 | 1994-95 | 1995-96 |
|---|---|---|---|

*Level 1 Schools: above 5 percentage points of the district minority level*

| | 1993-94 | 1994-95 | 1995-96 |
|---|---|---|---|
| King* | 64.2% | 65.6% | 66.4% |
| Longfellow* | 63.3% | 64.4% | 65.7% |
| Maynard* | 59.8% | 67.9% | 64.9% |
| Fletcher | 58.5% | 64.7% | 62.5% |
| Kennedy* | 52.7% | 55.7% | 62.5% |

*Level 2 Schools: within 5 percentage points of district minority level*

| | | | |
|---|---|---|---|
| Morse* | 67.2% | 64.5% | 61.2% |
| Fitzgerald | 57.0% | 59.9% | 61.1% |
| Graham & Parks* | 54.4% | 57.4% | 57.3% |
| Haggerty | 61.9% | 59.4% | 53.3% |
| Peabody | 48.6% | 47.9% | 52.4% |
| Tobin | 52.0% | 52.4% | 52.1% |

*Level 3 Schools: below 5 percentage points of the district minority*

| | | | |
|---|---|---|---|
| King Open | 47.7% | 47.4% | 51.8% |
| Harrington* | 48.0% | 48.8% | 51.8% |
| Agassiz | 48.3% | 44.9% | 48.7% |
| Cambridgeport | 41.3% | 46.4% | 46.8% |
| | | | |
| District Minority Percentage | 55.2% | 56.6% | 57.1% |

* Indicates school with a bilingual education program which frequently enrolls a minority student population: G&P—Haitian Bilingual; Harrington—Portuguese Bilingual; Kennedy and Maynard—Amigos Two-Way English/Spanish Bilingual; King—Chinese Bilingual; Longfellow—Spanish Bilingual; Morse—Korean Bilingual.

simultaneously. Our recommendations are designed to achieve these simultaneous goals.

## PLANNING GOALS

1. All Cambridge residents shall have equal access to all public schools.

2. Bilingual and Special Education (SPED) programs shall be distributed among Cambridge schools equitably. Transitional bilingual education programs for people of color, if needed, shall be placed in schools that do not have a strong record of attracting minorities into their student bodies.

3. In developing racial fairness guidelines for student assignments, each racial/ethnic group with a proportion of one-fifth of public school students in Cambridge will be identified and named. All groups with a critical mass less than 20 percent will be combined into a single category specified as "Other."

4. Each school shall be a coherent learning community with its own principal and faculty, its own building, and adequate physical space to accomplish its educational mission.

5. Each school shall develop goals and objectives for the purpose of fulfilling its mission, which may include a variety of complementary learning strategies for the total student body designed to enhance the school as an attractive learning environment.

6. To promote efficient and equitable use of space and resources, student capacity and program location decisions shall result in approximately similar classroom utilization in each school building.

7. All proposals in this planning project shall have desegregative and school improvement effects that simultaneously enhance students, schools, and the school system.

8. Proposed improvements in facilities and programs must be fair to all population groups and shall be achieved in the least disruptive way, avoiding unnecessary movement of students.

9. System-wide recommendations are for the purpose of promoting socioeconomic diversity in all schools.

## SYSTEM-WIDE RECOMMENDATIONS

1. Cambridge should reaffirm and continue to implement the objectives of the 1981 Controlled Choice student assignment plan, which makes all schools available to all students in an equitable way.

2. Cambridge should rescind the March 1989 policy that gives priority in school assignments to students by residential neighborhoods.

3. A walk zone priority for some student assignments may be limited to residents who live not more than one-eighth mile from a school.

4. Racial fairness guidelines for the assignment of students to schools should recognize by name and plan for any population group that is 20 percent or more of the city-wide student body.

5. To guarantee equitable access to all educational opportunities that the school system provides, racial or socioeconomic fairness guidelines may be used, and they should be applied, without exception, to the student bodies of all schools.

6. School student bodies may vary from system-wide racial or socioeconomic proportions of public school students by plus or minus 10 percentage points.

7. Minority bilingual education students who are people of color should be counted as part of the minority proportion of a school's student body.

8. A system-wide grade structure such as K–8 should be adopted for all schools (with the exception of schools that are not large enough for eight grades).

9. If feasible, schools should be able to accommodate two or three classes per grade with a maximum enrollment of 660 students.

10. Assess and upgrade the procedures of the Family Information and Student Assignment Center with new and fair policies to govern student assignments.

11. The system's "assignable capacity" should be determined and adhered to in order to promote efficient and equitable use of space and resources. This process will eliminate overcrowding in some schools and underutilization of space in other schools.

12. Schools, rather than programs, should be the primary basis for student choice and assignment.

13. Waiting lists for students who choose a school but are not assigned to it should be maintained for not more than one year and, preferably, for a shorter period of time.

14. All available seats should be posted in the Family Information and Student Assignment Center, and all students should be eligible to request a transfer to fill available seats under the rules of the Cambridge Controlled Choice student assignment plan.

15. Require that each school improvement plan include the listing of distinctive features and educational offerings that lead to a clear identity of purpose. Each plan should also indicate how a school will accommodate a diverse student body.

16. A proposed middle school curriculum should be included in the sixth, seventh, and eighth grades of all K–8 schools. By doing this, the benefits of the Intensive Studies Program (I.S.P.) in middle school grades will be offered to all students.

## GENERAL DISCUSSION OF REMEDIES

The Cambridge Controlled Choice student assignment plan adopted in 1981 was "designed to provide maximum choice for parents in selecting the schools their children will attend within the constraints imposed by available space [and] the requirements of racial balance and special needs of children" (Cambridge School Department, no date: 16). This plan still offers great promise because, if implemented properly, it will guarantee school desegregation, promote school improvement, and provide choice of school of enrollment. In Cambridge, the choice component is real since all schools are supposed to be available to all students; all students have the privilege of filing rank-ordered lists of schools preferred; and all school assignments are made according to racial fairness or socioeconomic fairness guidelines that apply without exception to every student.

Fifteen years have passed since Cambridge adopted this bold, new plan that other school districts now use. With the passage of time, the plan has become frayed around the edges and some of the basic tenets have been forgotten. Although the Cambridge public school system operates today without any racially isolated schools in which 80 percent of the student body consist of one race only, the number of racially imbalanced schools has increased from one-fifth to three-fifths of all schools since the neighborhood student assignment policy was restored. And the number of racially balanced schools diminished from four-fifths shortly after Controlled Choice was launched to two-fifths of all schools today, as seen in Table 4.1. This fact demonstrates the negative impact of a neighborhood student assignment policy on student body diversity.

With reference to socioeconomic status, most of the Cambridge schools today are imbalanced or isolated. Only two of its fifteen schools may be classified as socioeconomically balanced with low-income students (46 percent of the total school system) varying not more nor less than 5 percentage points around the system-wide percentage, as seen in Table 4.2.

A decade and a half after attaining equity in the availability of educational opportunity for most students, Cambridge was drifting away from this goal as manifested by the disparity in student average achievement scores among its schools. Kennedy, the school with the lowest average achievement score in reading and mathematics on the California Achievement Test in 1995, had the highest proportion of children affiliated with low-income families. Moreover, proportions of low-income children in Cambridge public schools varied in 1995 from a low of 23 percent in Agassiz, its highest-performing school, to a high of 72 percent in Kennedy, its lowest-performing school. These data indicated that a review of Cambridge's Controlled Choice plan should be undertaken and that such a review should determine how to make all schools available to all students regardless of economic status.

Because Controlled Choice continues to be the best way to make educational opportunities available to all students in ways that are fair, we proposed that the 1981 plan should be revised to accommodate contemporary issues that may not have been present or recognized a decade and a half ago. Our investigation reveals that the Controlled Choice student assignment plan in Cambridge was not broken, but it needed a few changes to become once more efficient, effective, and fair in assigning students to public schools.

**Table 4.2** Three-Year Distribution of Low-Income Students by Schools That Are above, within, and below Five Percentage Points of the District-wide Percentage of Low-Income Students, Cambridge Public Schools, 1995–96

| | Cambridge Public Schools: 1993-94 - 2001-02 | | | |
|---|---|---|---|---|
| | 1993-94 | 1994-95 | 1995-96 | 2001-02 |
| Level I Schools: above 5 percentage points of the district-wide low-income average | | | | |
| Kennedy | 69.8% | 75.9% | 71.5% | *47.0% |
| Harrington | 66.5% | 83.3% | 70.8% | 72.0% |
| Maynard | 47.6% | 42.8% | 60.2% | 55.0% |
| King | 52.6% | 52.2% | 59.8% | 63.0% |
| Fletcher | 55.2% | 52.4% | 53.4% | 55.0% |
| Ftizgerald | 58.6% | 65.9% | 48.1% | 45.0% |
| Level 2 Schools: within 5 percentage points of the district-wide low-income average | | | | |
| Longfellow | 48.8% | 41.9% | 47.3% | 42.0% |
| Morse | 55.0% | 48.7% | 45.9% | 45.0% |
| Level 3 Schools: below 5 percentage pointc of the district-wide low-income average | | | | |
| Graham & Parks | 35.1% | 39.8% | 38.2% | 33.0% |
| Haggerty | 45.9% | 45.8% | 33.3% | 27.0% |
| Tobin | 29.8% | 30.4% | 31.4% | 42.0% |
| Peabody | 30.1% | 31.8% | 28.9% | 23.0% |
| King Open | 17.7% | 20.1% | 23.9% | 21.0% |
| Cambridgeport | 19.6% | 21.8% | 23.4% | 20.0% |
| Agassiz | 17.8% | 18.9% | 23.1% | 29.0% |
| District Low-Income: | 45.7% | 47.3% | 45.7% | 41.0% |

\* Kennedy's reduction in percentage of low-income students in 2001-02 is due to placement of Amigos Two-Way Language Immersion Program in the Kennedy School Building.

*Source*: Cambridge Public Schools Student Data Report, Part I: 1995–96—Students Eligible for Free and Reduced-Cost Lunches.

We were impressed with concerns expressed by the school committee, the superintendent, and many parents of children about the racial and socioeconomic imbalance in several schools and the socioeconomic isolation seen in some schools. Much of our study was devoted to understanding what caused these deviations from the original plan and how to reverse their adverse effects. Following is a general discussion of our proposals for the achievement of greater diversity in all Cambridge public schools.

## THE 1989 SCHOOL POLICY FOR STUDENT ASSIGNMENTS

One might ask how a school system that wanted all of its schools to be available to all students could have a disproportionate number of low-income students in some schools and a disproportionate number of affluent students in other schools. We believe that the answer is associated with the new student assignment policy adopted in 1989, which gave priority of assignment to all students according to neighborhood districts that were used prior to desegregation but abandoned in 1981 when Controlled Choice was adopted.

Neighborhoods in most urban areas, including Cambridge, tended to be more or less homogeneous in the racial and socioeconomic characteristics of their residential populations. When neighborhood location was given priority in the assignment of students to schools, such a practice built in a racial and socioeconomic bias that is part of the social ecology of residential living. Our analysis revealed that the 1989 school committee policy on student assignment priorities reversed the 1981 policy that made all schools equally available to all students. The 1989 policy limited the enrollment of students in several schools to the kinds of people who live near them. This policy reduced student body diversity in several schools.

We recommended that Cambridge should return to the original policy of Controlled Choice which made all schools available to all students in an equitable way and which gave priority of assignment only to siblings and a few students who lived within a one-eighth-mile radius of a school.

A brief review of the history of school segregation in Cambridge revealed that racial balance could not be achieved in all schools if neighborhood districts in which students lived determined the assignment process. An open enrollment plan adopted by the school committee in 1972 assigned students to schools by neighborhood districts but also permitted students to attend schools outside their districts. Since transportation was not provided, only a few students took advantage of this option. Thus, several schools remained segregated. In 1979, the school committee retained neighborhood districts as the primary basis for assigning students to schools, but reaffirmed the open enrollment plan and provided transportation for students who chose to transfer to a school outside their neighborhood district. With this plan, several schools continued to be racially isolated but some were desegregated. In 1981, the school committee adopted Controlled Choice that abolished neighborhood districts as the basis for student assignment and made all schools in the city available to all students. Initial implementation of this policy balanced all schools racially and none was racially isolated (Cambridge School Department, no date: 12). With the change in school committee policy in 1989 that reinstated neighborhood districts as a priority component in the assignment of students (Cambridge School Department, no date), several schools by 1994–95 had racially imbalanced student bodies and some were socioeconomically isolated. This policy was harmful educationally and ignored research findings that integrated schools help weaker students perform better but do not harm stronger students.

## LOCATION OF BILINGUAL EDUCATION PROGRAMS

Our analysis also revealed that a higher proportion of students enrolled in bilingual education programs, including the Amigos two-way bilingual program, also participate in the federally subsidized lunch program. If bilingual education programs are placed most frequently in schools in which there is a high concentration of minority students, an equitable distribution of low-income students among all schools in the system will be more difficult to achieve.

## DEVELOPMENT OF GENERAL EDUCATION PROGRAM AND UNIQUE SCHOOL FOCUS

The development of a strong and attractive general education mission and school focus is more likely to attract a diversified student body than any other approach, including the placement of magnet attractor programs within schools.

Encouraging a school to create a whole-school focus by developing a general education mission that embraces all enrolled students is sound educationally. The whole-school focus regards each school as a basic educational unit of the system. Activities to fulfill a general education whole-school mission contribute to the development of a unified school culture. It is school culture that supports and sustains education. Of course, a general education mission may be a many-splendored mission. But all that is done should be for the purpose of advancing and enhancing the school culture that supports and sustains all students enrolled. This approach identifies schools and not individual programs as the basic units of an educational system. Students, therefore, should be offered the privilege of choosing schools, rather than special, self-contained programs within schools.

Comprehensive general education need not be the same in all schools. Indeed, there is beauty and benefit in having schools with different concentrations and foci. They encourage and guarantee diversity and genuine school choice. Such a policy places greater responsibility on school building leaders to work with parents, teachers, staff, community groups, and other institutions to design a common educational mission that is worthy and to which all are committed because all have participated in its development. By following this course of action, the era of special magnet programs within part of a school that is designed to attract a special population group will be phased out as general education and whole-school programs are strengthened.

The whole-school approach contributes to stability and continuity as well as to innovation and change in education. Moreover, it overcomes the potential harmful practice of favoring one racial, ethnic, or socioeconomic group over another by installing magnet programs that are designed to attract some but not all students.

An analysis of students who received first-choice school assignments in Cambridge indicated that general education programs, including those that have a particular focus for the whole school, are programs of choice for most students; and that the highest proportion of students in the system apply to schools with general education programs rather than to school-within-a-school programs that are limited to part of a school's student body.

A study sponsored by the U.S. Department of Education and authored by Laurie Steele and Marian Eaton, titled *Reducing, Eliminating and Preventing Minor-*

*ity Isolation in American Schools* (1996), discovered that "achieving desegregation objectives proved to be more difficult in ... program-within-a-school magnets
... since such programs can affect only a portion of the school's enrollment"
(60–61). The study found that dedicated magnets, otherwise known as whole-
school magnets where all students are subject to enrollment fairness guidelines,
were more effective in achieving desegregation (44).

All of this is to say that better ways of achieving racial and socioeconomic diversity in all schools are needed, and that the development and judicious placement of magnet programs in part of a school is not likely to be the best way to
achieve genuine diversity and full interaction between students of different racial,
ethnic, and socioeconomic backgrounds. Although the program-within-a school
has attracted students in the past, this approach is experiencing diminishing pop-
ularity today in Cambridge.

## FAMILY INFORMATION CENTER

The Family Information Center (FIC) in Cambridge in 1995 was hard to find and
did not have convenient parking. Hours of operation did not meet the needs of
some working parents, especially parents working one or more jobs or parents who
did not have flexible work hours. Outreach services to parents of limited resources
and to parents for whom English is not their first language needed to be upgraded.
Also, we found in 1995 that the counseling and advising program of the FIC was
not as strong as it should have been. Today, Cambridge has reorganized the FIC to
coordinate a wide range of services.

Ways of establishing a more direct link between each of the elementary schools
and the FIC are necessary; one possibility is to require parent liaison staffs in all
schools to work in the FIC one day per week as counselors and advisors. In general, our investigations have revealed that the FIC continues to be essential in the
operation of Controlled Choice but that its methods of rendering service should be
reviewed and revamped from time to time. The Center should be placed in a more
accessible location with adequate parking and public transportation accessibility.

## SCHOOL SIZE AND ASSIGNABLE CAPACITY

Cambridge schools come in a wide variety of sizes and styles. Built and rebuilt
over the past ninety years, the system's thirteen school buildings range in capacity from 343 students at Morse to 788 at Tobin. The buildings themselves also vary
greatly in appearance, from the angular, fortress look of the early 1970s Tobin
School to the more bucolic, pavilion style of Morse and the colorful, contextual
appearance of the new Agassiz School. Each building has its unique character, setting, and combination of program spaces.

By national standards, Cambridge's school buildings are not large. In the pre-1960
period of educational reform, larger schools became the norm in educational planning. In *The American High School Today* (1959), James Bryant Conant made a per-
suasive argument for consolidation of smaller schools into larger, more efficient

schools. At that time, large schools were thought to be cost-effective and able to offer a wider range of specialized teaching services and spaces. However, in *Big School, Small School*, a 1964 study of very large and very small schools, psychologists Roger Barker and Paul Gump provided evidence that smaller schools offer students greater opportunities to excel. Since the 1950s and the 1960s, studies have equated smaller school size with a lower incidence of violence and increased responsibility and participation on the part of students. Some studies have indicated that smaller schools are particularly effective for students who are academically challenged and who come from lower socioeconomic backgrounds.

In a 1989 study for the District of Columbia, the Public Education Association recommended that schools be downsized to between 500 and 600 students. In the January 1997 issue of its newsletter *Horace*, the Coalition of Essential Schools recommended that schools be broken down into "units" of 500 students.

By national standards, Cambridge's schools are not large. Considering only the thirteen school buildings owned by the system, the average school size in Cambridge was 460 students. In 1995–96, only three (Harrington, Longfellow, and Tobin) of all fifteen schools, in owned and rented buildings, exceeded this number. Three schools were under 300, and seven under 400.

In our recommendations, we have suggested that the size of any Cambridge elementary school should not exceed 660 students. This maximum capacity is derived from a K–8 school model in which there are three classes per grade and in which the maximum number of children in a kindergarten class is 20 and in grades 1–8 is 25. Cambridge's policy on class size calls for a maximum of 21 to 23 students. This policy effectively reduces the three-strand school model to 582 students. Even in the larger schools, smaller learning communities could be established within clusters of elementary and middle school grades. Our recommendations were intended to balance the advantages of small school size with the school system's need to use its existing facilities in a cost-effective way.

Table 4.3 indicates the maximum and target capacity of each school building after implementation of our recommendations and the planned renovation of both Morse and Fitzgerald. The target capacity is a planning tool established in a 1991 space-needs study for Cambridge by John Calabro. The target capacity is derived from an analysis of space size for each teaching room in the school.

We recommend an assignable capacity for each school. The assignable capacity would be based on a ratio of the available capacity in the system and an estimate of the K–8 enrollment. For example, if there were 1,000 available seats in the system and 800 students, the system would operate at 80 percent utilization and each school's assignable capacity would be 80 percent of its actual capacity. In this way, the notion of assignable capacities assures that all schools are utilized equally.

Because most students are assigned to schools at kindergarten or first grade, the use of assignable capacities will require several years before the results of more equitable utilization of each school are realized. The long-term effect will be to achieve equity among all schools in their teaching loads, availability of special ed-

**Table 4.3** Comparison of Existing and Proposed Enrollment Capacities by School

| School Building | Existing | | | | Proposed | | |
| | Oct-96 Enrollment | Maximum Capacity | Target Capacity | Utilization | Maximum Capacity | Assignable Capacity | Utilization |
| --- | --- | --- | --- | --- | --- | --- | --- |
| Tobin | 709 | 788 | 727 | 90% | 788 | 648 | 82% |
| King | 661 | 769 | 742 | 86% | 769 | 633 | 82% |
| Harrington | 702 | 643 | 638 | 91% | 702 | 578 | 82% |
| Longfellow | 546 | 504 | 459 | 108% | 504 | 415 | 82% |
| Fitzgerald | 448 | 549 | 494 | 82% | 715 | 588 | 82% |
| Peabody | 426 | 436 | 400 | 98% | 436 | 359 | 82% |
| Kennedy | 377 | 687 | 430 | 55% | 687 | 565 | 82% |
| Graham-Parks | 371 | 408 | 368 | 91% | 408 | 336 | 82% |
| Maynard | 363 | 455 | 446 | 80% | 455 | 374 | 82% |
| Agassiz | 339 | 452 | 407 | 75% | 452 | 372 | 82% |
| Fletcher | 306 | 419 | 388 | 73% | 419 | 345 | 82% |
| Haggerty | 263 | 355 | 317 | 74% | 355 | 292 | 82% |
| Morse | 255 | 343 | 317 | 74% | 575 | 473 | 82% |
| Cambridgeport | 206 | | | | | | |
| Total | 5,908 | 6867 | 6,138 | 86% | 7,265 | 5,977 | 82% |

*Source*: Maximum and target capacities are from the 1992 Calabro Report and 1996 CPS Annual Budget Report. Total assignable capacity is the average of projected annual K–8 enrollment for 1998–2001.

ucation resources, class size, and space utilization. Of course, policies such as lower teacher-student ratios in classrooms with severely disabled students should remain in effect and serve to create program-driven differences among schools.

Assignable capacity, based on average enrollment projections, would result in no Cambridge school having over 660 students. One school would still be about 300 students; four schools would be less than 400 students, four less than 500, and two less than 600. These changes would serve to reduce the number of very large and very small schools in the system.

By equalizing the utilization factor in each school through the use of an as signable capacity figure, each building would have some available, unprogrammed space. This space, could be utilized productively for small group study, confer ence, project space, and staff space. These types of spaces are desirable for current teaching methods which emphasize individualized learning and require more space for a variety of concurrent learning activities. In addition, space should be avail able in all schools for parent activities and preschool programs. We also recommended a universal prekindergarten program for Cambridge. Such a program is widely recognized for its effectiveness in preparing young children for school.

Our 1997 report urged Cambridge to include socioeconomic status in its enrollment fairness guidelines for schools. However, the school board was not ready to do this. Superintendent Bobbie D'Alessandro who arrived after our report had been presented to the community, during the latter half of the 1990s, declared during the year 2001 that now is the time to use socioeconomic status as a diversity factor, especially since courts today seem to be less favorable to the use of race as a diversity factor. Eligibility to participate or not participate in the free and reduced-price lunch program is used as the indicator of socioeconomic status. According to the superintendent's proposal, "each grade in each school [should] be within a range of plus or minus 10 percentage [points] of students who are eligible for free and reduced-[price] lunch." The policy adopted in 2001 expanded the variation to 15 percentage points the first year, 10 percentage points the second year, and 5 percentage points the third year and thereafter.

According to the new rules, race may be used as a diversity factor only if the applicant pool for a school and its grades varies around the district-wide proportions for racial groups more than 10 percentage points (Cambridge Public Schools 2001: 7–10).

Edward Fiske concluded that "controlled choice has for the most part succeeded in its primary objective of fostering racial diversity in Cambridge Schools" and "that using socioeconomic status as a basis for prompting diversity through controlled choice could have more of a positive impact on academic achievement than was the case with a similar policy based on race" (Fiske 2002:168–170).

## REFERENCES

Alves, Michael. 1984. "Cambridge Desegregation Succeeding." *Integrateducation* 21, nos. 1–6: 178–185.

Alves, Michael, and Charles V. Willie. 1987. "Controlled Choice Assignments: A New and More Effective Approach to School Desegregation." *The Urban Review* 19, no. 2: 67–88.

Barker, Roger, and Paul Gump. 1964. *Big School, Small School*. Stanford, CA: Stanford University Press.

Cambridge School Department. No date. *The Cambridge Controlled Choice School Assignment Plan*. Cambridge, MA: Cambridge Public Schools.

Cambridge Public Schools. October 10, 2001. *Controlled Choice Plan* (Working Draft). Cambridge, MA: Office of the Superintendent.

Coalition of Essential Schools. 1997. *Horace Newsletter* (January).

Conant, James Bryant. 1959. *The American High School Today*. New York: McGraw-Hill.

Fiske, Edward B. 2002. "Controlled Choice in Cambridge, Massachusetts," in The Report of the Century Foundation Task Force on the Common School. *Divided We Fail*. New York, NY: The Century Foundation Press, 167–208.

Steele, Laurie, and Marian Eaton. 1996. *Reducing, Eliminating and Preventing Minority Isolation*. Washington, DC: U.S. Government Printing Office.

# 5

# ELEMENTS OF EFFECTIVE PARENT INFORMATION CENTERS

This chapter discusses how a Parent Information Center (PIC) can facilitate the implementation of an effective Controlled Choice student assignment plan. We will indicate information that should be made available to parents so they can choose the schools that are best suited for their children. We also will explore how school districts can ensure that all parents and students are being given an equal opportunity to participate in the school choice application process. Moreover, we will suggest how school districts may ensure that students are assigned to their preferred schools in accordance with the plan's enrollment fairness guidelines. Our experience designing, implementing, and studying Controlled Choice student assignment plans over the past twenty years indicates that these and other important issues can be addressed by establishing an effective Parent Information Center.

## WHY A PARENT INFORMATION CENTER SHOULD BE ESTABLISHED

Establishing an effective Parent Information Center has been recognized as an essential element of successful Controlled Choice student plans for many years (Alves, 1983: 178–185; Alves and Willie, 1987: 76–81; Fiske, 1991: 171–180; Rasell and Rothstein, 1993: 35–47, 76–78; and Willie and Alves, 1996: 38–39). In Cambridge a Parent Information Center was considered essential for ensuring equity and integrity in the implementation of its new Controlled Choice plan in the early 1980s. Prior to adopting the nation's first Controlled Choice plan in 1981, the Cambridge public schools had a neighborhood school attendance policy that mandatorily assigned students to public schools solely on the basis of the students' home addresses. The only "information" that parents needed to know under this decentralized residential-based assignment policy was the location of the school that their child was supposed to attend. However, the central administration provided little if any oversight or assistance in helping parents locate the school their child should attend and responsibility for actually enrolling students in their neighborhood schools was left up to principals and school secretaries who rarely verified students' home addresses. These procedures resulted in hundreds of students enrolling in schools outside of their attendance area, including students from other communities at Cambridge's expense.

Cambridge also had an "open enrollment" policy that was adopted in 1965 following the passage of the Massachusetts Racial Imbalance Act. Under this policy, which was intended to promote voluntary desegregation, the district was supposed to identify available or unused seats in its neighborhood schools and encourage minority and majority race students to make desegregative transfers. However, the open enrollment policy was never implemented as designed, and in 1978 the Massachusetts Department of Education identified hundreds of students who were transferred in violation of the state's desegregation law (Alves, 1983). Cambridge also had several magnet schools and alternative programs that operated their own admissions policies. Although most of these schools and programs of choice had desegregated student enrollments, many of the White students who were admitted to some of these schools had been recruited from the district's minority-imbalanced schools (Alves, 1983). In light of the above deficiencies in the district's traditional student assignment policy, Mary Lou McGrath, the then superintendent of Cambridge public schools, declared that "the Parent Information Center was needed to ensure that the assignments of all elementary students meet the requirements of the Controlled Choice Desegregation Plan. Centralizing information about schools and student assignments was strongly encouraged by parents, faculty, students, and community representatives" (Cambridge Public Schools Student Assignment and Elementary School Application Information, 1986: 1).

The importance of having a Parent Information Center was also acknowledged by the St. Lucie County School Board when it created two PICs as part of its Controlled Choice plan in the early 1990s. A published statement indicates that

> the District believes that parental choice is a vital part of a child's education. The District realizes that parents do not always have the information necessary to make informed choices. Therefore, it is the responsibility of the District to provide information and assistance to parents as they make choices for their children. Parent Information Centers will be maintained in at least two locations [and] additional sites may be established as the need arises. It is the responsibility of the District to provide information and assistance to all parents as they make choices for their children. (St. Lucie County School District Controlled Choice Student Assignment, Part V, 1992: 133)

A Parent Information Center has also played a crucial role in implementing the Controlled Choice plan in the Lee County School District since the plan was

adopted in 1997. According to this school district, "the function of the Parent Information Centers is to assist parents and guardians in maximizing the options of
school choice for their children. Parent Information Centers will be maintained in
convenient locations in each choice zone" (School District of Lee County, Florida,
Controlled Choice Plan for Student Assignment, 1987: 8–9).

Each of these plans charged the PIC with responsibility for carrying out parent
outreach activities and for collecting and disseminating information to parents
about the rules and regulations of the Controlled Choice student assignment plan.
The plans also specified how the PIC would be staffed and how it would coordinate the school choice application and assignment process.

## INITIATING AN EFFECTIVE PARENT INFORMATION CENTER

We believe the process that was recently used to create an effective PIC in Champaign, Illinois, may provide a useful planning model for communities and school
districts in other sections of the nation. The Champaign School District adopted
a Controlled Choice student assignment plan in 1997 in response to a threatened
federal desegregation lawsuit. Before implementing the plan, the district con-
vened a broad-based multiracial Parent Information Center planning committee
that included parents, students, principals, teachers, school board members, business and community leaders, and central office administrators responsible for
student transportation, public relations, data processing, and management information services, special education, bilingual education, and other programs. The
committee met over a three-month period and considered a host of organizational
and policy issues that would affect the proposed Parent Information Center. The
committee drafted an operational plan for the PIC that included recommendations and suggestions for where a PIC should be located, how it should be staffed,
hours for doing business, cost, and how it should be evaluated. The committee
also made recommendations on information that should be made available to
parents about schools and programs of choice, how information should be disseminated to parents, and other parent outreach activities that should be offered
by the center. The committee's recommendations expedited the creation of the
Champaign Family Information Center and the successful implementation of a
Controlled Choice plan.

The PIC operational plan is updated each year in relation to the following matters: (1) assessing the results of school choice application and assignment process;
(2) establishing a time line for the following school year's entry-grade assignments;
(3) processing new student assignments and transfers during the school year;
(4) developing strategies to improve outreach efforts to parents who did not participate in the early application period; (5) reviewing and updating the information that is being made available to parents and students about schools; and
(6) identifying the professional development needs of PIC staff and other district
staff involved in the implementation of the student assignment plan. The major

lesson to be learned from Champaign is that the development of an effective Parent Information Center is an integral part of the Controlled Choice planning process.

## HOW MANY PARENT INFORMATION CENTERS SHOULD BE ESTABLISHED TO ENSURE THE EFFECTIVE IMPLEMENTATION OF A CONTROLLED OPEN ENROLLMENT PLAN?

Deciding on exactly how many Parent Information Centers should be established and where they should be located will depend primarily on the geographic size of the school district and the number of students that will be directly impacted by the Controlled Choice plan on a yearly basis. Experience with Controlled Choice student assignment plans in Florida and other states suggests that a single PIC should be centrally located within a student attendance zone or service delivery area that enrolls up to 30,000 students in grades K–12. A PIC's service delivery area could encompass an entire school district if it enrolled less than 30,000 students. Since most students assigned to schools in a Controlled Choice plan are students in the entering grades for elementary, middle, and high schools, the number of students annually assigned by the PIC is substantially less than the district's total student population. Others who may need the services of the PIC are students who enroll in the district during the school year and students already enrolled who wish to be transferred to another school. The number of students who will likely enroll in kindergarten, grade 6, and grade 9, if these are the entry grades of the district's elementary, middle, and high schools, usually represent about 20 percent of the district total enrollment. The district can also estimate the number of new students that will likely enroll during the school year by analyzing its yearly mobility rate, which is defined as the percentage of the district's total enrollment that enters and leaves the school district during a school year. The number of newly enrolled students in the district is usually about one-half of the district's total mobility rate, which is about 15 percent in most Florida school districts. Experience suggests that less than 10 percent of the students enrolled in the district will request voluntary transfers under a Controlled Choice student assignment plan. This figure is usually less than 10 percent because generally most parents are satisfied with their children's school of enrollment when they have been assigned under Controlled Choice. The above discussion suggests that about 40 percent of a district's student population should be directly affected by the implementation of a Controlled Choice plan on a yearly basis. This means that a school district with 30,000 students should have a PIC that is capable servicing approximately 12,000 students during the course of the school year.

Where Parent Information Centers are located is an essential issue. The Malden public school system in Massachusetts, which enrolls approximately 5,000 students, has one PIC that is centrally located in the district's only high school. It has plenty of free parking and is accessible to public transportation. The Champaign Community School District in Illinois enrolls about 9,000 students and has one PIC located in a rented facility in the middle of the district with ample parking and access to public transportation. The Lowell public schools in Massachusetts enroll over 16,000 students and have two school choice attendance zones and one PIC, which is located in the district's central administration building in downtown Lowell. The Rockford School District in Illinois enrolls about 26,000 students and has three school choice attendance zones and one PIC. The Rockford PIC is located in a former junior high school in the district's West Zone, which is predominantly African American. This single center is solely responsible for enrolling students in the district's thirty-nine elementary schools, eight middle schools, and four high schools. The St. Lucie County School District in Florida enrolls nearly 30,000 students and has three school choice attendance zones and two PICs. One PIC is located in a building adjacent to the district's central office in Ft. Pierce. It provides office space for the PIC director and staff who implement the district's Controlled Choice student assignment plan. The other PIC is a one-person satellite office located in a county-owned building near the district's transportation facility in Port St. Lucie. It serves parents who reside in the southern part of the district. Both centers have ample free parking but are not readily accessible by public transportation.

When the St. Lucie County Controlled Choice Plan was initiated in the early 1990s, parents were required to register their children at the Parent Information Centers. However, in the mid-1990s the district began allowing parents to register for Controlled Choice at local schools instead of the Parent Information Center. This practice, instituted for the convenience of parents, has created problems for the district's Transportation Department because of inaccurate information given by parents on school choice application forms.

The Lee County School District in Florida enrolls about 53,500 students in grades K–12 and has three Controlled Choice attendance zones and only one Parent Information Center. The Lee County PIC, which has been in operation since 1998, serves over 25,000 students yearly. The PIC is very busy in August and September with hundreds of parents registering their children at the start of the school year. During this peak enrollment period, the PIC allows some parents to complete the student registration and school choice application forms at local public schools. However, as in St. Lucie, this practice of decentralizing the student registration process has caused problems with incomplete and inaccurate school choice applications submitted to the PIC.

The Boston public schools enroll approximately 65,000 students. When its Controlled Choice Plan was initiated in 1989, the district had three school choice attendance zones for elementary and middle school students and a district-wide zone for Boston's seventeen high schools. Each elementary and middle school attendance zone had its own PIC. Also, Boston operated a separate PIC for high school students and a satellite center in the district's central headquarters.

School districts that enroll less than 30,000 students may effectively implement a Controlled Choice Plan with one centrally located Parent Information Center. A single PIC with maybe one or more satellite centers for students who reside in outlying areas could serve the needs of parents in these medium- to small-size school districts. Districts that enroll between 30,000 and 60,000 students may require two PICs with satellite centers if needed. A ratio of one PIC for every 30,000 students is a useful way of determining the number of PICs required to render efficient and effective service.

## MANAGING A PARENT INFORMATION CENTER

A Parent Information Center needs a full-time administrator who is responsible for supervising personnel and managing the day-to-day operations of the center. The director should have strong managerial and interpersonal skills and should be compensated at a level comparable to other senior noninstructional administrators with district-wide duties. The PIC director should be responsible for all student assignment decisions and should be held accountable for ensuring the integrity of the school choice application and assignment process. The PIC directors should report directly to the superintendent or to a cabinet-level administrator who has direct access to the superintendent. This reporting relationship is important because the PIC director should have the authority to enroll students and make other decisions regarding school attendance that are limited to principals and other high-level administrators in some school districts.

Some school districts have appointed professional educators with advanced degrees and individuals with strong community-based experience to manage their PICs. Both experiences are helpful prerequisites for a PIC director since this person must have credibility with school officials as well as parents from all segments of the community.

## STAFFING A PARENT INFORMATION CENTER

PIC directors usually supervise staff persons who may be characterized as parent liaisons, school choice specialists, and data management specialists. The *parent liaison* is responsible for conducting parent outreach activities to ensure that parents from all segments of the community participate in the school choice application and assignment process. This staff member may also help register new students, coordinate parent visitations to schools, and organize informational workshops to explain the school choice application process, including the dissemination of information about individual schools and programs with special attention given to parents and students in low-income populations.

The *school choice specialist's* primary duty is to help parents make informed decisions about schools and programs they want their children to attend. The choice specialist serves as a counselor to parents who may have difficulty understanding the information that is available. The choice specialist is an advocate for parents and students and should not steer parents into or away from certain schools. The choice specialist is responsible for providing parents and students with accurate and useful information about the district's schools and programs.

Providing parents with accurate and timely information about individual schools and programs is a huge task that involves reaching out into the entire school district. Over the years, PICs have developed a number of creative ways to reach parents who may not know how to effectively participate in the school choice application and assignment process. In Cambridge, which established the nation's first Controlled Choice PIC in 1981, the director and staff set up student registration booths in the city's low-income housing projects and went door to door to get parents to register their children for kindergarten. In Lowell, Massachusetts, few Southeast Asian parents were participating in the "early" Controlled Choice application period until the PIC hired Vietnamese and Cambodian staff, who disseminated student registration information in churches, grocery stores, and homes throughout the Southeast Asian community. Boston PICs conduct an annual "showcase of schools" in one of the city's major convention centers. In Rockford, Illinois, the PIC puts school choice application information on billboards throughout the city and has a regular program on cable television. Cambridge also adopted a school choice "open-door" policy and was a pioneer in the practice of allowing parents and students to visit schools when schools are in session. The school tours are coordinated by the PIC in cooperation with principals, teachers, and parent volunteers who already have children enrolled in the school. Community outreach and family-counseling services are enhanced when the PIC staff reflects the racial, ethnic, linguistic, and socioeconomic diversity of the community that it serves.

The other kind of staff required in a PIC can be characterized as a data management specialist. The person in this position is responsible for processing student registration and school choice application forms and maintaining all records and documents pertaining to student assignments. Since maintaining accurate records and assigning students in an objective and tamper-free manner is essential to ensuring the integrity of the Controlled Choice plan, the data management specialist must have extensive knowledge of the district's computer operations and must report directly to the PIC director.

The PIC should also have access to district personnel who are knowledgeable about the district's student transportation services so that parents may get information on whether or not their children need transportation to attend their preferred schools. The PIC staff should also have information on the time and distance of bus routes, and they should know if transportation services are available for afterschool programs. The PIC should have staff who can communicate with non-English-speaking parents and who can translate school choice application forms and all other documents that pertain to Controlled Choice into the major languages that are spoken in the district.

The Brockton, Massachusetts, PIC recently added another PIC staff member who is responsible for coordinating the school district's parent involvement program. This staff member has upgraded and expanded the role of the PIC in the delivery of services to parents that support student learning, health and nutrition, home/school communications, volunteering, school-based decision making, and community outreach. This Parent Involvement Program has been in operation for three years and has sponsored events involving more than 33,000 parents and students, conducted over 500 school tours, and trained over 300 volunteers who have logged more than 8,000 academic tutoring hours in the district's fifteen elementary schools and four junior high schools.

## HELPING PARENTS MAKE INFORMED SCHOOL CHOICES

The PIC staff should be responsive to the needs of parents and students at each educational level of the district. While PIC staff should have a general knowledge about all of the schools and programs in the school district, at least one choice specialist should have extensive knowledge about kindergarten classes and elementary schools and another should have extensive information about the district's middle schools and high schools.

The PIC staff should also develop a relationship with middle and high school guidance counselors. PIC staff and guidance counselors should develop and maintain a cooperative relationship in all schools so that students and parents do not receive conflicting information.

Support for a diversified staff and a diversified approach to providing parent information services is strongly suggested by the results of recent surveys of how and why parents choose schools in two Illinois school districts that are implementing Controlled Choice. One survey was conducted in Rockford, Illinois, in 1998 and a similar survey was conducted in Champaign, Illinois, in 1999. Both surveys were carried out under the direction of D. Garth Taylor and the Metro Chicago Information Center.

The Rockford survey, titled *Rockford Parent Attitudes toward Controlled Choice*, found that parents selecting an elementary school for a kindergarten child were most concerned with small class size, meeting the educational needs of children, and discipline. Rockford parents choosing a seventh-grade school placed the highest values on preparation for high school, preparation for college, and discipline. And Rockford parents choosing a first-choice ninth-grade school placed the highest values on preparation for college, discipline, and assigning homework. The Rockford survey also found that the reputation of the school in terms of safety and educational quality was a top priority for parents at all grades, and it discovered that only a small group of parents (ranging from a low of 13 percent at grade 9 to a high of only 17 percent at kindergarten) indicated that having their child walk to school was their top priority in selecting a school as their first choice. The following are some of the major conclusions of the Rockford survey that may have important implications for parents choosing schools in other school districts.

- Parent satisfaction with the implementation of the Controlled Choice plan is very high in all racial, ethnic, and income groups who live in all geographic sectors.

- There is a large constituency of parents with school-going children who choose schools for reasons other than nearness of the school to their child's home. This constituency is a majority of all racial, ethnic, and socioeconomic groups.

- Public information sources are very important for parents who are trying to learn more about schools that are distant from their homes and that family members have not previously attended.

- Black and Hispanic parents rely a great deal on the services provided by the Parent Information Center.

- Safety at the school, around the school, and on the way to and from school is a great concern for most parents.

- The teaching staff is the single most significant asset a school has for attracting students.

- Parents tend to select a school that has a reputation for teacher openness to communication with parents.

- Black and Hispanic parents believe an integrated school has better resources and better enforcement of discipline than a minority-isolated school.

- Black and Hispanic parents are more highly satisfied than Whites with the educational opportunities provided to them by Controlled Choice.

- Whites seem to be more dissatisfied with the quality of education throughout a school district than with its student assignment plan (Taylor and Alves, 1999: 18–28).

D. Garth Taylor conducted a similar survey of the reasons why parents of kindergarten students select an elementary school under a Controlled Choice student assignment plan in Champaign, Illinois, in 1999. That survey, titled *Champaign School District 1999 Kindergarten Choice Survey*, found that the majority of both Black and White parents indicated that the way school staff treats students is the most important factor in selecting a school. Also, Champaign parents of all racial groups were concerned with school safety, the quality of teachers, and the reputation of the school. The Champaign survey also found that in selecting a first-choice school for their children, a majority of Black parents placed top priority on the way school staff treats *parents*. These findings strongly indicate that the creation of a school culture that is friendly, open, and responsive to parents and students of all racial groups is an important feature of an attractive elementary school (Taylor, 1999).

As in Rockford, a relatively low percentage of Champaign parents (26 percent) selected their first-choice school because it was located near their home. Both surveys also found that Blacks were more likely to use the services of the Parent Information Center than Whites. In Champaign, 39 percent of the Black parents say they rely "a great deal" on the information obtained from the PIC in selecting their first-choice school as compared to only 14 percent of the White parents. When asked how the PIC could be improved, 59 percent of the parents responded that they need more information about the curriculum in the schools, the qualifications of teachers, special programs, and extracurricular activities.

The Rockford and Champaign parent surveys strongly indicate the needs of students and parents that PICs should fulfill. A major conclusion that can be drawn from these surveys is that parents want to know about teaching and learning in schools and how their child will be treated when enrolled in a particular school. Helping parents select schools that fulfill the unique needs of their children is a major mission of the PIC.

The findings of Illinois surveys of parents in two Controlled Choice school districts are similar to the results of a parent survey that was conducted in the Boston Public Schools in 1995. That survey, which was conducted by Bain and Company, an independent research firm, found that 44.2 percent of parents in kindergarten, grade 1, grade 6, and grade 9 selected their first-choice school because of the quality of education as opposed to 20.4 percent who selected a school because of its location (Bain and Company, 1995).

## HELPING SCHOOLS REACH OUT TO PARENTS

The Parent Information Center should also assist individual schools in developing their own parent outreach programs. Each school should be encouraged to develop its own marketing strategy that would include samples of student work and a description of a school's curriculum, programs, and extracurricular activities. This information should be on display at the PIC and also should be made available to parents and students who visit a school.

## CONTROLLED CHOICE ENROLLMENT
## FAIRNESS GUIDELINES

In addition to providing information about schools, the Parent Information Center should also inform parents about the Controlled Choice plan's enrollment fairness guidelines and how the school choice application process and student assignment procedures will be implemented in the district.

### Stability of Assignment

Although a Controlled Choice plan seeks to maximize school choice, the plan should also promote continuity and predictability by allowing students to remain in their assigned school until they complete that school's highest grade. This stability of assignment provision should apply to all students who are already enrolled in a school when a new Controlled Choice plan is approved, and it should apply to all students who are assigned to a public school by the plan. Once enrolled in a Controlled Choice school district, no student should be mandatorily reassigned to another school. However, a district may require students to obtain a new school assignment in accordance with Controlled Choice if they move out of their attendance zone. If a change of residence occurs during the school year, the students should be allowed to remain in their currently assigned schools until the end of the school year. Students may also have to be reassigned in accordance with Controlled Choice enrollment fairness guidelines if their school is closed.

## Rank-Ordered Schools of Choice

All students who need or desire a new school assignment should be allowed to choose the schools they want to attend by their own rank-order of preference. While the exact number of schools that parents and students can select will vary from district to district, our experience strongly suggests that they should select at least three schools of choice. The district's school choice application form should clearly identify the rank-ordered preferences of each applicant as indicated by their first-, second-, and third-choice schools. No school choice application form should be processed unless it contains at least two rank-ordered school choices. The applicant's parent or legal guardian should sign all school choice application forms. These enrollment fairness procedures should help minimize assignments to schools other than those that are a student's first or second choice.

## Facilities Use Fairness Guidelines

Parents need to know if their preferred schools have any available seats *before* they submit their school choice application form. Parents should also know if the school is overcrowded and how many students are likely to enroll in their child's classes. Principals should know how many students will be assigned to their school and teachers should know how many students they will be expected to teach in a given school year. The school board and other stakeholders need to know if the district has enough instructional space to accommodate the educational needs of all of its students. Therefore, the district must establish grade-specific enrollment capacities and identify available seats in all its schools within each school choice attendance zone before applications for school choice are distributed to parents and students. The district should know and share with the public each school's enrollment capacity with reference to regular or general education students as well as bilingual and special education students.

## Identifying Available Seats

The Parent Information Center must maintain accurate and up-to-date information about available seats, and it should disseminate this information to parents in a timely manner. Being able to identify available seats in an accurate and timely manner is an essential matter in Controlled Choice plans, and strongly supports the practice of having the PIC serve as the only unit in the school district responsible for student assignments. To maintain an accurate record of available seats, the PIC must keep track of students who enter and leave the district on a daily basis by school and grade. Computer programs can perform this enrollment tracking activity very well.

## Equalizing and Reducing Class Size Enrollments

Our experience also strongly suggests that establishing "grade-specific" enrollment capacities in accordance with Controlled Choice enrollment fairness guidelines before students are assigned can also help equalize and possibly reduce class size enrollments throughout the school district. For example, a school district that has ten elementary schools and enrolls 1,000 first-grade students in forty classrooms would have a district-wide average class size of twenty-five students. If the first grade is the official entry grade of this district's elementary schools, then each first grade in each elementary school should have twenty-five students. However, some schools may have more than twenty-five students in each class because the school is over-enrolled at that grade. By using the district's average class size as the basis for determining each elementary school's first-grade enrollment capacity under Controlled Choice, a school that had three first-grade classes would have an enrollment capacity for seventy-five first-grade students with twenty-five students per class. A school that had five first-grade classes would have an enrollment capacity for 125 first-grade students—also with twenty-five students per class. By using this approach to set the enrollment capacities in all of this district's ten elementary schools, each school and classroom receives its proportional share of first-grade students. No school should be over-enrolled.

Prior to implementing its Controlled Choice plan in 1995, the number of students enrolled in first-grade classrooms in the Brockton, Massachusetts, public schools ranged from thirteen to over forty students in different neighborhood schools. After the first year of Controlled Choice, each elementary school had approximately twenty-six students in every first-grade classroom, which is the entry-grade of the district's elementary schools. Brockton achieved these results by utilizing the district's average class size as a basis for determining the enrollment capacities for Controlled Choice assignments in all its elementary schools.

## Sibling Fairness Guidelines

Students with a brother or sister already enrolled in their first-choice school should be assigned to that school before other applicants. This sibling-preference enrollment guideline has worked well in many Controlled Choice plans, provided that parents verify the sibling relationship and submit a timely application. Sibling assignments may also be granted for children who reside with a legal guardian.

## Racial Fairness Guidelines

School districts that have achieved unitary status or have never been under a federal court order to desegregate their schools have a moral, if not legal, obligation not to intentionally segregate students by race. As documented earlier in this book, the State of Florida's own school report cards show that minority-group students receive educational benefit from attending racially diverse schools. Therefore, minority-group students and majority-group students should be guaranteed their proportional share of seats in the district's highest performing schools and all other schools and programs of choice.

## Socioeconomic Fairness Guidelines

Controlled Choice school districts can also maximize opportunities for all students to learn by ensuring that students from different income levels have equal access to their rank-ordered schools of choice. This can be accomplished by ensuring that students who qualify for the federal free and reduced-cost lunch program are allocated their fair share of available seats in each school based on their proportion of the district's total enrollment at each grade. In this way, each income group would be guaranteed its proportional share of seats in every school, and no student would be denied opportunity to enrollment in a school of choice because of family income.

## Random Lottery Assignments

In the event that a school has more applicants than available seats, the district should assign students by a random lottery that is weighted in accordance with the Controlled Choice plan enrollment fairness guidelines. In this way, all of the students who are eligible to attend a school of choice will be given a fair chance (a random chance) of being admitted.

## Mandatory Assignment Fairness Guidelines

If a student cannot be assigned to a rank-ordered school of choice, the student should be assigned to the school that is closest to his or her home in accordance with the enrollment fairness guidelines of the Controlled Choice student assignment plan. Our experience with Controlled Choice indicates that only a small percentage of students will not be assigned to a school of choice. This fact has been well established in Florida by the St. Lucie County and Lee County Controlled Choice plans and by Champaign, Illinois, Malden, Massachusetts, and other school districts that have consistently assigned over 90 percent of their entry-grade students to a school of choice for several years.

Experience suggests that "mandatory" assignments may occur during the early application period for entry-grade Controlled Choice assignments when certain schools are significantly overchosen and applicants select only one or two schools of choice. When this situation occurs, the students should be assigned to a school as discussed above. Mandatory assignments are less likely to occur when students enter the district during the school year since these "new" students usually are not competing with other students for available seats when they register at the Parent Information Center.

However, all students who are mandatorily assigned should be placed on a waiting list for their first-choice school. Students who are not assigned to a school of choice should also be given the opportunity to return to the Parent Information Center and select a school of enrollment that has an available seat in accordance with the enrollment fairness guidelines of the district's Controlled Choice plan.

## Waiting List Fairness Guidelines

All students who are not assigned to their first-choice school should be placed on a waiting list for that school. Waiting lists should only be maintained for the entry-grades of the district's elementary, middle, and high schools. When a seat becomes available in a school that has an entry-grade waiting list, the seat should be filled in accordance with the district's enrollment fairness guidelines. An effective Controlled Choice plan also allows parents who are dissatisfied with their child's assigned school to request a voluntary transfer prior to and during the school year. Therefore, waiting lists have a limited purpose and should be eliminated at the end of the first marking period of the academic year.

## Voluntary Transfer Fairness Guidelines

Students who are already enrolled in a school district but are dissatisfied with their current school should be given the opportunity to request a transfer to another school in accordance with the enrollment fairness guidelines of the district's Controlled Choice plan. However, voluntary transfers should be limited to one transfer per school year and should not be encouraged after the end of the first marking period. Students who want to transfer to a school in the following school year should be required to submit their requests at the end of the school year. Voluntary transfer procedures such as those mentioned above should help stabilize student enrollments while also accommodating students who want to attend another school.

## Hardship Assignments

Because the Controlled Choice plan provides parents and students with opportunities to choose the schools they want to attend, few situations will materialize in which a child's attendance at an assigned school may be construed as a hardship. The district should consider "hardship" reassignments on a case by case basis and should only grant such reassignments when the district's enrollment fairness guidelines have been violated or when the physical well-being of the student is clearly at risk. Districts should consider creating a committee to act on hardship requests the same way a jury is assembled.

## Early Entry-Grade Application and Assignment Period

All application forms must be submitted to the PIC by a certain date, and the PIC usually has about one month to process the assignments. Our experience with Controlled Choice plans indicates that an application and assignment process can be effectively implemented over a three-month period from January to March. A school district should be able to early assign 75 to 85 percent of its expected kindergarten students and up to 90 percent of its expected grade 6 and grade 9 students, which are usually the district's entry-grades, during a three-month period.

## Late Entry-Grade Assignments

After the three-month early assignment period ends, all "late" entry-grade applicants should be assigned on a first-come-first-served basis at the PIC. Due to the fact that seats, especially in the most attractive schools, will be filled during the early assignment period, the district should make every effort to make sure that all parents and entry-grade students are made aware of the application deadline in January or February.

## Walk-In Assignments

Students who enroll in the school district during the school year should also be assigned on a first-come-first-served basis at the PIC in accordance with the Controlled Choice enrollment fairness guidelines. The "walk-in" registration and assignment procedures should also apply to students requesting voluntary transfers during the school year.

## SUMMARY

By centralizing all Controlled Choice student assignments in the Parent Information Center, the school district will help ensure that all parents have an equal opportunity to participate in the choice process and make informed school choices. It will help to ensure that the students' school choice applications are submitted in an accurate and timely manner, and that all assignments will be made in accordance with the Controlled Choice plan's enrollment fairness guidelines. A centralized student enrollment process will also provide increased accountability in the management and integrity of student records, and will facilitate the delivery of efficient student transportation services. Finally, it will help ensure the appropriate testing and placement of bilingual students and students with special educational needs. And it will help equalize and reduce class size enrollments throughout the school district.

## REFERENCES

Alves, Michael J. 1983. "Cambridge Desegregation Succeeding." *Integrateducation* (January): 177–187.

Alves, Michael J., and Charles V. Willie. 1987. "Controlled Choice Assignments: A New Approach to School Desegregation." *The Urban Review*, 19, no. 2: 67–86.

Bain and Company. 1995. "Student Assignment Process: Parent Survey Results." Boston: Boston Public Schools.

Cambridge Public Schools. Student Assignment and Elementary Application Information. 1986.

Fiske, Edward B. 1991. *Smart Schools, Smart Kids: Why Do Some Schools Work?* New York: Simon and Schuster.

Rasell, Edith, and Richard Rothstein (eds.). 1993. *School Choice: Examining the Evidence.* Washington, DC: Economic Policy Institute.

St. Lucie County School District Controlled Choice Assignment. 1992. Part V.

School District of Lee County, Florida, Controlled Choice Plan for Student Assignment. 1987.

Taylor, D. Garth. 1998. *Rockford Parent Attitudes toward Controlled Choice.* Rockford, IL: Metro Chicago Information Center.

———. 1999. *Champaign School District 1999 Kindergarten Choice Survey.* Champaign, IL: Metro Chicago Information Center (unpublished.)

Taylor, D. Garth, and Michael J. Alves. 1999. "Controlled Choice: Rockford Illinois Desegregation." *Equity and Excellence in Education*, 32, no. 1: 18–30.

Willie, Charles V., and Michael J. Alves. 1996. *Controlled Choice: A New Approach to Desegregated Education and School Improvement.* Providence, RI: Brown University, The Education Alliance.

# PART II

# SCHOOL REFORM STRATEGIES AND STUDENT IMPROVEMENT

# 6

# EFFECTIVE INSTRUCTIONAL PROGRAMS

School improvement is a basic goal of the Controlled Choice concept. Indeed, it is our position that choice options for students can be maximized only by making all schools effective schools. Therefore, school systems should regard student assignment mandates as wake-up calls for improving school effectiveness.

In our experience, however, this seldom happens. The range of immediate issues that accompany a district's Controlled Choice deliberations (e.g., fairness guidelines, attendance zones, transportation, etc.) tend to dominate a dialogue that is generally disconnected from the system's instructional goals. In our opinion, this should change. While the assessment of educational progress is an ongoing task, school improvement initiatives should be intensified during consideration of a new Controlled Choice policy.

District officials should provide unbiased feedback to individual schools while assessing the efficacy of the district's own's efforts to improve schools. The content of this feedback may be drawn from a periodic in depth review of each school's instructional quality (i.e., a School Quality Review, or SQR). SQRs, which should be scheduled over time for each district school, are generally preceded by a period of self-study conducted by the school itself. SQR findings are highly detailed and include specific recommendations for school improvement.

Controlled Choice mandates also provide opportunities for facilitating other educational goals, such as eliminating overcrowded schools and reorganizing the school district. The number of students assigned to schools could be regulated in part by class-size limits, which the district might include in its enrollment guidelines. Thus, student capacity could be capped not only by space (sometimes called instructional capacity), but also by the educational goal of making classes smaller, particularly in the early childhood grades.

With respect to district reorganization in which attendance zones are created to expand choice options for students, those zones might also serve as the district's

administrative units, thereby decentralizing the system and providing a more efficient span of control over it. District superintendents, or directors, could be appointed to head the zones. Central authorities should make the equitable distribution of resources and programs among these units an ongoing priority. By doing
so, all student attendance and administrative zones in a district will be equivalent
in the quantity and quality of educational services and opportunities offered.

In the event, however, that a school district does not have a comprehensive instructional strategy, we recommend that the system's superintendent, with the
school board's guidance, should begin the process of developing one. In our experience, there seem to be two general approaches for doing this. One is called
"strategic planning" and features the deliberate and systematic involvement of
broad educational and community constituencies. Typically, under this format,
goals are established and prioritized by the assembled participants after a needs-
assessment survey has been conducted by the district. Subcommittees, often chaired
by persons of vision and general knowledge of the community, are formed to address specific areas of school reform. Superintendents eventually receive final reports from the subcommittees, select recommendations from the reports, then prepare and submit a coherent plan of action to school boards for approval.

The process is often a long one, sometimes taking more than a year to complete.
In this instance, in fact, the process is as important as the product itself. Its aim is
to get all major stakeholders in the project's success safely "on board," thereby reducing the likelihood of serious political opposition to the plan once implementation has begun.

This process is clearly articulated in the 1984 volume of the American Association of School Administrators (AASA) titled "Planning for Tomorrow's Schools."
In it, the authors stress that educational planning "may reside less in its technical
adequacy or vision than in the processes it conditions and the political environment within which it functions. By bringing together all of the groups who have
an interest in a district's educational plan (and by letting them shape the plan
through their discussion and debate) the district gains support for the resulting
plan" (p. 9). Strategic planning of this nature may be employed to address a range
of educational issues, including curriculum, facilities, human resource development, and student assignment itself. In a 1999 AASA publication, "Preparing
Schools and School Systems for the 21st century," guidance is provided on how
to use strategic planning for revitalizing the educational mission of school districts
as they enter the twenty-first century. Themes of equity, standardized curriculum,
high expectations of student performance, shared leadership, and the importance
of technology are among the sixteen characteristics of effective twenty-first-
century school systems that the volume identifies. School districts are advised in
the volume to convene up to sixty representatives with school and community affiliations who will launch well-publicized planning sessions for infusing these
themes into the district's educational offerings.

While strategic planning is of value, we nevertheless offer a cautionary note
drawn from a study we conducted of school politics in Boston (Edwards and Willie,

1998). While the extended duration of the strategic planning process can have the advantages of consolidating political support and postponing judgments about instructional progress, such advantages may come at a price. For example, if the district's most urgent academic challenges are not being conspicuously addressed during this planning period, they may come back to haunt a superintendent and his or her administration. This occurred in the Boston public schools during the 1985–90 administration of superintendent Laval Wilson. Dr. Wilson spent close to a year developing a strategic plan through a process that was broadly inclusive. When the plan was submitted to the school committee in 1987, it quickly received approval. However, shortly thereafter, when major funding by a local business consortium was scheduled for renewal, the system's failure to improve student achievement was strongly criticized by business elites and other education stakeholders, despite the fact that Dr. Wilson's plan was in its early stages of implementation and was designed to deal with this matter in the future. In the end, Wilson lost the support of the school committee's voting majority, and his administration's inability to raise student achievement during the planning period contributed importantly to this outcome. One learns from this that while long-term strategies are certainly important, short-term results, particularly in urgent matters like student achievement, are indispensable for retaining public support.

These considerations were carefully taken into account, we feel, by the Hillsborough County, Florida, school district when it was engaged in creating a strategic education plan. It would be instructive, we believe, for districts contemplating a similar effort to study how Hillsborough did it. The plan is separated into three parts, each requiring school board approval. Part 1 focuses heavily on the district's core values and its educational priorities, the foremost of which is the improvement of reading skills. This initial segment, which received school board approval, outlines the programs, strategies, time frames, and measurement procedures related to meeting the district's instructional goals. Part 2 will address how the district plans to align its resources for this purpose, while Part 3 will provide details of implementation. Parts 2 and 3 were both under preparation at the time of our study and will be presented for school board approval later.

However, during this planning stage, the district's central office instructional team focused intently on student achievement, particularly in the areas of reading and literacy. The district employs such reading approaches as "balanced literacy," "Reading Recovery," "reading across the curriculum," 2–3 hour literacy blocks during morning sessions in elementary schools, and block scheduling in selected high schools to maximize literacy opportunities for students. It is important to note that identical programs are used in Santa Rosa County, which ranked first in the state academically during the most recent assessment period. Hillsborough, which also has commendable ranking for a large school district, is implementing some school improvement programs now while engaging in a long-range planning project. In addition, Hillsborough's assistant superintendent for instruction is taking the lead in designing a whole-school effectiveness model for the system that will be used to assess and facilitate each school's progress in implementing the principles of "More

Effective Schools" and "Unusually Effective Schools." These principles, which will be briefly discussed later, are drawn from the research of Edmonds (1979), Brookover and Lezotte (1979), Stedman (1987), Good and Brophy (1986), Firestone (1991), Levine and Lezotte (1990), and others. Hillsborough, then, is being careful to address long-term goals and short-term priorities in simultaneous and rigorous detail. The latter effort, moreover, is derived from and is being coordinated with the district's long-range plans. An example of Hillsborough's attention to short-term matters is the superintendent's promise to the school board that Hillsborough will have no "F" schools in the state's annual academic ratings.

Strategic planning in this and most instances, in fact, results from policy decisions by school boards. This fact is a reminder of the powerful potential school boards hold for setting policies that directly enhance school improvement. For cogent examples, we turn again to the two Florida school districts cited above, Santa Rosa and Hillsborough. As noted, Santa Rosa attained the state's highest academic ranking during the 1999–2000 school year's assessment period. When we visited the county to learn more about its educational offerings, we were struck by how a major policy decision had contributed to the district's academic successes. We learned that the district's school board had decided it would concentrate its accumulated resources mainly on instruction, with emphasis on low-achieving schools. One strategy it had used to accumulate resources was to privatize certain services (e.g., maintenance, food service) and assign the savings gained to instructional purposes. It was also pointed out that the district had decided against building "showcase" schools in favor of erecting simpler yet structurally sound ones, at lower costs. These savings, too, we were informed, had been directed toward instruction. Thus, the district has deliberately pruned its budget to maximize its instructional options. In Santa Rosa one finds a strong commitment to the professional development, training, and mentoring of teachers and administrators; the use of highly successful reading approaches (some of which have been mentioned); and regular attendance by professional staff at national and regional conferences to keep abreast of scholarship and best practices.

In Hillsborough County, a major decision by the school board was to concentrate substantial district resources on attracting and retaining high-quality teachers. The decision is reflected in the district's statement of core values and in its strategic plan, where a substantial segment of Part 1 is devoted to the details of accomplishing this goal. New teachers in Hillsborough who hold only bachelor's degrees earn starting salaries of $30,000, among the highest in the state. From these examples, it would seem advisable for school boards in general to periodically review their expenditures and deliberately realign them with instructional priorities.

The other general approach districts sometimes use for developing comprehensive educational strategies is conducted with much less fanfare than occurs during a traditional strategic-planning process. Having articulated an overall educational vision that the school board has approved, the superintendent of the district quietly begins to assemble the resources and people (including school professionals, university researchers, foundation support, parent and community stakeholders) to translate the vision into action. The ultimate goal of the effort is to create a single coherent instructional strategy for the system and a unified framework for implementing it. In the end, the district's schools are on the same instructional page, so to speak, and a common educational focus permeates the system.

In addition to Hillsborough's whole-school effectiveness model, which is still being developed, another example of this process in action is Boston's "Whole School Change" program, which influenced Hillsborough's effort. Spearheaded by an educational foundation, the Boston Plan for Excellence, "Whole School Change," began as a pilot program three years ago involving twenty-seven of the city's public schools. The program employs a single instructional model, with literacy as its common initial focus. It also uses six explicit, research-based strategies called "essentials" for reaching the district's educational goals. Details of the program are available, as are those of similarly promising programs being conducted in Chicago, San Diego, Pittsburgh, New York City, and elsewhere. The point we are making is that school districts can create effective instructional strategies through a more focused, less politically conscious process than the initial one cited. Since both processes have important advantages, districts should select or create planning formats appropriate to their particular circumstances.

In this chapter, the following additional elements of school improvement will be discussed: (1) the principal as instructional leader; (2) teacher recruitment and retention; (3) theory and research pertaining to school improvement; and (4) lessons regarding school improvement.

## PRINCIPAL AS INSTRUCTIONAL LEADER

The most fundamental tenet of any school effectiveness paradigm is that successful schools require strong leadership from their principals (see, especially, Edmonds, 1979). Yet, the roles and responsibilities of principals are quite extensive. Cuban (1988) has divided those functions into three general categories: instructional, managerial, and political. Managerial imperatives, he notes, tend to dominate the demands upon a principal's time. And because political demands are so integral to the job, Cuban asserts that "there is no such phenomenon as nonpolitical behavior" where principals are concerned (Cuban, 1988: 72). But since the delivery of instruction is a school's main function, how then do principals provide the leadership for meeting this basic responsibility? On the face of it, two steps appear to be needed to answer this question. First, principals have to gain control over the non-instructional demands upon their time. Then they must decide exactly how their instructional time will be used. Accomplishing either step is not generally easy. Indeed, it is a mistake, we believe, for school reformers, who are understandably focused on instruction, to trivialize the managerial burdens of school leadership. Unless these burdens are adequately addressed, principals will remain seriously and permanently distracted from instructional tasks.

Moreover, the performance of these instructional tasks brings its own managerial demands. These include classroom observations, the supervision of curriculum, the promotion of best-practices, testing and test-taking preparation, staff professional development, the evaluation of personnel and programs, and a host of other instructional leadership functions for which principals hold bottom-line responsibility. The very meaning of instructional leadership, in fact, is the ability to sustain these functions while making significant personal contributions to the school's academic success.

Our own solution to the instructional leadership challenges principals face has two aspects. First, we recommend that principals impose a conscious level of structure on their work, and we will offer one example for doing this momentarily. Then, we strongly advise a process of ongoing personal reflection for them, under the guidance of a mentor where feasible. In other words, we believe that the "reflective practice" model Schon (1983) recommends for teachers is equally valid for principals—perhaps more so, since principals are more isolated than teachers from their colleagues during working hours and, therefore, have fewer immediate opportunities for reflective professional dialogue. We shall elaborate briefly on both recommendations.

The model created by Cuban (1988) that divides the principalship into managerial, instructional, and political functions is useful for conceptualizing the position. For long-range planning and daily practice, however, performance planning that reflects explicit behavioral objectives has more practical application. It is important to report that this is precisely the framework being employed in Santa Rosa County. There, performance planning is the principal formal mechanism that drives the instructional system. Principals, in consultation with their directors, design both yearly and long-term performance plans that articulate specific objectives and time-framed action plans for reaching them. Directors in turn submit similarly structured plans of their own to the deputy superintendent, and the deputy must submit a personal performance plan to the superintendent. One is impressed by the collegial and informal atmosphere among the county's academic leaders. But the instructional system itself rests upon a solid base of careful planning and review. We regard this framework as feasible for organizing the work of principals and would urge other districts to consider it if they wish to alter their present accountability structures.

The recommendation that principals be given opportunities for guided reflection derives from the personal experience of the member of our team responsible for this section of the chapter. He has served in recent years as a mentor to individual principals and as a co-facilitator of a principals' network, both for the Boston Plan for Excellence, which conducts programs of professional development in the city's schools. The author found strong receptivity among principals for reflective dialogue with a person they could trust, one who understood their professional circumstances, and who held no supervisory authority over them. He also found strong interest among them to meet as a group on at least a monthly basis to exchange ideas about professional challenges, particularly regarding instruction. One should distinguish between this program and traditional professional development opportunities that teach principals important "skills" about literacy, for example, and other instructional priorities. Here, the dialogue is conducted mostly in the form of individual conferences. Its focus is on the self-analysis of leadership behavior and on collegial professional concerns. The outcomes are not necessarily measurable in terms of student gains, but principals have been assisted by this process in meeting their performance goals and have learned from it how to function with greater confidence and authority. School districts might wish to consider this or some other form of professional development whose basic purpose is to promote reflective practice and focused leadership dialogue among administrators.

## Teacher Recruitment and Retention

The classroom is the fundamental building block of any school system. And classrooms are successful only insofar as teachers are competent. Darling-Hammond (2001) cites the research of Ferguson (1991) whose analysis of data from 900 Texas school districts found teacher quality to be the most important measurable cause of increased student learning. Referring to that research, Darling-Hammond states: "Holding socioeconomic status constant, the wide variation in teachers' qualifications in Texas accounted for all of the variations in Black and White students' test scores. That is, after controlling for SES, Black students' achievement would have been closely comparable to that of Whites if they had been assigned equally qualified teachers" (Darling-Hammond, 2001: 14). This fact has profound implications for, among other things, closing the notorious achievement gap between White and minority students, particularly in heavily minority, urban settings, where poor students in low-achieving schools are often taught by under-prepared, uncertified teachers.

The urgency of the situation is intensified by special circumstances in the current teacher market: a generation of veteran teachers is retiring; student populations, generally, are growing; high-stakes testing has significantly increased diploma standards for students; and states, accordingly, have raised teacher certification requirements. Thus, teacher shortages are occurring at the precise moment when intensive new learning and teaching pressures are being applied in the nation's schools. Moreover, for a range of reasons (e.g., uncompetitive salaries, the absence of professional support, pressures to improve student performance), nearly one-third of newly hired teachers leave the profession within the first five years (National Center for Educational Statistics, 1997).

Clearly, then, school districts are well advised to pursue the goals of teacher recruitment and retention through a process of careful planning and review. We have already cited Hillsborough County's efforts in this regard and will briefly expand upon them now. As noted earlier, Hillsborough's teacher recruitment plan was created at the direction of the district's school board. A central figure in the plan's implementation is a full-time recruiter whose responsibility it is to organize and spearhead outreach efforts to prospective teachers. Other major elements of the plan include creating a teacher recruitment team; preparing a recruitment guide; holding annual recruitment fairs; visiting college campuses across the country for recruitment purposes; providing housing and relocation services for newly hired teachers; offering pre-contract binders (guarantees of employment) to selected teacher recruits; and creating a teacher retention committee for developing retention strategies. In addition, the plan calls for annual reviews of the district's recruitment efforts and follow-up revisions of the plan where indicated.

We regard Hillsborough's teacher recruitment plan as one model other districts might draw upon, since it addresses the four major components of personnel processes often cited in the literature, that is, recruitment, selection, induction, and personnel development (see, for example, Castetter, 1992). Under each component, there are key activities districts are advised to pursue within the context of an overall plan for organizational staffing. For example, recruitment requires establishing qualification standards; preparing long- and short-term budgets based upon the assessment of a district's teaching needs; selecting recruiters; planning broadly based, geographically diverse searches; and integrating the recruitment process with those of selection, induction, and development.

Teacher selection, of course, is a most critical step in the process since it determines the quality of teaching personnel to whom children will be exposed (see statement above by Linda Darling-Hammond). In New York City, for example, where the need for qualified teachers is especially acute, the city's board of education was placed under a court order during the summer of the year 2000 that required that only certified teachers be newly assigned to the city's ninety-four lowest performing schools (*New York Times*, September 5, 2000). In this instance, the court was protecting the equity interests of students in greatest educational need. As noted, such students often attend schools that are least able to attract qualified teachers, particularly during teacher shortages.

However, all school systems, even those achieving high academic performance, need competent teachers, and the availability of such teachers is closely tied to a system's recruiting successes. Teacher selection, in turn, is contingent upon pre-established criteria that assure the proper fit between candidates and a system's most vital needs. In Santa Rosa County, for example, where the system's reputation assures a continuous pool of qualified candidates, the principals and faculties of individual schools are closely involved in the selection of new teachers. Their intimate familiarity with their schools' needs and the high level of confidence placed in principals by the district's school board and superintendent make such involvement natural. Still, Santa Rosa and other districts must assure that teacher selection is fair and that candidates are protected against biases, such as those of race, gender, and age. Perhaps the first official step taken in this direction by a school district is the issuance of an employment policy statement declaring the district's intention to follow federal, state, and local equal employment opportunity (EEO) guidelines; to promote affirmative action with respect to race, gender, age, and disability; and, in general, to be fair in its hiring practices. In addition, districts often assign a staff member to oversee legislative compliance with EEO and the other copious employment legislation and regulations dating back as far as the civil rights laws of 1866 and 1871 (see Castetter, 1992: 10–11).

Our personal experience, however, has been that, notwithstanding official declarations and legal safeguards, a district's fair employment policies are no more meaningful than the effectiveness of the individual responsible for implementing them. In some districts, this person reports directly and regularly to the superintendent, an arrangement that assures direct access to power and that sends a signal to all concerned that the district is serious about its equal opportunity commitments.

Even with the best of intentions, however, substantial challenges still confront many school districts in the areas of teacher diversity, quality, and, in the end, sufficient numbers. In Hillsborough County, for example, where a promising recruitment plan is being implemented in a district that enjoys a fine reputation, the 2000–01 school year began with a notable teacher shortage. Santa Rosa County, while not experiencing a teacher shortage, faces the important challenge of diversifying its teaching force. The county has a minority student population of 10 percent, while minority teachers comprise less than 8 percent of a teaching force whose minority candidates total less than 5 percent of each year's applicant pool. Gadsden County, by contrast, where student achievement is the lowest in the state, has a 92 percent minority pupil population (almost entirely African American) and a 60 percent African American teaching force, more than four out of five of whom are female. Having recently visited Gadsden, we are encouraged by the educational changes the district is planning and by the optimism of central administrators, and the grass-roots activists we met. Nevertheless, we are more persuaded than ever by Darling-Hammond's work (2001), reporting that the success of Gadsden's school improvement efforts will depend heavily on the district's ability to attract and develop top-notch teachers, regardless of their ethnicity. All of this is to say that a school district like Gadsden may need special help in developing and financing a plan to recruit and retain fine teachers. Probably several school districts in the United States could use this kind of help.

Returning to the subject of teacher certification, while in most cases it would appear to be a minimal selection criterion, school districts often hire promising uncertified candidates, then assist them in meeting state requirements. This occurs most commonly during periods of teacher shortages in systems like New York City's, where substantial numbers of teachers are at various stages of the certification process. The ability of school systems, in fact, to prepare promising candidates to meet certification, promotional, and professional development needs is a clear example of how intimately the recruitment, selection, and induction processes are related.

Induction is a key step in the personnel process because it addresses the critical issue of retention. Its goal is to assist teachers in adjusting to new assignments and to the overall environment in which they have to work. This means that veteran teachers, too, have induction needs when, for example, they have been reassigned, transferred, or have just returned from leave. Induction needs, for new teachers especially, include not only professional development supports, such as mentoring by experienced teachers and preparation for certification exams, but also a range of mundane necessities, like finding housing, opening bank accounts, and becoming familiar with the geography and culture of the area to which they have relocated. Hillsborough County's teacher recruitment plan is a promising one largely because it addresses these and similar induction needs in appropriate detail.

Finally, we would like to include just a word about personnel development. Personnel development is, in fact, an extension and continuation of the induction process. It addresses the continuous professional development of all staff and becomes the vehicle to their career development. Personnel development is also concerned with the values and mores of a system and with engendering a sense of loyalty and ownership among those who work within it. It is a process through which the system's morale is sustained and continuous organizational growth is assured. In our opinion, personnel development in Santa Rosa and Hillsborough counties has reached high levels of proficiency.

### Theory, Research, and Observed Practice

Upon reviewing the main features of current school improvement models, it becomes clear that the basic strategies for school reform continue to be drawn from the More Effective Schools research of the late 1970s and early 1980s. Cuban (1998) notes that while policy makers today speak less explicitly about this research, its school reform tenets have become "nationalized while dropping the brand name" (p. 403). In the pages that follow, we will (1) list the characteristics of More Effective Schools and Unusually Effective Schools; (2) cite examples of selected traits in action, ones observed during our recent visits to Santa Rosa and Hillsborough counties, and from our experience with Boston's Whole School Change model; and (3) comment briefly on school improvement patterns in middle and high schools.

### *Characteristics*

Led by Ron Edmonds (1979) and others (e.g., Brookover and Lezotte, 1979; Stedman, 1987; Levine and Lezotte, 1990; Firestone, 1991), More Effective Schools research identified five basic characteristics of effective schools that seem to have found permanent acceptance among researchers:

• strong leadership by the principal, especially in instructional matters
• high expectations by teachers for student achievement
• an emphasis on teaching basic skills
• a safe and orderly school environment
• frequent and systematic evaluation of student progress

Levine and Lezotte supplemented this list with additional traits they found to distinguish "Unusually Effective Schools." These traits include: practice-oriented staff development, the use of instructional support personnel, an emphasis on higher order thinking skills, unusually effective organizational arrangements for low-achieving students, an emphasis on guidance and personal development in secondary schools, and the use of distinctly manageable intervention strategies.

## Examples

The school effectiveness trait that has perhaps been most salient in the current standards-based reform climate is the careful attention now being given to student progress. (For a discussion of standards-based education, see Tucker and Codding, 1998.) Attention to student progress has become increasingly diagnostic, prescriptive, and individualized. In Santa Rosa, for example, each elementary school student has an Academic Improvement Plan. The teachers (and principals) are trained in the use of special software, which provides individualized practice for students based upon the results of each child's curriculum inventory. The software is correlated with Florida State Standards and is designed to "fill in" learning gaps, but is not a substitute for a school's basic instructional program. A somewhat similar approach is found in Boston's Whole School Change model where, perhaps, the most prominent of the model's six "essentials" for improving classroom instruction is looking at student work (LASW). Under this model, baseline writing samples, for example, are collected from each student. Teachers are trained to analyze these samples in order to discover common and specific strengths and weaknesses in students' work. Instruction is then jointly planned by the teachers to address common needs among groups of children and to assist them individually.

In the area of mathematics, Santa Rosa County employs a diagnostic and prescriptive strategy that has assisted it in consistently leading the state in this subject on annual examinations. Early in the school year, Santa Rosa's coordinator of mathematics and science distributes a mathematics pre-test to each student in the district who is scheduled to be tested on the state examination later that year. The pre-test is based upon the skills that the state examination will measure. After the pre-tests have been administered, the coordinator and his staff collect and score them. They then develop prescriptive exercises for each student, based upon individual test results, and distribute the exercises to the students' teachers. Thus, students receive supplemental, individualized mathematics practice in addition to their regular mathematics curriculum, which is itself carefully monitored by district and school staff. We were also impressed by how seamlessly the activities of this central office specialist meshed with those being conducted at school sites.

Another More Effective Schools characteristic currently receiving strong attention is the teaching of basic skills. Again, the standards-based movement has reinforced the importance of this trait by setting specific criteria against which student progress can be measured. The basic skills area most often focused upon in this connection is literacy. In both Santa Rosa and Hillsborough counties, elementary schools schedule two-hour morning literacy blocks devoted to concentrated, reading-related activities. We visited one elementary school in Hillsborough that devotes three hours to this activity on selected mornings. This particular school has just been reconstituted to combat a condition of entrenched educational failure and is now being led by a dynamic young minority principal. For literacy blocks to be effective, however, strong teacher professional development is mandatory, and both counties provide this training at the school sites concerned. As mentioned previously, on-site professional development is a trait of Unusually Effective Schools.

Further evidence of Santa Rosa's strong focus on literacy is found in programs of reading and writing across diverse subject areas. During our visit to the county's King Middle School, we witnessed a seventh-grade writing lesson being conducted during a science period and did not realize at first that the teacher's specialty was physics, rather than language arts. At this particular school (one with a low-SES student population that had recently achieved "A" status in the state's school-grading system) literacy is taught in every subject class at least one period during the week. It is also extremely important to note that while comprehensive data on achievement gaps among the school's subgroups were not available during our visit, we learned that the highest scores on the previous year's writing examinations had been achieved by African American girls. The school itself had come in second that year in the state's annual writing examinations. Elsewhere in the district, one notes that high school teachers are receiving training in how to teach reading, and that high school scheduling blocks are arranged to double the availability of literacy and mathematics classes for students who have fallen behind.

Literacy, as noted earlier, is the initial priority of Boston's Whole School Change model, a priority that is reflected in the use of single literacy models at each of the city's schools, that is, schools are required to avoid "projectitis" by selecting a singular, manageable, and schoolwide literacy focus. This policy, too, is consistent with the principles of Unusually Effective Schools, one of which is the use of distinctly manageable intervention strategies.

Regarding safe and orderly environments, every high-achieving school we have ever visited possessed them. While this fact might appear axiomatic, there are important inferences to be drawn from it. First, it seems clear to us that good pedagogy may contribute to school safety by keeping students actively and constructively engaged—that is, classroom disruptions in general are minimized, first, by good teaching. And in high-achieving schools good teaching is the rule rather than the exception. Therefore, teacher professional development that includes a strong focus on effective classroom management should be one priority for creating safe and orderly schools. An alert school administration stays "on top of" student dynamics to prevent the outbreak of conflicts, including those that might erupt between racial groups or among local gangs. Besides prevention, schools can provide mentoring programs, conflict resolution training, social skills training, and parent and community involvement programs to address school conflict (Padilla, 1992; Parks, 1995). Another conflict resolution strategy is peer mediation. Johnson and Johnson (1994) describe a notable example of this strategy involving elementary school students, and Sanchez and Anderson (1990) report on a peer mediation effort in which serious problems among gang members were resolved, resulting in a dramatic reduction in gang-related violence. Peer mediation procedures, typified by those described in the Johnson study (1994), include (1) joint descriptive definitions of problems; (2) an exchange of proposals between opposing sides for solving them; (3) the reversal of perspectives among participants (seeing problems through the eyes of the other); and (4) reaching mutual agreement on resolutions.

In Santa Rosa County, Florida, we observed an excellent guidance program at Hobbes Middle School. Administered by a retired marine colonel (whose compassionate, yet firm, demeanor with students immediately caught our attention), the guidance program at Hobbes is credited by the principal with significantly contributing to the school's recent academic successes. (One is reminded that attention to adolescent guidance is an important characteristic of Unusually Effective Schools.) Both Hobbes and King are Santa Rosa middle schools with significant low SES populations that became state "A" schools during the most recent evaluation period. Both schools stress student discipline and both employ dress codes; yet, student and teacher morale at both schools are extremely high.

Where secondary schools are concerned, we would like to cite the successful leadership at Boston's Burke High School. Here an effective student discipline program has clearly contributed to the school's academic improvement. A common lament among some high school principals is that they are seriously burdened by student discipline problems and, largely for this reason, cannot attend properly to instruction. We have heard this complaint often in Boston and elsewhere, but we have also witnessed how principals, at times, seem to be drawn to such problems. For example, we have seen principals preside over disciplinary hearings that their assistants might well have handled; we have observed them intervening in classroom situations that others might have addressed just as well; and we have even seen one veteran high school principal become involved in a protracted mediation effort at his school around an internal dispute among immigrant nationals whose children happened to be attending the school.

At Burke High School, none of this occurs. The only hearings conducted by Burke's principal are expulsion hearings, and these are rare because the school is under effective disciplinary control. We have observed Burke's principal pass by classrooms in which students were misbehaving and report what he saw to the appropriate assistants, who immediately handled the matters. At Burke, discipline is handled consistently and through an effective chain of command. Classroom teachers, of course, are the first link in the chain. Then team leaders of the small learning communities (SLCs) into which the school is organized assume disciplinary responsibility; next comes the school's dean and then the appropriate assistant principal. Burke's principal takes pride in pointing out that nobody in the chain, especially assistant principals, wants discipline problems to reach the principal's office. Given how well this system works, we can appreciate why Burke's principal has become one of the district's strongest instructional leaders.

Finally, a brief word about the More Effective Schools trait of high teacher expectations for student success is in order. In its fall 2000 edition, the *Harvard Educational Review* published a reprint of a classic study on this topic: Ray Rist's 1970 article, "Student Social Class and Teacher Expectations: The Self-Fulfilling Prophesy in Ghetto Education." In the article, Professor Rist describes how a kindergarten teacher placed children into reading ability groups based primarily on their social class status and how membership in those groups persisted over the early years of the children's schooling. The study has come to provide a classic example of how low teacher expectations for early student success can help to assure future academic problems for children. Since the time of Rist's study, a sufficient body of scholarship on this general topic has been produced (see, for example, Ginsberg, 1986; Ogbu, 1986; Delpit, 1988) to convince the school reform community and, perhaps, the general public that high teacher expectations contribute critically to successful learning. During our observations of schools in Santa Rosa County, Hillsborough County, and Boston, teacher expectations for student success were extremely strong in high-achieving schools.

It is true, of course, that successful student performance can induce strong teacher expectations, but the reverse is also true, which leads to the concluding point we wish to make on this subject. During his tenure as the principal of a Harlem elementary school, the author of this segment of the chapter encountered a learning disabilities specialist who had visited his school to conduct a teacher workshop. After the workshop had ended, the author and specialist held a lengthy and somewhat intense conference in his office about teaching strategies that worked for poor children. At one point, tired, perhaps, of having to explain matters at such length, the specialist turned to the principal and declared, "There is no child I will ever meet that I could not personally teach how to read and write." This remark has remained salient in our memory since it was spoken over twenty years ago. It suggests another side of teacher expectations: the expectations teachers have for themselves as teachers, as well as for their students as learners. Years later we encountered this concept in the literature under the heading "teacher efficacy" (see, for example, Hoy and Woolfolk, 1990, 1993; Grusky and Passaro, 1994). Teachers who possess self-efficacy, Woolfolk found, work harder at student success because they believe in themselves as much as they believe in their students (Woolfolk, 1998). If they have not already done so, teacher education and professional development programs ought to incorporate this finding immediately into their offerings.

## School Improvement in Middle and High Schools

Based mainly upon elementary school research, the early effective schools movement had little impact on middle, junior high, and high schools (Firestone and Herriott, 1982). The latter were different from elementary schools in important ways. For example, they generally had far more students and were usually located in much larger buildings. In addition, curricula at the upper levels were more sharply differentiated and faculties there specialized in explicit subject-area disciplines, unlike their elementary school counterparts. As one consequence of these features, upper school students had to relate to a far greater range of adults on a daily basis than was the case at the elementary level. It is useful, moreover, to distinguish between middle and junior high school designs, the latter being more deliberately based upon the high school's organizational image. Beginning in the early 1960s, middle schools were introduced to provide a more compatible educational environment for pre- and early adolescent children (grades 5–8), who educators felt were not yet mature enough for the rigidities of a junior high school format (Romano and Georgiady, 1994). From their inception, middle schools were centers for developing innovational strategies to meet the learning needs of early adolescence. Among those strategies are flexible scheduling of classes (as opposed to the rigid blocks employed in junior high schools); team teaching; student-centered (as opposed to teacher-centered) instruction; multi-materialed teaching approaches; individualized guidance; on-going attention to basic skills; the use of small learning communities (SLCs); and common planning time for teachers (Romano and Georgiady, 1994; Ames and Miller, 1994).

The last two strategies—SLCs and common planning time—have become especially popular and are widely employed, even in high schools. In small learning communities, limited numbers of students (generally, about 100) are taught all the basic subjects by the same four or five teachers who plan together, review the academic progress of students, and get to know them on a personal basis. Providing common planning time for these teachers is an integral part of the SLC strategy. The success of this strategy has prompted junior high schools and, as noted, high schools as well to adopt it.

Where high schools are concerned, educational reformers have long felt them to be too large, too impersonal as far as students are concerned, and, in general, over-burdening for teachers (Goodlad, 1984; Sizer, 1992; Cuban, 1998). Also, high schools seldom seemed to employ some of the useful and adaptable strategies cited above, like flexible scheduling and team teaching. Recognizing these shortcomings, school systems have been restructuring their high schools for some time now. In 1994, for example, Maryland's State Department of Education designated all low-achieving high schools in Baltimore for radical reorganization. And in 1998, Boston's school system adopted a resolution requiring all of its fifteen high schools to develop and implement plans for restructuring themselves. The typical high school restructuring format in Boston calls for assigning students to SLCs in grade 9, then allowing them to select a career "pathway" program in grade 10. Career pathways focus instruction from grades 10 to 12 around occupational interests, which students select from a limited range of options, such as the health professions, media arts and communication, and computer technology. Undergirding Boston's high school restructuring effort, however, is a set of mandated instructional practices that schools are expected to follow. These practices (such as implementing multiple and ongoing assessments, and using time flexibly) unmistakably derive from the literature on More Effective Schools and Unusually Effective

Schools (for a discussion of high school restructuring in Boston, see Edwards, 1999).

What we discovered, therefore, is that notwithstanding any early resistance to the More Effective Schools movement, middle and secondary schools now seek to employ the movement's basic tenets. Indeed, research conducted on Unusually Effective Schools has facilitated this change since much of it has been focused at the middle and secondary levels (see, for example, Levine, Levine, and Eubanks, 1984; Levine and Sherk, 1990). Another facilitating influence has been, again, the standards-based movement, which has significantly sharpened the instructional focus of the entire educational community. Improving instruction, we found, has now reached an unprecedented level of priority.

In light of this priority status, it was refreshing (for us) to discover that some instructional leaders have begun to challenge certain "sacred cows" of the school reform paradigm. At Santa Rosa's King Middle School, for example, where dramatic educational advances among low-SES students attracted our attention, we expected to find exemplary small learning communities. But, we did not. "What we discovered to be more important [than small learning communities]," King's principal told us, "was 'sequencing.' Our grade level teachers work together a lot, but we don't exactly have small learning communities. We're more into departmental planning: sequencing and subject continuity."

Hearing this, we immediately recalled that when we met with the system's deputy superintendent and his instructional leadership team, we were informed that a major, system-wide "curriculum-mapping" project would soon begin. Its aim would be to assure the highest quality of comprehensive and continuous instruction in each major K–12 subject in the district. Curriculum mapping is a strategy for doing this—for examining explicit objectives, practices, and student outcomes in a particular subject at each grade level. In the end, the entire K–12 scope and sequence for a subject is evaluated on the basis of actual performance, revised where needed, and connected to achieve grade-to-grade continuity. At King Middle School, we learned, this process was already occurring, but on an ongoing, almost daily basis. Planning time is at a premium in all schools, and at King this precious commodity was being devoted primarily to subject-area meetings. It seemed to make sense to us. The school appeared to enjoy a highly collegial atmosphere; teachers and administrators seemed to be working in close harmony. Therefore, some of the advantages that SLCs offer (like following individual student progress, collectively) might be gained through informal contacts and, where appropriate, at department meetings. Moreover, as King's principal informed us, "We tried small learning communities, but they didn't quite work for us. We like each other here, and we work together well. But we found out that we still wanted walls and doors; that's how we prefer it. And so far, what we're doing seems to be working."

This encounter supports our hope that educators in the field are beginning to think and act for themselves. King's principal is familiar with the literature on school reform, but she is even more familiar with the hard lessons of daily practice. Those lessons, in this instance, suggest, perhaps, a reappraisal of certain school reform tenets. She and her staff are uniquely qualified to guide us in such matters because they actually inhabit the often murky zone between theory and practice. And because they do, and are more prone now to illuminate this area for us, they have become the most authentic school reformers we have.

## Lessons Regarding School Improvement

In this concluding segment on school improvement, we will list a number of suggestions on the topic that are drawn from the preceding narrative, from our own general experience, and from a range of literature, some of which has been cited in this book. Where literature and scholarship in general are concerned, we wish to emphasize how important we think it is for educational practitioners (particularly principals and superintendents) to be conversant with both past and current research in their field. Plans for the improvement of one's own district or school should be developed, regularly assessed, and, where appropriate, revised with conscious regard for existing scholarship. Local decisions about educational initiatives will, thereby, become informed by the best knowledge available. Herewith, then, we offer a few suggestions:

- Districts should develop strategic plans for addressing their comprehensive educational mandate, and school improvement should be the central component of those plans. Hillsborough County's strategic plan, and the process through which it was developed, is one model worthy of replication.

- Strategic planning should be sure to include teacher recruitment as a matter of the first importance. School boards should regard the development and implementation of teacher recruitment plans as a major policy concern. This is precisely what occurred in Hillsborough County.

- Where principals are concerned, opportunities for guided, personal reflection on their overall leadership efforts should be carefully built into the district's professional development plans for them. Principals should also be given opportunities to meet regularly as a group for the purpose of sharing common leadership concerns and solutions, particularly around issues of instruction.

- It is better to begin new district projects for school improvement on a small scale, utilizing, perhaps, one or two schools in selected attendance or service delivery zones during the first year. By doing so, districts will be able to identify some of the program's early, unanticipated problems and address them. In addition, through this strategy, the district will develop a cadre of professionals who are experienced in the new program and able to help others as the program expands. For a thoughtful discussion on how to expand promising programs and practices in school districts, see "Getting to Scale with Good Educational Practice" by Richard Elmore, in the *Harvard Educational Review* (1996).

- Similarly, a district's school reform efforts are better initiated through a single, sustained academic focus (for example, literacy) during the first year or two. A good example of this strategy in action is seen in Boston's Whole School Change program cited earlier in this chapter.

- At the individual school level, a single, distinctly manageable instructional focus should be employed as opposed to using an array of models (also known as "projectitis").

- Not only should school leaders learn and promote best instructional practices, but those practices should be deliberately aligned with state curriculum standards. This would help to assure that, at the minimum, all students are exposed to the basic information they are expected to know.

- Professional development for teachers and principals should be deliberately planned to meet the needs of the district's instructional focus, as well as self-identified teacher and administrator needs.

- Schools should be encouraged to create small learning communities (notwithstanding the experiences of Santa Rosa's King Middle School) in which teachers work together in instructional teams and are given common planning time. We still feel this strategy should be given every opportunity to work because it has been largely successful in a range of settings.

- Districts should provide the essential resources needed for school reform (i.e., money, people, time) in a manner that avoids waste and duplication. In other words, districts should be efficient in their allocation of resources, without being insensitive to the needs of particular programs. To ensure efficiency, districts should conduct periodic audits of their educational offerings. Similarly, school boards should, from time to time, review their budgetary spending and deliberately adjust it, where necessary, to better support the district's instructional priorities.

Finally, a few comments about magnet schools and related thematic strategies, such as "attractor" programs. The magnet school concept came into prominence mainly around the issue of school desegregation. Employing courses of study centered upon particular themes (e.g., the creative and performing arts), magnet schools usually aim to attract students of all races from all areas of a school district or attendance zone. Thus, magnets provide one means of achieving voluntary school desegregation. This segment of the chapter, however, has been focused on general strategies for school improvement, notwithstanding the type of school involved. It is our position that the research we have cited regarding school effectiveness applies to most schools, including those with magnet themes. Santa Rosa County, in fact, does not presently operate magnet schools, preferring, instead, to concentrate on achieving maximal instructional effectiveness in each of the more-or-less traditional schools for general or regular education that comprise the district's system. Nevertheless, the authors of this book do support the magnet concept when it is appropriately and thoughtfully applied. We do so, because to the extent that magnet arrangements promote racial and socioeconomic balance in schools, we feel they enhance prospects for higher student achievement. Elsewhere in this book, we discuss the important relationship we found between academic achievement, on the one hand, and racial and socioeconomic diversity, on the other. We are also curious to learn more about the dynamics of that relationship and plan to follow up on this concern in subsequent research. In addition, we support equitable magnet arrangements when they offer students valuable learning opportunities that might otherwise be denied them—for example, when they offer arts programs in situations where districts might have reduced them, due to budgetary cutbacks. For all of the reasons cited above, we feel that magnet arrangements have value. However, in our opinion, the most valuable school arrangements are those that provide research-based, comprehensive strategies to effectively instruct all students.

## REFERENCES

American Association of School Administrators (AASA). 1984. *Planning for Tomorrow's Schools*. Arlington, VA: AASA.

———. 1999. *Preparing Schools and School Systems for the 21st Century*. Arlington, VA: AASA.

Ames, N., and E. Miller. 1994. *Changing Middle Schools*. San Francisco, CA: Jossey-Bass.

Brookover, W., and L. Lezotte. 1979. *Changes in School Characteristics Coincident with Student Achievement*. East Lansing: Michigan State University.

Castetter, W. 1992. *The Personnel Function in Educational Administration*. New York: Macmillan.

Cuban, L. 1988. *The Managerial Imperative and the Practice of Leadership in Schools*. Albany: State University Press of New York.

———. 1998. "How Schools Change Reform." *Teachers' College Record* (Spring).

Darling-Hammond, L. 2000. "New Standards and Old Inequalities: School Reform and the Education of African American Students." *Journal of Negro Education* 69, no. 4.

Delpit, L. 1988. "The Silenced Dialogue: Power and Pedagogy in Educating Other People's Children." *Harvard Educational Review* 58: 280–298.

Edmonds, R. 1979. "Effective Schools for the Urban Poor." *Educational Leadership* 37, no. 10.

———. 1999. "High School Restructuring and the Instructional Leadership Role of Principals: An Interim Report on the Boston Experience." Paper prepared for the conference of the American Association of School Administrators (AASA), New Orleans, LA, February.

Edwards, R., and C. Willie. 1998. *Black Power/White Power in Public Education*. Westport, CT: Praeger.

Elmore, R. 1996. "Getting to Scale with Good Educational Practice." *Harvard Educational Review* (Spring).

Ferguson, R. 1991. "Paying for Public Education: New Evidence on How and Why Money Matters." *Harvard Journal of Legislation* 28, no. 2: 465–498.

Firestone, W. 1991. *Rethinking Effective Schools*. Englewood Cliffs, NJ: Prentice-Hall.

Firestone, W., and R. Herriott. 1982. "Prescriptions of Effective Elementary Schools Don't Fit Secondary Schools." *Educational Leadership* 3: 51–53.

Ginsberg, H. 1986. "The Myth of the Deprived Child: New Thoughts on Poor Children." In U. Heisser (ed.), *The School Achievement of Minority Children*. Hillsdale, NJ: Erlbaum.

Good, T., and J. Brophy. 1986. "School Effects." In N. Wittrock (ed.), *Handbook of Research on Teaching*. New York: Macmillan.

Goodlad, J. 1984. *A Place Called School*. New York: McGraw-Hill.

Guskey, T., and P. Passaro. 1994. "Teacher Efficacy: A Study of Construct Dimensions." *American Educational Research Journal* 31: 645–674.

Hog, W., and A. Woolfolk. 1990. "Organizational Socialization of Student Teachers." *American Education Research Journal* 27: 279–300.

————. 1993. "Teachers' Sense of Efficacy and the Organizational Health of Schools." *Elementary School Journal* 9: 355–372.

Johnson, D., and L. Johnson. 1994. *Learning Together and Alone: Cooperation, Competition and Individualization*. Boston, MA: Allyn and Bacon.

Levine, D., R. Levine, and E. Eubanks. 1984. "Characteristics of Unusually Effective Inner-City Intermediate Schools." *Phi Delta Kappan* 65, no. 10: 707–711.

Levine, D., and L. Lezotte. 1990. *Unusually Effective Schools*. Bloomington, IN: Phi Delta Kappan.

Levine, D., and J. Sherk. 1990. *Effective Implementation of a Comprehensive Development Approach in Secondary Schools*. Kansas City: University of Missouri at Kansas City.

National Center for Educational Statistics. 1997. *Characteristics of Stayers, Movers and Leavers: Results from the Teacher Follow-up Survey, 1994–5*. Washington, DC: U.S. Department of Education.

Ogbu, J. 1986. "The Consequences of the American Caste System." In U. Neisser (ed.), *The School Achievement of Minority Children*. Hillsdale, NJ: Erlbaum.

Padilla, R. 1992. *The Gang as an American Enterprise*. New Brunswick, NJ: Rutgers University Press.

Parks, C. 1995. "Gang Behavior in the Schools: Myth or Reality?" *Educational Psychology Review* 7: 41–68.

Rist, R. 1970. "Student Social Class and Teacher Expectations: The Self-Fulfilling Prophesy in Ghetto Education." *Harvard Educational Review* (August).

Romano, L., and N. Georgiady. 1994. *Building an Effective Middle School*. Madison, WI: Brown and Benchmark.

Sanchez, F., and M. Anderson. 1990. "Gang Mediation: A Process That Works." *Principal* (May).

Schon, D. 1983. *The Reflective Practitioner*. New York: Basic Books.

Sizer, T. 1992. *Horace's School*. Boston, MA: Houghton Mifflin.

Stedman, L. 1987. "It's Time We Changed the Effective Schools Formula." *Phi Delta Kappan* 69.

Tucker, M., and J. Codding. 1998. *Standards for Our Schools*. San Francisco, CA: Jossey-Bass.

Woolfolk, A. 1998. *Educational Psychology*. 7th ed. Boston, MA: Allyn and Bacon.

# 7

# THE RELATIONSHIP BETWEEN STUDENT BODY DIVERSITY AND STUDENT ACHIEVEMENT

In 1967, the United States Commission on Civil Rights presented a report to the president of the United States that included the following conclusion: "Racial isolation damages [African American] students by adversely affecting ... their achievement" (U.S. Civil Rights Commission, 1967: 190). James Coleman, senior author of the study *Equality of Educational Opportunity* (1966), reported a similar finding: "If a minority pupil from a home without much educational strength is put with school mates with strong educational backgrounds, his [or her] achievement is likely to increase" (Coleman et al., 1966: 22). Coleman and his associates sincerely believed that "the composition of the student bod[y] has a strong relationship to the achievement of [Black students] and other minority pupils" (22).

In 1968, James Comer and his associates at the Yale Child Study Center Schools Program introduced a school improvement initiative at Baldwin and King elementary schools in New Haven, Connecticut (Comer, 1980: 54). Comer reports that more than 90 percent of the families in these schools were Black and had low to lower-middle incomes (61). Major goals of the initiative were "to modify the climate ... of the school in a way that facilitates learning" and "to improve the achievement of basic skills" (67–68).

Ten years after the intervention, Comer reported these results:

> The King School fourth grade ranked twentieth in reading and thirty-first in mathematics among thirty-one schools on the Metropolitan Achievement Test in 1969.
> ... The Iowa Test of Basic Skills was used for the first time in 1978–79. The King fourth grade ranked tenth in reading and mathematics [among thirty-one schools

and was] behind only the highest socioeconomic schools in the city and ahead of
a few. (Comer, 1980: 74–75)

In general, Comer reported a good response to the intervention program, particularly in King School. He said, "These developments moved both schools toward
one of the best attendance records in the city, greatly reduced student problems,
minimized parent-staff conflict and achieved near grade-level academic performance" (Comer, 1980: 73). Comer acknowledged that some of these assessments
are "subjective and inconclusive" since a more formal evaluation was not designed
as part of the project.

The Baldwin and King schools remained racially isolated before and during the
intervention. And this condition, apparently, was associated in some way with the
lack of high average achievement scores for their students. Comer said, "Student
achievement on the Metropolitan Achievement Test was up [toward the end of the
project] in both schools, but not at a statistically significant level or in all categories" (Comer, 1980: 189–90). The project's mental health team had accomplished
the goal of making these schools "a decent place for children" (Comer, 1980: 107).
But this alone was insufficient because the achievement scores of the minority students were not raised as much as one would wish.

For this reason, the findings by the U.S. Civil Rights Commission and James
Coleman and his associates require further study to determine if there is a continuing relationship today between student achievement among minorities and student body composition. It is important to study this matter to prevent irreparable
harm to minority students if there is an association, since "[a] trend toward resegregation is manifest across the country," according to Gary Orfield (1996: 359),
and since racial isolation is harmful to African American children, according to the
U.S. Civil Rights Commission.

Elaine Jones, an attorney whose hometown is Norfolk, Virginia, has observed
in Norfolk the trend of resegregation (mentioned above by Orfield) and shares with
us this information: "After ... a declaration of 'unitary status' ... the Norfolk school
district sought and was allowed to return to neighborhood schools which means a
return to segregated school[s]" (1996: viii). Jones further said, "The school board's
promise ... of increased test scores ... and resources for minority schools [has]
gone unfilled as the predictable consequences of racially and economically segregated schools have crushed equal opportunity" (1996: viii). In Jones's opinion, the
Norfolk schools were better when they were integrated.

Coleman offers an interesting conjecture about why integrated schools enhance
achievement among minority students. Coleman discovered that "a pupil attitude
factor, which appears to have a strong ... relationship to achievement ... [is
whether] an individual feels that he [or she] has some control over [one's] own
destiny" (Coleman et al., 1966: 23). He goes on to say that "[African Americans]
in schools with a higher proportion of [White students] have a greater sense of control" (Coleman et al., 1966: 23). He explained that "[Black] children in integrated
schools come to gain a greater sense of their efficacy to control their destiny ...

due to the fact that they ... see that they can do some things better than [W]hites ... a knowledge which they never had so long as they were isolated in all [B]lack schools" (Coleman, 1968: 25). This is an interesting hypothesis that merits both psychological and sociological study.

Coleman's explanation echoes the experience reported by Benjamin Elijah Mays, the esteemed Black educator, former president of Morehouse College, and former president of the Atlanta School Board. Mays began his college education at Virginia Union, a predominantly Black school in Richmond, Virginia, in 1916. Richmond exhibited the same racial practices that he had experienced in South Carolina, his home state (Mays, 1971: 52). Although he enjoyed his year at Virginia Union, Mays said he left and transferred to Bates. He was determined to go to a New England college (53).

Mays said that he wanted to go to New England primarily for one reason—to prove his worth and ability (1971: 50). The environment in which he grew up "proclaimed that [African Americans] were inferior people" (50). Although he never accepted this assessment, Mays said he would never know whether he was inferior to Whites without having a chance to compete with them, an opportunity that was not available in the racially segregated South in 1916 and 1917.

If he could compete effectively with White college students in New England, Mays believed, he "would have *prima facie* evidence that [Blacks] were not inferior" (1971: 50). At the conclusion of his Bates College career in 1921, Mays was pleased to report in his autobiography, *Born to Rebel* (1971), that he "conced[ed] academic superiority to no more than four in his class" (60). Enumerating the ways in which he had prevailed, Mays stated: "I had done better in academic performance, in public speaking, and in argumentation and debate than the vast majority of my classmates" (60).

Because of his Bates College experience, Mays "finally dismissed from [his] mind for all time the myth of the inherent inferiority of all [African Americans] and the inherent superiority of all [W]hites—articles of faith to so many in his pervious, [segregated] environment" (60).

Coleman found that integrated schools have "[a positive] effect ... on the reading and mathematics achievement of [Black] pupils" (Coleman et al., 1966: 29), and that "the achievement of minority pupils depends more on the schools they attend than does the achievement of majority pupils" (22).

We bring to your attention data derived from pilot studies we conducted in Boston and Cambridge (Massachusetts), Charleston County (South Carolina), and Hillsborough County (Florida) that demonstrate an association between student body diversity and achievement. Each of these studies directly or indirectly suggests that public school integration is beneficial academically for minority students.

In 1996, Michael Alves, George Hagerty, and Charles Willie published an article, "Multiracial, Attractive City Schools: Controlled Choice in Boston," in the journal *Equity and Excellence in Education* (Willie et al., 1996: 95–102). Boston has had a Controlled Choice student assignment plan since 1989. Students in each school (until 1999) were assigned to their schools of choice in one of three large attendance zones that reflected the racial and ethnic proportions of Black, White, Hispanic, and other groups in the city-wide public school–going population. When the racial and ethnic composition of the student body in a school reflects the population of an attendance zone, such a school is classified as racially balanced.

An "attractive" school is one in which the proportion of students in all racial and ethnic groups chose it as their first- or second-choice school, if this proportion is larger than the proportion of seats allocated for each group in that school. Such a school also is designated as "overchosen."

During a ten-year period, thirty to thirty-five of 117 schools in Boston each year were attractive, overchosen schools. Our research revealed that these schools were better than other schools in significant ways. Their students had higher average achievement test scores and lower suspension and drop-out rates than students in other schools (Willie et al., 1996: 5–19).

In Cambridge, Massachusetts (using 1995–96 data), we discovered that Agassiz—the school with the highest achievement score—had a balanced student body of 51 percent White students and 49 percent Black, Hispanic, and other minority student, while Kennedy—the school with the lowest achievement score—was imbalanced with a student body 63 percent Black, Hispanic, and other minorities and only 37 percent White (Willie, 2000: 204–205).

These findings caused us to formulate a hypothesis that there probably is an association between student achievement and student body diversity. Evidence that such a hypothesis is worthy of testing was derived from an analysis of 1995–96 data obtained from the Charleston, South Carolina, public school system that does not have an equitable Controlled Choice student assignment plan but that, nevertheless, was declared to be a unitary public school system by a U.S. District Court. In Charleston, several schools were imbalanced with some consisting of a single racial group ranging from 90 to 100 percent of the school student body. Indeed, the school in Charleston with the lowest achievement score—Fraser—was 99 percent Black and only 1 percent White. We classified it as a racially isolated school. A correlation coefficient for these two variables—(1) proportion of Blacks in a student body, and (2) proportion of students achieving above the national norm—was $-.81$, revealing that two-thirds of the variance in average achievement scores for students in Charleston schools may be associated with the racial composition of public school student bodies (Willie, 2000: 205). This finding is a tentative confirmation of the Coleman hypothesis that student body composition is associated with the achievement of minority students.

This finding, however, was not applicable to Cambridge, Massachusetts, which has had a Controlled Choice student assignment plan since 1981. Because of the racial fairness guidelines of this plan, no racial group in Cambridge exceeds two-thirds of the student body in any school. Consequently, only 48 percent of the variance in average achievement scores by schools in Cambridge may be explained by the racial composition of student bodies; this fact means that more than half of the variance in achievement scores by schools in Cambridge may be attributed to other circumstances. Several Cambridge schools are racially balanced; a few are imbalanced; but none is racially isolated. By desegregating most of its schools, Cambridge has diminished the association between race and achievement scores found in Charleston County, South Carolina, and in schools elsewhere in the United States.

Hillsborough County, Florida, has a draft plan to delineate its school district into seven relatively large racially balanced regions with each region including several elementary, middle, and high schools. Based on the 1991 School Improvement and Accountability Act, the 1999 Florida Legislature enacted new laws that increase standards and accountability for students, schools, and educators. All schools, for example, will receive grades based mainly on student performance. Since these grades are widely publicized, we thought it appropriate to test our hypothesis about student achievement and student body diversity in a pilot study of Region 1 in Hillsborough County.

Awarding schools grades from "A" to "F," the new accountability system enables the public to see how well a school is performing relative to state standards. School grades are based on Florida Comprehensive Assessment Test (FCAT) performance data.

In general, a majority of the students perform at Level 3 or above in "A" and "B" schools. Level 3 performance indicates student capacity for partial success with challenging test content, answering many of the questions correctly but less successful and inconsistent with questions that are most challenging. Level 4 performance indicates student capacity for success in handling challenging test content, answering most of the questions correctly but unable to answer all questions, especially the most challenging. Level 5 performance indicates student capacity for success in handling the most challenging test content, answering most of the questions correctly, including those that are most challenging. In most "A" and "B" schools, 50 percent or more of the students score at or above Level 3 in reading and mathematics in elementary, middle, and high schools. For writing, 67 percent of the students in elementary school, 75 percent in middle school, and 80 percent in high school tend to score at or above Level 3 in "A" and "B" schools.

A few additional criteria factored into the grading of schools are the proportion of eligible students who actually take the FCAT, their demonstrated improvement in reading from their performance of the previous year, and no substantial decline in mathematics or writing. Finally, the grading of schools is affected by absenteeism, suspension, and high school student dropout rates, if these exceed the state average by more than one standard deviation and have not improved from the previous year.

"A" schools must test 95 percent of their students eligible to take the test. All other schools with grades of "B" or less must test at least 90 percent of their eligible students. "C" schools meet the minimum criteria in reading, writing, and math. "D" schools are below the minimum criteria in reading or writing or math. "F" schools are below the minimum criteria in reading and writing and math. In summary, a majority of students score at or below Level 3 in reading and math in "C," "D," and "F" schools, while a majority score at or above this level in "A" and "B" schools.

The boundaries of Region 1 in Hillsborough County encompass seventeen elementary schools, five middle schools, and four high schools. Because we wanted to analyze both racial and socioeconomic student body compositions, high schools were eliminated from this pilot study. The analysis of socioeconomic status is based on the number of students eligible or ineligible for free and reduced-cost lunch. There is general consensus among educational administrators that such data are less reliable for high school students. Thus, this analysis focused on elementary and middle school students only. Because this is a pilot study, we compared schools at extreme ends of the hierarchy and not all schools in Region 1. There were no "F" schools in Hillsborough County in 1999. All eight "A" elementary and middle schools were compared with all four "D" elementary and middle schools in Region 1.

The proportions of White and minority students in Hillsborough County more or less balance each other; 54 percent are White and 46 percent are minorities. Included in the minority category are Hispanics, African Americans, Asians, and Native Americans. There are several ways of defining "balance" or school integration. Because the majority and minority populations are so similar in numbers, we defined a balanced school in Region 1 as any school in which the majority or minority population was not more than 60 percent or not less than 40 percent. Variations in minority and majority populations in any school between 61 percent and 79 percent or 21 percent and 39 percent cause such a school to be classified as racially imbalanced. And finally, variations in minority and majority populations between 80 percent and 100 percent or between 0 percent and 20 percent cause such a school to be classified as imbalanced and racially isolated.

Five of the eight "A" schools in this Region 1 pilot study in Hillsborough County are balanced racially, as seen in Table 7.1. This fact means that only three of the eight "A" schools are imbalanced racially. In the three imbalanced schools (including one school that is isolated racially), Whites range from 59 percent to 65 percent of the student body in two imbalanced schools and minorities are 87 percent in the racially isolated school. Thus, most of the high-achieving "A" schools in this pilot study are racially balanced; they are diversified and, therefore, racially integrated.

The "D" schools in Region 1 have student bodies with racial compositions that are the opposite of most "A" schools, as seen in Table 7.1. All four of the elementary and middle schools performing at this level were racially imbalanced with minorities as the prevailing population and two of these four were so severely imbalanced with minorities that they merited the classification of racially isolated. None of the "D"-graded schools were balanced and, therefore, racially integrated. Whites in these schools ranged from 4 percent to 37 percent and minorities ranged from 63 percent to 96 percent.

Minorities are the prevailing population in all "D" schools. In the "A" schools, the prevailing population is shared among Whites and minorities—Whites being the prevailing population in nearly two-thirds of the eight "A" schools and minorities being the prevailing population in slightly more than one-third of the eight

**Table 7.1** "A" and "D" Elementary and Middle Schools by Race, Socioeconomic Status of Students in Region 1, Hillsborough County, Florida, 1999–2000 School Year

| "A" Schools | Student Body | Race | | | | Free, Reduced-Cost Lunch | | | | Racial Composition of School | | | | | SES Composition of School | | | | |
|---|---|---|---|---|---|---|---|---|---|---|---|---|---|---|---|---|---|---|---|
| | | White | | Minority | | Ineligible | | Eligible | | Balanced | Imbalanced | | Isolated | | Balanced | Imbalanced | | Isolated | |
| | | # | % | # | % | # | % | # | % | | W* | M* | W* | M* | | I* | E* | I* | E* |
| Anderson (E.S.) | 484 | 289 | 60 | 195 | 40 | 217 | 45 | 267 | 55 | X | | | | | X | | | | |
| Ballest Point (E.S.) | 423 | 244 | 58 | 179 | 42 | 167 | 39 | 256 | 61 | X | | | | | | | X | | |
| Grady (E.S.) | 565 | 270 | 48 | 295 | 52 | 272 | 48 | 293 | 52 | X | | | | | X | | | | |
| Mabry (E.S.) | 714 | 535 | 75 | 179 | 25 | 571 | 80 | 143 | 20 | | X | | | | | | | X | |
| Roosevelt (E.S.) | 540 | 319 | 59 | 221 | 41 | 317 | 59 | 223 | 41 | X | | | | | X | | | | |
| Tampa Bay Blvd (E.S.) | 669 | 90 | 13 | 579 | 87 | 163 | 24 | 506 | 76 | | | | | X | | | X | | |
| West Shore (E.S.) | 417 | 172 | 41 | 245 | 59 | 72 | 17 | 345 | 83 | X | | | | | | | | | X |
| Coleman (M.S.) | 803 | 523 | 65 | 280 | 35 | 588 | 73 | 215 | 27 | | X | | | | | X | | | |
| TOTAL | 4615 | 2442 | 53 | 2173 | 47 | 2367 | 51 | 2248 | 49 | | | | | | | | | | |
| "D" Schools | | | | | | | | | | | | | | | | | | | |
| Franklin (M.S.) | 746 | 164 | 22 | 582 | 78 | 60 | 8 | 686 | 92 | | | X | | | | | | | X |
| Williams (M.S.) | 921 | 278 | 30 | 643 | 70 | 206 | 22 | 715 | 78 | | | X | | | | | X | | |
| Lanier (E.S.) | 554 | 207 | 37 | 347 | 63 | 140 | 25 | 414 | 75 | | | X | | | | | X | | |
| West Tampa (E.S.) | 693 | 25 | 4 | 668 | 96 | 49 | 7 | 644 | 93 | | | | | X | | | | | X |
| TOTAL | 2914 | 674 | 23 | 2240 | 77 | 455 | 16 | 2459 | 84 | | | | | | | | | | |
| State | | | 54 | | 46 | | 53 | | 47 | | | | | | | | | | |

W*=White; M*=Minority; I*=Ineligible; E*=Eligible.

"A" schools. While there seems to be an overwhelming association between the concentration of minorities in a school and its low level of performance, the opposite is not true—that a high-performing school always has a majority of White students. In three of the high-performing "A" schools, minorities range from 52 to 87 percent.

When all "A" schools are analyzed as a group, balance in racial composition is clearly revealed; 53 percent of students in the combined student bodies of the eight "A" schools are White and 47 percent are minorities. However, when student bodies are combined for the four "D" schools, an imbalance weighted toward minorities is seen; 77 percent of their combined student bodies consist of minorities and only 23 percent are White students. A majority of the high-performing "A" schools are balanced but all low-performing "D" schools are imbalanced racially.

Educators frequently talk about the value of diversity in learning environments but seldom demonstrate how it is associated with achievement. Experts in population genetics have found that "polymorphic populations [are], in general, more efficient in the exploitation of ecological opportunities of an environment than genetically uniform ones" (Dobzhansky, 1951: 132–133). This principle seems to be applicable to teaching and learning environments as well as to ecological systems as revealed in the pilot study of Hillsborough County public schools. Racially, most "A" schools, the better schools in Region 1 of Hillsborough County, have polymorphic student bodies and are balanced racially.

Data on FCAT scores by schools were complete for seven of the eight "A" schools and three of the four "D" schools (see Table 7.2). A majority of the students in Anderson, Ballest Point, Grady, Mabry, Tampa Bay Blvd., and Coleman (the "A" schools with complete data) had scores on the reading and math sections of the FCAT at or above Level 3. In reading, the scores ranged from 56 percent to 83 percent; and in math, the scores ranged from 51 percent to 83 percent. For all seven "A" schools (for which data were available) the change in reading scores increased between 1999 and 2000 from +7 percentage points to +27 percentage points, averaging out at +13 percentage points. For the same "A" schools grouped as a collectivity, the change in math scores between 1999 and 2000 ranged from +4 percentage points to +12 percentage points, averaging out at +8 percentage points.

Among "D" schools, data were complete and available for three of the four schools: Franklin, Williams, and Lanier. A majority of students were at or above Level 3 in reading in only one of the 3 "D" schools (for which data were available in the year 2000). None of the "D" schools experienced this level of achievement in the math section of the FCAT in the year 2000. In two of the three "D" schools, the proportion scoring above Level 3 in reading was a paltry 12 and 22 percent. And these low proportions represented a decrease of 6 to 7 percentage points in reading scores for these schools between 1999 and 2000; only in math was there an increase in the proportion of students scoring at and above Level 3 in the year 2000 compared to 1999. Nevertheless, the year 2000 scores in math were relatively low in the three "D" schools, ranging from 27 to 34 to 49 percent, and, of course,

**Table 7.2** Reading and Mathematics Scores on the FCAT for "A" and "D" Elementary and Middle Schools in Region 1, Hillsborough County, Florida, 1998–99 and 1999–2000 School Years

| "A" Schools | Proportion of Students Scoring at or above Reading Level 3 | | Difference Between 1999 and 2000 proportions | Proportion of students Scoring at or above Math Level 3 | | Difference Between 1999 and 2000 proportions |
|---|---|---|---|---|---|---|
| | 1999 | 2000 | | 1999 | 2000 | |
| Anderson | 39 | 66 | +27 | 53 | 60 | +7 |
| Ballest Point | 57 | 66 | +9 | 59 | 63 | +4 |
| Grady | 69 | 79 | +10 | 62 | 66 | +4 |
| Mabry | 71 | 78 | +7 | 72 | 83 | +11 |
| Roosevelt | 71 | 83 | +12 | 64 | 76 | +12 |
| Tampa Bay Blvd. | 38 | 56 | +18 | 45 | 51 | +6 |
| West Shore | DATA | | NOT | | | AVAILABLE |
| Coleman | 58 | 65 | +7 | 69 | 80 | +11 |
| "D" schools | 1999 | 2000 | | 1999 | 2000 | |
| Franklin | 19 | 12 | -7 | 23 | 27 | +4 |
| Williams | 28 | 22 | -6 | 25 | 34 | +9 |
| Lanier | 39 | 52 | +13 | 38 | 49 | +11 |
| West Tampa | DATA | | NOT | | | AVAILABLE |

were quite different from the range of scores in math (51 to 83 percent) in "A" schools.

An analysis of the year 2000 scores in reading for "A" schools indicates that excellence manifests itself in a variety of circumstances. Mabry Elementary School, which is 75 percent White and affluent-concentrated, with only 20 percent of its student body eligible for free and reduced-cost lunch, has achievement scores that are similar to those of Roosevelt Elementary School, which is 59 percent White and socioeconomically mixed with 41 percent of its students eligible for free and reduced-cost lunch. Despite these differences in the personal circumstances of the students enrolled in these two "A" schools, their indicators of excellence are similar with 78 percent of Mabry's student body scoring at or above Level 3 in reading and 83 percent scoring at or above Level 3 in math compared with Roosevelt, in which 83 percent of its students scored at or above Level 3 in reading and 76 percent scored at or above Level 3 in math. Of the seven "A" schools for which data were reported, Mabry had the highest math score in Region 1 and Roosevelt had the highest reading score in the Region 1 pilot study.

This analysis also demonstrates the beneficial effects of diversity with regard to academic achievement. While Tampa Bay Blvd. Elementary School with a high proportion of minority students (87 percent) and a high proportion of low-income students (76 percent) should be congratulated for moving into the ranks of "A" schools, it nevertheless lags 10 to 27 percentage points behind the four racially balanced "A" schools for which data are available in reading (Anderson, Ballest Point, Grady, and Roosevelt) and 9 to 25 percentage points behind the same schools in math. Tampa Bay Blvd. Elementary School, although an "A" school, also lags 10 to 27 percentage points in reading behind the three "A" schools that are socioeconomically balanced (Ballest Point, Grady, and Roosevelt), and 9 to 25 percentage points in math behind these same schools. The racially and socioeconomically balanced schools have achievement scores consistently at or above the 60th percentile, ranging from 66 to 83 percent in reading and 60 to 76 percent in math.

While some "A" schools may not have caught up with other fast-track "A" schools, such schools as Tampa Bay Blvd. Elementary School and West Shore Elementary School in Region 1 of Hillsborough County should be intensively studied as case illustrations of how to overcome predisposing circumstances that usually result in limited achievement. The latter school has a 59 percent minority population and 83 percent of it student body is eligible for free and reduced-cost lunch. It, too, like Tampa Bay Blvd. School, is an "A" school. The schools mentioned above break stereotypes and, therefore, should be examined fully to determine how to replicate their achievements.

These findings indicate that while we are trying to learn specifically what enhances and promotes high levels of achievement, one feature—diversity—stands out as an important factor according to findings derived from this analysis of one region in the Hillsborough County public school system.

We conducted another study with 1996–97 Charleston County data. Again, our focus was on the composition of the student body. These data are exhibited in Tables 7.3, 7.4, and 7.5. Since Coleman (1968) concluded that the racial composition of a school's student body was related to the achievement of students, we wanted to know if minority students and majority students of high and low achievement responded in the same way to similar learning environments.

The data in Tables 7.3 and 7.4 reveal that the highest proportion of White students with achievement scores above the national norm on the Metropolitan Achievement Test (91 percent) attend schools that are White racially isolated and affluent-concentrated. But the highest proportion of Black students with achievement scores above the national norm (51 percent) attend schools that are racially mixed and affluent-concentrated. On the other hand, the learning environments with the lowest proportion of White students scoring above the national achievement norms (43 percent) are racially mixed, poverty-concentrated schools. For Blacks, however, their least hospitable learning environments in terms of achievement above the national norm (22 percent) are Black racially isolated, poverty-concentrated schools.

**Table 7.3** Proportion of White Public School Students Achieving above the National Norm on the Metropolitan Achievement Test, Charleston County, South Carolina, 1996–97

| Composition of School Student Body | Number of Schools | Percent of Whites Above National Norm | Rank | % of Whites in System |
|---|---|---|---|---|
| White Racially Isolated/ Affluent-Concentrated | 3 | 91 | 1 | 10 |
| Racially Mixed/Affluent-Concentrated | 8 | 87 | 2 | 31 |
| Racially Mixed/Socioeconomically Mixed | 20 | 64 | 3 | 49 |
| Black Racially Isolated/ Poverty-Concentrated | 23 | 60 | 4 | 4 |
| Black Racially Isolated/ Socioeconomically Mixed | 2 | 46 | 5 | 2 |
| Racially Mixed/ Poverty Concentrated | 4 | 43 | 6 | 4 |
| TOTAL | 60 | 65 | | 100 |

Actually, Black racially isolated, poverty-concentrated schools are harmful as learning environments to students in all racial groups but are more harmful to Blacks than to Whites. However, the opposite is not true for all racial groups. White racially isolated, affluent-concentrated schools are settings that support the highest proportion of White students who score above the national norm (91 percent), whereas the highest proportion of Black students who score above the national achievement norm (51 percent) are found not in these kinds of institutions but in racially mixed, affluent-concentrated schools.

While the absence of concentrated poverty in a student body seems to provide a contextual effect for enhancing the achievement of majority and minority students, Whites tend to do better in White racially isolated schools while Blacks tend to do better *not* in Black racially isolated schools but in racially mixed schools. These differences between minority and majority populations are substantial.

There were no schools with Black-isolated, affluent-concentrated student bodies in Charleston. So we are not able to determine if Black students would respond to a Black racially isolated, affluent-concentrated learning environment similar to the way White students responded to a White racially isolated, affluent-concentrated learning environment; neither were there White-isolated,

**Table 7.4** Proportion of Black Public School Students Achieving above the National Norm on the Metropolitan Achievement Test, Charleston County, South Carolina, 1996–97

| Composition of School Student Body | Number Of Schools | Percent of Blacks above National Norm | Rank | Percent of Blacks in System |
|---|---|---|---|---|
| Racially Mixed/Affluent-Concentrated | 8 | 51 | 1 | 7 |
| Racially Mixed/ Socioeconomically Mixed | 20 | 31 | 2 | 33 |
| Black Racially Isolated/ Socioeconomically Mixed | 2 | 31 | 3 | 5 |
| White Racially Isolated/ Affluent-Concentrated | 3 | 29 | 4 | 1 |
| Racially Mixed/ Poverty-Concentrated | 4 | 25 | 5 | 7 |
| Black Racially Isolated/ Poverty-Concentrated | 23 | 22 | 6 | 47 |
| TOTAL | 60 | 31 | | 100 |

poverty-concentrated schools in Charleston. This absence eliminated another comparative analysis between majority and minority racial groups that would have been interesting.

We do know that White racially isolated, affluent-concentrated schools in Charleston in which Whites achieve at their best accommodate only 10 percent of all White students. But in the schools in Charleston in which Black student achievement is the worst (Black racially isolated, poverty-concentrated institutions), 47 percent or nearly half of all Black students are enrolled. We have concrete evidence of what actually harms many Black students now, since nearly half of these students in Charleston attend Black racially isolated, poverty-concentrated schools and have low achievement scores. We also know that the achievement of Blacks tends to increase in schools that are racially mixed but not poverty-concentrated or in socioeconomically mixed schools that are not racially isolated; most Blacks in Charleston do not attend such schools today. Finally, we know that White students in Charleston perform quite well in racially mixed schools that are not poverty-concentrated. While they do not perform at their highest level in mixed

**Table 7.5** Variation Gap between Achievement Scores for Minority and Majority Students on Metropolitan Achievement Test by Student Composition of Learning Environment, Charleston County, South Carolina, 1996–97

| Composition of School Student Body | Number of Schools | Percent of Whites Above National Norm | Percent of Blacks above National Norm | Point Difference In Race Percentage | Percent of Students in System |
|---|---|---|---|---|---|
| Black Racially Isolated/ Socioeconomically Mixed | 2 | 46 | 31 | 15 | 4 |
| Racially Mixed/ Poverty-Concentrated | 4 | 43 | 25 | 18 | 6 |
| Racially Mixed/ Socioeconomically Mixed | 20 | 64 | 31 | 33 | 39 |
| Racially Mixed/ Affluent-Concentrated | 8 | 87 | 51 | 36 | 17 |
| Black Racially Isolated/ Poverty-Concentrated | 23 | 60 | 22 | 38 | 30 |
| White Racially Isolated/ Affluent-Concentrated | 3 | 91 | 29 | 62 | 4 |
| TOTAL | 60 | 65 | 31 | 34 | 100 |

schools, nearly two-thirds of the White students in these kinds of schools achieve at or above the national norm. This figure represented a relatively large proportion of White students who currently experience achievement success in racially or socioeconomically mixed schools.

Since racially mixed schools that are not poverty-concentrated and socioeconomically mixed schools that are not racially isolated are helpful to both majority and minority populations, the occasion is set to broker an honest and honorable compromise. To make an equity decision that helps most minority students but does not jeopardize the achievement of most majority students, we advocate this action strategy after an analysis that reveals that more than 80 percent of all White students in Charleston County already are enrolled in the mixed schools mentioned above but only 40 percent of Black students are so enrolled. So the equitable thing to do is to increase the proportion of minority-group individuals who receive education in multiracial and multicultural settings until they reach parity in this experience with majority-group students.

As seen in Table 7.5, the point spread or gap between the proportion of Blacks and the proportion of Whites in Charleston County with achievement scores above the national norm is greater in the schools that are not racially or socioeconomically mixed. The point spread in these kinds of schools ranges from 38 to 62 percentage points while it gets as low as 15 to 18 percentage points in some of the schools with racially and socioeconomically mixed student bodies. Thus, the mixed schools seem to be learning environments that tend to promote equity.

Returning to the Coleman study and his finding that "the achievement of minority pupils depends more on the schools they attend than does the achievement of majority pupils" (Coleman et al., 1966: 22), we now are bold to declare, based on the Charleston County and Hillsborough County studies, that the kinds of schools that will benefit minority students most are racially mixed and socioeconomically mixed schools. The Hillsborough County pilot study of Region 1 revealed that 47 percent of the students in this region's elementary and middle "A" schools are minorities; they balanced well the majority population, which is 53 percent. However, in the region's "D" schools, minority students are 77 percent of their combined student bodies while White students are only 23 percent. Based on these data and earlier presentations, we believe that, along with leadership, staff development, and curriculum improvements, the achievement of students may be further advanced by diversifying their learning environments.

Because all of the four "D" elementary and middle schools in the Region 1 pilot study of Hillsborough County were homogeneous (that is, racially and socioeconomically imbalanced), we did a study of all seventeen elementary and middle "D" schools in the county to determine if the same pattern held when all low-performing schools were considered. Data are presented in Table 7.6. Sixteen of the seventeen "D" schools (or 94 percent) were racially imbalanced in favor of minorities and half of these racially imbalanced schools were racially isolated with minorities constituting 82 to 97 percent of their student bodies. In none of the "D" schools were Whites a majority.

All seventeen of the "D" schools in Hillsborough County (100 percent) were socioeconomically imbalanced as is shown in Table 7.6. These imbalanced schools favored minorities of limited income, with slightly more than three-quarters (76 percent) of them being socioeconomically isolated or poverty-concentrated—in which children from low-income families ranged from 81 percent to 97 percent.

With only one of the seventeen "D" schools racially balanced and the remainder racially isolated or at least racially imbalanced with minorities, and, simultaneously, with all seventeen schools being poverty-concentrated or at least socioeconomically imbalanced, one may conclude that the county-wide study of all low-achieving "D" schools in Hillsborough revealed findings similar to those that were seen in the pilot study of Region 1 in Hillsborough. The "D" schools are a cluster of institutions that are more or less homogeneous in the social attributes of the members of their student bodies.

Diversified student bodies share experiences and learn how to negotiate with peers from a range of cultural backgrounds. Louis Kriesberg states that "the American tradition of local control in many areas of life has been strengthened as previously excluded groups are included" (Kriesberg, 1979: 431). We believe that school reform and its twofold goal of excellence and equity has a greater possi-

**Table 7.6** The 17 "D" Elementary and Middle Schools by Number of Students, Percentage White and Minorities and Percentage Eligible and Ineligible for Free/Reduced-Cost Lunch, Hillsborough County, Florida, 1999–2000 School Year

| The "D" Schools By Name | Number of Students | Race of Students | | Eligibility of Students For Free/Reduced-Cost Lunch | |
|---|---|---|---|---|---|
| | | % White | % Minority | % Eligible | % Ineligible |
| Clair-Mel (ES) | 834 | 17 | 83 | 87 | 13 |
| Egypt Lake (ES) | 946 | 27 | 73 | 76 | 24 |
| Kenley (ES) | 592 | 49 | 51 | 81 | 19 |
| Lanier (ES) | 554 | 37 | 63 | 75 | 25 |
| Lockhart (ES) | 617 | 5 | 95 | 94 | 6 |
| Lomax (ES) | 227 | 3 | 97 | 86 | 14 |
| Mort (ES) | 1011 | 22 | 78 | 92 | 8 |
| Oak Park (ES) | 658 | 18 | 82 | 94 | 6 |
| Palm River (ES) | 569 | 31 | 69 | 89 | 11 |
| Robles (ES) | 748 | 3 | 97 | 95 | 5 |
| Shaw (ES | 1077 | 14 | 86 | 91 | 9 |
| Sulphur Spring (ES) | 991 | 9 | 91 | 97 | 3 |
| West Tampa (ES) | 693 | 4 | 96 | 93 | 7 |
| Franklin (MS) | 746 | 22 | 78 | 92 | 8 |
| Oak Grove (MS) | 985 | 23 | 77 | 78 | 22 |
| Van Buren (MS) | 747 | 22 | 78 | 81 | 19 |
| Williams (MS) | 921 | 30 | 70 | 78 | 22 |

bility of being achieved by making all educational programs and offerings available to a broader range of individuals and groups.

Student body diversity does not guarantee that the average achievement score of students in such schools will be high. But the absence of diversity in schools with large numbers of low-income minority students is often associated with average achievement scores that are low. This finding means that school context is an important variable that impacts teaching and learning and has to be considered in school reform strategies designed to improve the academic performance of students.

Having been alerted to the significance of diversity and social context, school system policy making and administrative structures that ignore this fact and continue to implement student assignment plans that contribute to racial and socioeconomic isolation for minorities commit unethical (if not illegal) actions that harm and hamper the education of specific student groups. As stated by Joe Feagin, professor of sociology at the University of Florida in Gainesville, "ethical concerns can be part of social science" (Feagin, 2000: 8). In addition to prescribing high standards for students and having high expectations that all can learn, we must also give attention to the learning context and ensure that it will be diversified. Our study reveals that diversity offers a more favorable environment for effective learning for most students than school settings that are homogeneous in the characteristics of their students.

Kriesberg offers other reasons for achieving a better balance in all institutions in society. Among the institutions he discusses, we would include the schools. He writes that "extreme power differences almost invite domination and repression as an outcome" (Kriesberg, 1982: 240). Moreover, Kriesberg states that "when the power differences are not extreme, the outcome is more likely to be a compromise than an imposition" (Kreisberg, 1982: 240).

We encourage schools to make student body diversity an important goal in educational reform because we know that school buildings and school communities are not self-contained islands. It is important for the planners in school reform to recognize that "any specific conflict between parties is embedded in a larger set of social relations" (Kriesberg, 1982: 245). Thus, discrimination, diversity, and desegregation are issues of the day in the community-at-large that must be embraced and solved to the extent possible in our school reform solutions. We close with this strong statement because we believe that the majority and minority populations in schools and society exist in a reciprocal relationship from which mutual advantages flow when they are educated in each other's presence.

Finally, our study reveals that there is an association between race and socioeconomic status, but that the two variables are not mirrors of each other. The high-achieving "A" schools are more apt to be racially balanced than socioeconomically balanced schools. The racial composition of a school's student body in terms of minority and majority students seems to be more strongly related to high achievement scores than the socioeconomic composition of a school's student body. At the bottom end of the hierarchy of average achievement scores, socioeconomic imbalance, including a preponderance of poverty-concentrated schools, seems to be more strongly related to low achievement than minority racial imbalance and racial isolation. Thus, we see that racial heterogeneity and socioeconomic homogeneity have different effects at high and low ends of the achievement hierarchy. At the high end of the achievement hierarchy, racial balance seems to have a primary effect and socioeconomic balance seems to have a secondary effect on achievement. At the lower end of the achievement hierarchy, socioeconomic iso-lation seems to have a primary effect and racial isolation seems to have secondary effect on achievement. These findings contribute to a puzzlement that deserves fur-ther study.

A conclusion derived from these studies of student body composition and stu-dent achievement is that schools, their surrounding communities, school districts, and state education agencies have a compelling interest in maintaining diversified learning environments. Data analyzed in these pilot studies demonstrated that school student bodies in high-ranking "A" schools are more frequently racially and socioeconomically balanced than imbalanced.

Another conclusion derived from these studies is that schools, their surround-ing communities, school districts, and state education agencies have a compelling interest in eliminating learning communities that are poverty-concentrated and racially isolated with many minorities. Data analyzed in these studies demonstrate that student bodies in low-ranking "D" schools are more frequently imbalanced, racially and socioeconomically, and more often isolated or segregated in the char-acteristics of their student bodies than they are integrated, socioeconomically or racially.

## REFERENCES

Coleman, James. 1968. "Equality of Educational Opportunity." *Integrated Education* 6, no. 5 (September–October): 19–28.

Coleman, James S., et al. 1966. *Equity of Educational Opportunity*. Washington, DC: U.S. Government Printing Office.

Comer, James. 1980. *School Power*. New Haven, CT: Yale University Press.

Dobzhansky, Theodosius. 1951. *Genetics and the Origin of Species*. New York: Columbia University Press.

Feagin, Joe. 2000. *Racist America*. New York: Routledge.

Jones, Elaine. 1996. "Foreword." In Gary Orfield and Susan Eaton (eds.), *Dismantling De-segregation*. New York: The New Press, pp. vii–viii.

Kriesberg, Louis. 1982. *Social Conflict*. 2d ed. Englewood Cliffs, NJ: Prentice Hall.

———. 1979. *Social Inequality*. Englewood Cliffs, NJ: Prentice Hall.

Mays, Benjamin. 1971. *Born to Rebel*. New York: Charles Scribner's Sons.

Orfield, Gary. 1996. "Toward an Integrated Future." In Gary Orfield and Susan Eaton (eds.), *Dismantling Desegregation*. New York: The New Press, pp. 331–361.

U.S. Civil Rights Commission. 1967. *Racial Isolation in the Public Schools*. Washington, DC: U.S. Government Printing Office.

Willie, Charles V. 2000. "The Evolution of Community Education: Content and Mission." *Harvard Educational Review* 70, no. 2 (Summer): 191–210.

Willie, Charles V., George Hagerty, and Michael Alves. 1996. "Multiracial, Attractive City Schools: Controlled Choice in Boston." *Equity and Excellence in Education* 29, no. 2: 5–19.

# 8

# MULTIRACIAL, ATTRACTIVE CITY SCHOOLS: CONTROLLED CHOICE IN BOSTON

## CONTROLLED CHOICE STUDENT ASSIGNMENT PLAN

Since 1989, Boston has implemented a new student assignment plan that is called Controlled Choice. While school improvement is a central component of this plan, it actually has a threefold goal of providing student choice, guaranteeing school desegregation, and promoting school improvement. What is distinctive about this plan is that it achieves these three goals simultaneously, not singly or sequentially.

Because of the centrality of school improvement in this plan, it fulfills some of the goals identified by the National Education Goals Panel. However, it tries to avoid the pitfall of this federal initiative that focuses more on students and less on the school as a social system and learning environment. Also, desegregation is an essential requirement of the Controlled Choice student assignment plan.

Controlled Choice is a method of achieving school desegregation that was implemented by Cambridge, Massachusetts, in 1981. Since then, several school districts in Massachusetts have implemented versions of the plan. Boston, Fall River, Lowell, Somerville, and Brockton are examples of cities that have desegregated their schools with a Controlled Choice approach to student assignments. St. Lucie County, Florida, also has a Controlled Choice plan developed by Michael Alves and Charles Willie, two of the authors of this chapter.

There are three components that are essential in a Controlled Choice plan. It must diversify schools according to racial and socioeconomic characteristics of students, provide choice of schools selected for matriculation, and promote school improvement for the least attractive schools. Moreover, these components must be implemented simultaneously. Some plans that claim to be Controlled Choice are not because they do not deal with all components mentioned or do not deal with them simultaneously. Boston, which adopted Controlled Choice in 1989, failed to do this and had to revise the plan in 1992 to comply with all requirements.

Student attendance zones in Controlled Choice are designed to embrace heterogeneous populations. There may be several large zones, such as the three in Boston, or the total school district, such as in Cambridge. The student populations in each school are expected to be the same proportions by race and ethnicity as those in the zones or the total district. However, they may vary from the ideal or expectation by 5, 10, or 15 percentage points. Priority of assignment is given to siblings and to students who can walk to school. However, walk zone students are given priority according to the racial fairness guidelines mentioned above.

Students choose the schools they wish to attend and rank-order their choices. The choice data, in effect, is a referendum on the attractiveness of schools. School boards are obligated to give special attention to upgrading the least chosen schools. This is the aspect of Controlled Choice that has been most difficult to implement. School authorities usually have other criteria for rewarding schools and have been slow to use the reputational data of Controlled Choice as the basis for determining which schools to upgrade.

To stimulate school authorities to take seriously the reputational data, we added another feature to our Boston Controlled Choice plan. We publicized the schools that are overchosen and underchosen by students in all racial groups. This practice has encouraged some administrators of least chosen schools to take initiatives themselves in finding new and sound educational programs of enhancement. Their actions have contributed to educational improvement within the system, one school at a time.

Controlled Choice is a plan that guarantees all population groups proportional access to all of a school system's educational opportunities. It promotes excellence without compromising equity.

## DEFINITION OF ATTRACTIVE AND OTHER SCHOOLS

Implementation of the Controlled Choice student assignment plan is reported elsewhere. This chapter is limited to an analysis of attractive schools the plan has spawned, schools that are attractive in an extraordinary way. Schools are designated as extraordinarily attractive if students in all racial groups choose to enroll in them in numbers that exceed the proportion of seats reserved for each of the groups. Because Controlled Choice promotes school improvement as well as racial desegregation in public education, this student assignment method may be instructive and of some value to the National Education Goals Panel and others who ought to be interested in dealing with diversity.

The analysis that follows will attempt to answer several questions. Do attractive, fully desegregated schools prepare students to achieve at a higher reading level than students in other schools? How do learning environments in such schools differ from those in other schools? And finally, what effects, if any, do race and socioeconomic status have on the achievement of students in attractive and other schools? To fully understand how and why these Boston schools are attractive will require further study using qualitative methods. The results presented in this analysis examine how, in selected ways, attractive schools differ quantitatively from other schools.

## SCHOOL CHOICE AND ASSIGNMENT METHODS

Our method for selecting attractive schools differs from the method used to select exceptional urban schools in the *Phi Delta Kappan* study. In that study, "observation was restricted to schools in which the dependent variable fluctuates in a single direction, that is, student achievement levels in a school are rising" (*Phi Delta Kappan*, 1980: 4). In our study, racial fairness guidelines are developed for all schools. All schools within a large student attendance zone admit students into all grades according to these guidelines. We tabulate the number of students by race with homes in a student attendance zone who plan to attend public schools. The number in each group is converted into a proportion; proportions for the several different groups become our racial fairness guidelines. Students are permitted to choose any of several schools in a zone. They may rank-order their preferences. Students are admitted to their school of choice if their presence will not exceed the "ideal" or zone wide racial proportion for their group in a school's student body.

If one or two racial groups are uninterested in attending a school, the students in the racial group that prefer the school in greater numbers than seats allotted may occupy the unused seats up to 10 percentage points beyond their allotment. Under this student assignment arrangement school leaders are not permitted to cater to a racial group that they prefer.

Most students choose a school that attracts them because of an educational theme or because the school has a learning environment that will facilitate growth. Neighborhood schools under a Controlled Choice arrangement are preferred less often when schools elsewhere in a zone are more attractive. The school system provides transportation to and from any school in the zone for students who live more than one mile from their school of choice. While most students use transportation to go to and from school there is no forced busing in Boston because the students choose the schools to which they are transported. Satisfaction with Controlled Choice increases year by year in Boston as 90 percent of the students in all racial groups receive first-choice or second-choice schools.

Controlled Choice was proposed initially as a way of achieving permanent desegregation in the Boston public schools. However, the idea occurred to the architects of the plan that this method of student assignment could be used to determine school attractiveness, too. In effect, the choice process each year is a public referendum on the attractiveness of schools. We hypothesized that schools preferred by students in all racial groups in greater numbers than the seats reserved for these groups must be doing something right. Thus, we labeled these extraordinarily attractive schools as "overchosen schools." Other or "non-overchosen schools" are those that none or some but not all racial groups chose in numbers that exceeded their allotted proportion. We were particularly interested in discovering why overchosen, desegregated public schools were so attractive. Rather than using achievement as the dependent variable, we used desegregation. Then we sought answers to questions of whether achievement and features of the school's learning environment were higher, more, and better in desegregated overchosen schools than in other schools.

## CHARACTERISTICS OF OVERCHOSEN SCHOOLS

The Office of Planning, Research and Development of the Boston public schools provided data on schools by name and on students anonymously. These are the same data published annually in the *School Profiles* report (1994). Achievement scores for reading and math are taken from the Metropolitan Achievement Tests administered in the spring of 1994 to all students in grades 1 to 12. A student's score is based on the number of items that he or she answers correctly. The score is then converted into a percentile measure to facilitate comparative analysis (Office of Planning, Research and Development, 1994: xii). Data on the entering and exit grades for 114 schools in Boston were analyzed: data on first and fifth grades for all elementary schools; the sixth and eighth grades for all middle schools; and the ninth and twelfth grades for all high schools. (The examination schools—Boston Latin School, Boston Latin Academy, and the John O'Bryant Technical School—were excluded from this analysis.) Variables used in the study were student age, reading achievement score, mathematics achievement score, number of days absent per year, number of suspensions per year, proportion of dropouts, proportion of bus riders, proportion of students eligible for free lunch or lunch at a reduced price, staff attendance rate, proportion of teachers with doctorates or master's degrees, proportion of students who receive a first-choice school, proportion of students who are administratively assigned to a school, proportion of students who walk or who are transported to school, and the student promotion rate.

Boundaries of the Boston School District are coterminous with those of the city of Boston. There were 60,109 students enrolled in the Boston public schools in 1993–94. The entry- and exit-grades analyzed in this study were a sample of 21,685 students or 36 percent of the city-wide public school student body. By race, the total public school student population is 18.9 percent White, 0.4 percent Native American, 23.3 percent Hispanic, 48.1 percent African American, and 9.4 percent Asian.

During the choice process, thirty-three schools were overchosen in 1994; three are Early Learning Centers, seventeen are elementary schools, nine are middle schools, and four are high schools. The data in Table 8.1 indicate that these schools are not extraordinarily attractive because they disproportionately enroll any particular racial group. Collectively, the distribution of students by race in these thirty-three overchosen schools is more or less the same as the distribution for the city-wide public school student body. The students in overchosen schools are 18.3

**Table 8.1** Characteristics of the Student Body and Teaching Staff in Overchosen and Other Public Schools, Boston, 1993–94

Average Indicators in Overchosen Schools

| | Students | Teachers | Reading (0-99) | Math (0-99) | Absence | Suspension | Dropout | Bus ride | Walk | Promotion |
|---|---|---|---|---|---|---|---|---|---|---|
| Asian | 10.5% | 4.2% | 41.9 | 67.8 | 11 | 55 | 4.3% | 62% | 38% | 96.8% |
| Black | 45.9% | 21% | 44.7 | 45.7 | 17 | 48 | 3.4% | 82% | 18% | 91.6% |
| Hispanic | 25.1% | 7.5% | 35.5 | 42.9 | 20 | 52 | 3.5% | 67% | 33% | 92.3% |
| Native Am. | 0.3% | 0.3% | 52.1 | 53.9 | 11 | 55 | 3.4% | 81% | 19% | 95.2% |
| White | 18.3% | 67.1% | 60.6 | 64.5 | 17 | 40 | 2.9% | 56% | 44% | 95.4% |
| Averages | | | 45.3 | 50.9 | 17 | 48 | 3.4% | 71% | 29% | 93.0% |

Total students:  7 , 5 6 1
Total schools:  33
Grades:  *1 and 5 (elementary); 6 and 8 (middle); 9 and 12 (high)*

Average Indicators in Non-Overchosen Schools

| | Students | Teachers | Reading (0-99) | Math (0-99) | Absence | Suspension | Dropout | Bus ride | Walk | Promotion |
|---|---|---|---|---|---|---|---|---|---|---|
| Asian | 7.5% | 3.2% | 38.7 | 71 | 16 | 53 | 7.0% | 69% | 31% | 96.6% |
| Black | 51.5% | 29% | 42.4 | 44.2 | 21 | 85 | 6.4% | 58% | 42% | 92.3% |
| Hispanic | 25.3% | 8.6% | 34.9 | 44.9 | 22 | 84 | 6.7% | 54% | 46% | 92.4% |
| Native Am. | 0.4% | 0.2% | 45.2 | 41.3 | 31 | 55 | 6.0% | 47% | 53% | 91.2% |
| White | 15.3% | 59% | 58.3 | 60.5 | 23 | 68 | 6.4% | 42% | 58% | 94.7% |
| Averages | | | 43 | 49.2 | 21 | 79 | 6.7% | 55% | 45% | 92.6% |

Total students:  14 , 124
Total schools:  8 0 *(excluding Boston Latin, Latin Academy, and Boston Tech)*.
Grades:  *1 and 5 (elementary); 6 and 8 (middle); 9 and 12 (high)*

Note: Overchosen schools are those chosen by all racial groups in numbers that exceeded their allotted proportion. Other or non-overchosen schools are those that none or some but not all racial groups chose in numbers that exceeded their allotted proportion.

percent White, 0.3 percent Native American, 25.1 percent Hispanic, 45.9 percent African American, and 10.5 percent Asian. According to Controlled Choice procedures, schools are permitted to vary from the zonewide racial distribution (which is similar to the city-wide racial distribution) by plus or minus 10 percentage points. In overchosen schools as a collectivity, variations by racial groups from their city-wide proportions never exceed 3 percentage points.

Likewise, the other schools do not fail to achieve overchosen status because of the racial characteristics of their student body. As a collectivity, the racial distribution in the remainder of the Boston public schools over the racial distribution system-wide (excluding the three examination schools) varies less than 4 percentage points. The Controlled Choice method of assigning students to schools truly has desegregated all Boston public schools at the elementary and middle school levels. Yet some of these desegregated schools are more attractive than others. The remainder of this article will attempt to determine why this is so.

## Characteristics That Do Not Vary by School

We will try to solve this problem first by ruling out variables that do not seem to differentiate overchosen and other schools. Table 8.2 presents data by grades for these two groups of schools. Restricting the analysis to entering grades 1, 6, and 9 for elementary, middle, and high school levels, we see that age of student, student promotion rate, student absentee rate, staff attendance rate, and whether teachers have a doctorate are similar for overchosen and other schools. Teachers who

**Table 8.2** Characteristics of the Student Body and Teaching Staff in Overchosen and Other Public Schools by Entering and Exit Grades in Elementary, Middle, and High Schools, Boston, 1993–94

Average School Indicators by Grade Level in Over-chosen and Non-Overchosen Schools

| | Age | Reading (0-99) | Math (0-99) | Absence | Suspension | Dropout | Bus ride | Free Lunch | Staff Attend | Doctor | Master | 1st Choice | Admin. Choice | Walk | Promotion | Total Students |
|---|---|---|---|---|---|---|---|---|---|---|---|---|---|---|---|---|
| Grade 1: Overchosen | 6.05 | 61 | 65 | 16 | 2 | 4.2% | 70% | 62% | 95% | 0.2% | 43% | 91% | 2% | 30% | 96% | 1,099 |
| Non-Overchosen | 6.07 | 53 | 59 | 21 | 13 | 0.98% | 55% | 65% | 94% | 1.0% | 40% | 77% | 13% | 45% | 95% | 4,155 |
| Grade 3: Overchosen | 10.2 | 49 | 59 | 13 | 2 | 3.9% | 69% | 65% | 95% | 0.1% | 47% | 97% | 1% | 31% | 99% | 804 |
| Non-Overchosen | 10.2 | 44 | 53 | 14 | 12 | 1.2% | 56% | 70% | 95% | 1.0% | 41% | 95% | 2% | 44% | 99% | 2,937 |
| Grade 6: Overchosen | 11.2 | 50 | 55 | 17 | 48 | 1.5% | 65% | 71% | 95% | 1.8% | 45% | 83% | 2% | 35% | 93% | 2,047 |
| Non-Overchosen | 11.3 | 43 | 48 | 18 | 88 | 1.5% | 50% | 62% | 94% | 1.5% | 44% | 58% | 23% | 50% | 94% | 1,872 |
| Grade 8: Overchosen | 13.3 | 39 | 44 | 17 | 48 | 1.4% | 63% | 57% | 95% | 1.6% | 46% | 92% | 0.5% | 37% | 93% | 1,516 |
| Non-Overchosen | 13.3 | 37 | 39 | 18 | 84 | 1.5% | 47% | 48% | 94% | 1.5% | 46% | 86% | 4% | 53% | 92% | 1,317 |
| Grade 9: Overchosen | 14.4 | 39 | 37 | 27 | 76 | 6.7% | 84% | 34% | 95% | 2.4% | 64% | 84% | 2% | 16% | 84% | 1,093 |
| Non-Overchosen | 14.7 | 36 | 35 | 32 | 179 | 11.3% | 55% | 26% | 95% | 3.7% | 50% | 66% | 15% | 45% | 79% | 2,183 |
| Grade 12: Overchosen | 18.0 | 31 | 41 | 16 | 79 | 6.8% | 87% | 25% | 95% | 2.2% | 64% | 89% | 0.4% | 13% | 91% | 1,002 |
| Non-Overchosen | 17.9 | 29 | 40 | 19 | 179 | 11.3% | 63% | 26% | 95% | 4.0% | 49% | 89% | 0.5% | 37% | 94% | 1,656 |

Note: Overchosen schools are those chosen by all racial groups in numbers that exceeded their allotted proportion. Other or non-overchosen schools are those that none or some but not all racial groups chose in numbers that exceeded their allotted proportion.

121

have a master's degree are similarly distributed in both kinds of elementary and middle schools but are disproportionately distributed by type of school at the high school level; two-thirds of the teachers of ninth-grade students in overchosen high schools have master's degrees compared to only half of the teachers in other schools. With the exception of this difference at the high school level, teacher training, staff attendance, student age, student absentee rate, and student race at all other grade levels do not seem to make a difference in determining whether a school is overchosen.

Students eligible for a free lunch or lunch at reduced cost are classified as low income and other students are classified as non-low income. These data are less reliable for the upper grades because some low-income students in these grades are reluctant to declare their socioeconomic status. For the entering grade in elementary school where parents must declare their socioeconomic status, there is no difference in the proportion of poor children in overchosen and other schools. Income data for the first grade are more reliable than those for other grades, according to school officials.

## Characteristics That Do Vary by School

Factors that seem to vary substantially by school type—that is, by overchosen or other schools—are suspension rates, dropout rates, proportion of students who receive a first-choice school, and bus riders or walkers to school.

The suspension rate in other schools is slightly more than twice as high as that in overchosen schools, as seen in Figure 8.1, and the dropout rate in other schools is almost twice as high as the rate in overchosen schools, as seen in Table 8.1. It is

**Figure 8.1** Number of Suspensions in Overchosen and Non-Overchosen Schools, Boston, 1993–94

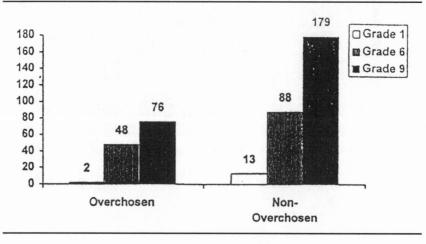

**Figure 8.2** Percentage of Students Who Are Enrolled by Their First-Choice Schools, Boston, 1993–94

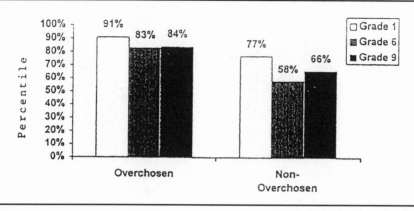

interesting to note that a significant proportion of the students in other schools that have relatively higher suspension and dropout rates are students in schools that were not their first choice. Apparently being in a school that one prefers to attend is something of value.

By entry-grade level, the proportion of students in a first-choice school varies from 91 percent in grade 1 to 83 percent in grade 6 to 84 percent in grade 9 in over-chosen schools. In contrast, the proportion of students with a first-choice school assignment in other schools varies for these three grades from 77 percent to 58 percent to 66 percent, as seen in Figure 8.2. Student response to an education in these two kinds of schools is likely to be different, when about eight out of every ten students in an overchosen school is in a school of preference compared to only about six out of every ten students in other schools.

It would appear that convenience is not the highest priority in the choice of which school to attend in Boston under the Controlled Choice plan. While a majority of the students require transportation, the proportion of students attending overchosen schools who elect to be transported exceeds the proportion of bus riders in other schools by approximately 15 to 30 percentage points, as seen in Figure 8.3. Apparently the convenience of walking to school is less valued by students in search of an education in an attractive learning environment.

## READING ACHIEVEMENT IN OVERCHOSEN AND OTHER SCHOOLS

We turn now to the issue of achievement. Our discussion focuses on reading test scores. As seen in Figure 8.4 and Table 8.2, the average reading score of students in grades 1, 6, and 9 of overchosen schools is consistently higher than the average for students in these grades in other schools. However, the difference is modest

**Figure 8.3** Percentage of Students Who Ride Buses in Overchosen and Non-Overchosen Schools, Boston, 1993–94

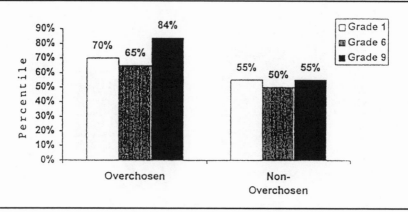

**Figure 8.4** Reading Achievement in Overchosen and Non-Overchosen Schools, Boston, 1993–94

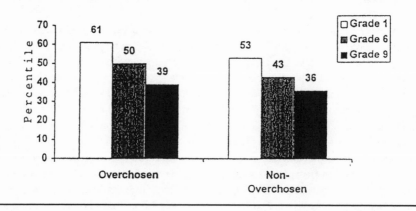

and never exceeds 8 percentile points at any grade level for the collectivity of over-chosen and other schools.

The fiftieth percentile represents the national norm in reading. Boston students in overchosen schools have an average score for entry-grades 1 and 6 at or above the national norm for reading in elementary and middle schools, as seen in Table 8.2, but below the national norm in high school. In the other schools, Boston students have an average score for the entry-grade of elementary school 3 percentile points above the national norm and an average score below the national norm for middle school and high school, as seen in Table 8.2.

**Figure 8.5** Reading Achievement Score, First Grade Students, in Overchosen and Non-Overchosen Schools, Boston Public Schools, 1993–94

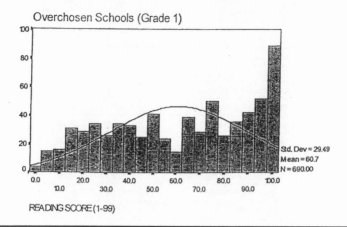

**Figure 8.6** Reading Achievement Score, First Grade Students, in Overchosen and Non-Overchosen Schools, Boston Public Schools, 1993–94

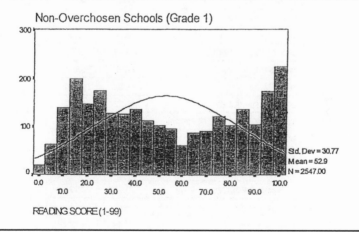

As mentioned earlier, the difference in average scores for reading in overchosen and other schools is modest; there is a difference of 8 percentile points in favor of overchosen schools in grade 1, 7 percentile points in favor of overchosen schools in grade 6, 3 percentile points in favor of overchosen schools in grade 9. While overchosen schools consistently have students who outperform the students in other schools in reading, the difference in performance is not great, as revealed in

**Table 8.3** Reading and Mathematics Average Test Scores of Students by Schools on the Metropolitan Achievement Tests in Overchosen Schools, Boston, 1993–94

| School Name | Reading | Math |
|---|---|---|
| ELC-NORTH ZONE | 79.79 | 70.69 |
| HAMILTON ELEMENTARY | 66.57 | 75.00 |
| BEETHOVEN ELEMENTARY | 65.76 | 59.89 |
| BATES ELEMENTARY | 64.92 | 68.80 |
| F ROOSEVELT ELEMENTARY | 63.86 | 71.11 |
| OHEARN ELEMENTARY | 60.87 | 71.21 |
| QUINCY ELEMENTARY | 59.92 | 69.37 |
| CONLEY ELEMENTARY | 54.90 | 62.43 |
| MOZART ELEMENTARY | 54.53 | 70.08 |
| GREW ELEMENTARY | 54.06 | 66.98 |
| OHRENBERGER ELEMENTARY | 53.41 | 56.58 |
| MURPHY ELEMENTARY | 52.95 | 61.33 |
| TIMILTY MIDDLE | 51.24 | 57.58 |
| IRVING MIDDLE | 50.61 | 54.66 |
| ELC-EAST ZONE | 50.50 | 50.64 |
| ROGERS MIDDLE | 49.66 | 55.37 |
| ELIOT ELEMENTARY | 49.20 | 59.49 |
| SNOWDEN INT SCH/COPLEY | 48.86 | 46.90 |
| CURLEY ELEMENTARY | 48.69 | 48.16 |
| LYON SCHOOL ELEMENTARY | 46.94 | 55.44 |
| MCCORMACK MIDDLE | 46.42 | 48.93 |
| MCKAY ELEMENTARY | 45.37 | 55.03 |
| ELC-WEST ZONE | 45.06 | 43.00 |
| LEWENBERG MIDDLE | 43.22 | 42.92 |
| HERNANDEZ TWO-WAY BILINGUAL | 43.12 | 49.21 |
| BARNES MIDDLE | 43.03 | 54.04 |
| R SHAW MIDDLE | 42.01 | 41.82 |
| TAFT MIDDLE | 41.55 | 50.41 |
| RUSSELL ELEMENTARY | 41.27 | 55.74 |
| EDISON MIDDLE | 38.66 | 50.10 |
| WEST ROXBURY HIGH | 36.19 | 41.79 |
| BOSTON HIGH | 32.40 | 32.73 |
| BRIGHTON HIGH | 30.24 | 35.78 |

Note: Overchosen schools are those chosen by all racial groups in numbers that exceeded their allotted proportion. Other or non-overchosen schools are those that none or some but not all racial groups chose in numbers that exceeded their allotted proportion.

**Table 8.4** Reading and Mathematics Average Test Scores of Students by Schools on the Metropolitan Achievement Tests in Other Schools, Boston, 1993–94

| School Name | Reading | Math |
| --- | --- | --- |
| ALIGHIERI ELEMENTARY | 74.94 | 80.23 |
| HOLMES ELEMENTARY | 71.05 | 61.45 |
| FULLER ELEMENTARY | 70.60 | 62.53 |
| ODONNELL ELEMENTARY | 69.08 | 76.52 |
| WINTHROP ELEMENTARY | 66.95 | 76.91 |
| ENDICOTT ELEMENTARY | 65.91 | 69.57 |
| KILMER ELEMENTARY | 64.72 | 67.15 |
| CHANNING ELEMENTARY | 64.33 | 71.94 |
| BRADLEY ELEMENTARY | 64.07 | 71.96 |
| MASON ELEMENTARY | 63.81 | 66.67 |
| CHITTICK ELEMENTARY | 61.07 | 63.80 |
| GUILD ELEMENTARY | 60.94 | 59.00 |
| STONE ELEMENTARY | 59.33 | 60.80 |
| FARRAGUT ELEMENTARY | 58.97 | 68.36 |
| FIFIELD ELEMENTARY | 57.31 | 57.54 |
| DEVER ELEMENTARY | 57.02 | 62.25 |
| KENT ELEMENTARY | 56.87 | 72.40 |
| P KENNEDY ELEMENTARY | 55.51 | 70.48 |
| E GREENWOOD ELEMENTARY | 55.48 | 53.22 |
| EMERSON ELEMENTARY | 55.38 | 69.47 |
| PERKINS ELEMENTARY | 55.14 | 52.72 |
| PHILBRICK ELEMENTARY | 54.75 | 62.10 |
| GARFIELD ELEMENTARY | 54.34 | 59.30 |
| DICKERMAN ELEMENTARY | 53.08 | 63.26 |
| SUMNER ELEMENTARY | 52.78 | 55.67 |
| ADAMS ELEMENTARY | 51.12 | 65.49 |
| HALEY ELEMENTARY | 50.37 | 59.47 |
| BALDWIN ELEMENTARY | 50.03 | 67.83 |
| TYNAN ELEMENTARY | 49.26 | 49.80 |
| WILSON MIDDLE | 49.07 | 51.18 |
| THOMPSON MIDDLE | 48.87 | 47.00 |
| LEE ELEMENTARY | 48.68 | 52.46 |
| HALE ELEMENTARY | 47.65 | 50.03 |
| HOLLAND ELEMENTARY | 47.54 | 56.23 |

**Table 8.4** *(Continued)*

| School Name | Reading | Math |
|---|---|---|
| TROTTER ELEMENTARY | 47.48 | 52.32 |
| MANNING ELEMENTARY | 47.40 | 57.70 |
| EVERETT ELEMENTARY | 46.52 | 53.13 |
| J KENNEDY ELEMENTARY | 46.33 | 61.63 |
| JACKSON MANN ELEMENTARY | 46.31 | 56.87 |
| OTIS ELEMENTARY | 46.00 | 69.19 |
| HENNIGAN ELEMENTARY | 45.94 | 56.95 |
| W PRESCOTT ELEMENTARY | 45.71 | 57.04 |
| PERRY ELEMENTARY | 44.94 | 59.91 |
| P A SHAW ELEMENTARY | 44.91 | 45.55 |
| GARDNER ELEMENTARY | 44.91 | 54.42 |
| HIGGINSON ELEMENTARY | 44.43 | 50.92 |
| CONDON ELEMENTARY | 43.51 | 52.84 |
| TAYLOR ELEMENTARY | 41.83 | 44.27 |
| LEWIS MIDDLE | 41.55 | 38.24 |
| KENNY ELEMENTARY | 41.37 | 39.85 |
| HURLEY ELEMENTARY | 41.30 | 49.99 |
| ELLIS ELEMENTARY | 41.22 | 44.05 |
| KING MIDDLE | 40.99 | 41.43 |
| WHEATLEY MIDDLE | 40.65 | 40.41 |
| DEARBORN MIDDLE | 40.41 | 39.01 |
| GAVIN MIDDLE | 40.18 | 47.84 |
| CLAP ELEMENTARY | 40.00 | 43.88 |
| MATTAHUNT ELEMENTARY | 39.79 | 46.51 |
| EDWARDS MIDDLE | 39.29 | 54.56 |
| BLACKSTONE ELEMENTARY | 39.18 | 49.01 |
| EAST BOSTON HIGH | 38.68 | 38.31 |
| SOUTH BOSTON HIGH | 38.53 | 40.51 |
| M CURLEY MIDDLE | 38.31 | 42.34 |
| TOBIN ELEMENTARY | 37.95 | 44.88 |
| MARSHALL ELEMENTARY | 36.70 | 43.50 |
| HYDE PARK HIGH | 35.92 | 34.10 |
| AGASSIZ ELEMENTARY | 35.78 | 49.25 |
| CLEVELAND MIDDLE | 35.53 | 39.21 |
| MENDELL ELEMENTARY | 34.76 | 42.57 |
| BURKE HIGH | 34.26 | 35.10 |
| MATHER ELEMENTARY | 34.19 | 60.18 |

Note: Other or non-overchosen schools are those that none or some but not all racial groups chose in numbers that exceeded their allotted proportion. Reading scores have been converted into percentiles from 1 to 99; the 50th percentile represents the national norm.

Figures 8.5 and 8.6 and Tables 8.3 and 8.4. When scores for all grades included in this study are combined, the average reading score for overchosen elementary, middle, and high schools is 45.3. This average is only 5 percent greater than the average reading score of 43 for these combined grades in all other schools.

One conclusion that may be derived from this analysis is that higher achievement in reading is probably one outcome of education in a school that is an attractive desegregated learning environment; our goal is to identify other experiences associated with an attractive, desegregated learning environment. Being in a desegregated school that one prefers to attend seems to be something of value. Also, being in a school that understands how to cope with student problems without excessive suspensions seems to be important, as suspensions in overchosen schools are less than those in other schools. And finally, being in a school that knows how to hold onto its students until they graduate and prevent them from dropping out is an educational enhancement factor, as the dropout rate is lower in overchosen schools than in other schools.

To triangulate our data and their analysis, we computed several correlation coefficients for distributions of overchosen and distributions of other schools to determine if the associations already discussed would continue to hold, using different methods of data manipulation. Correlation coefficients are presented in Tables 8.5a and 8.5b. At the 1 percent level of statistical confidence, the average score for reading by schools results in a correlation coefficient with school suspension and dropout rates that is significantly different from zero in both distributions. The correlation coefficients of −.80 and −.64 for suspension and dropout rates, respectively, among overchosen schools, and −.45 and −.61 for suspension and dropout

**Table 8.5a** Correlation Coefficient Matrix for Overchosen Schools, Boston, 1993–94

|  | READPC_1 | SUSPUPIL | DOPCT | RIDEBU_1 | FIRSTC_1 | FREELU_1 |
|---|---|---|---|---|---|---|
| READPC_1 |  |  |  |  |  |  |
| SUSPUPIL | -.8042<br>( 26)<br>p= .000 |  |  |  |  |  |
| DOPCT | -.6415<br>( 15)<br>p= .010 | .5012<br>( 15)<br>p= .057 |  |  |  |  |
| RIDEBU_1 | -.1333<br>( 33)<br>p= .460 | .2181<br>( 26)<br>p= .284 | .1464<br>( 15)<br>p= .603 |  |  |  |
| FIRSTC_1 | .3912<br>( 33)<br>p= .024 | -.4431<br>( 26)<br>p= .023 | -.2817<br>( 15)<br>p= .309 | .1037<br>( 33)<br>p= .566 |  |  |
| FREELU_1 | .1782<br>( 33)<br>p=.321 | -.3694<br>( 26)<br>p=.063 | -.4787<br>( 15)<br>p=.071 | -.2514<br>( 33)<br>p=.158 | -.0425<br>( 33)<br>p=.814 |  |

Note: Displayed first is the correlation coefficient; second, the number of schools; and third, the significance of the coefficient. Overchosen schools are those preferred by students in all racial groups in numbers that exceed the proportion of seats allocated for their group.

**Table 8.5b** Correlation Coefficient Matrix for Other Schools, Boston, 1993–94

| | READPC_1 | SUSPUPIL | DOPCT | RIDEBU_1 | FIRSTC_1 | FREELU_1 |
|---|---|---|---|---|---|---|
| READPC_1 | | | | | | |
| SUSPUPIL | -.4469<br>( 66)<br>p= .000 | | | | | |
| DOPCT | -.6049<br>( 20)<br>p= .005 | .5782<br>( 25)<br>p= .002 | | | | |
| RIDEBU_1 | -.1759<br>( 77)<br>p= .126 | .0574<br>( 66)<br>p= .647 | .2506<br>( 20)<br>p= .286 | | | |
| FIRSTC_1 | .2091<br>( 77)<br>p= .068 | -.3223<br>( 66)<br>p= .008 | -.0406<br>( 20)<br>p= .865 | .0793<br>( 77)<br>p= .493 | | |
| FREELU_1 | .2387<br>( 77)<br>p=.037 | -.4959<br>( 66)<br>p=.000 | -.7357<br>( 20)<br>p=.000 | .0739<br>( 77)<br>p=.523 | .1757<br>( 77)<br>p=.126 | |

Note: Displayed first is the correlation coefficient; second, the number of schools; and third, the significance of the coefficient. Other or non-overchosen schools are those that none or some but not all racial groups chose in numbers that exceeded their allotted proportion.

rates, respectively, among other schools indicate an indirect association between reading achievement and these variables. Schools that help their students become good readers are schools that tend to have students with low suspension and dropout rates. Actually, from 64 to 41 percent of the variance in suspensions and dropouts, respectively, is associated with the reading achievement experience of students in overchosen schools; and from 17 to 37 percent of the variance in suspensions and dropouts, respectively, is associated with the reading achievement experience of students in other schools. As stated above, these associations are statistically significant. The high correlation at .50 and .57 between suspension and dropout rates in distributions of overchosen schools and distributions of other schools means that both factors apparently tap into a common negative condition in schools. Thus, we consider these factors to be reflections of school culture. Apparently school cultures that generate a substantial number of suspensions and that do not discourage dropping out are incompatible with high levels of reading achievement. This analysis strongly suggests that school culture and individual achievement are interrelated. Efforts to improve education must deal with both.

## NEW PARADIGMS IN EDUCATION

For these reasons, we have been critical of the National Education Goals Panel for not emphasizing policy changes that could affect relationships between administrators, teachers, staff, and students, and program changes that could enrich the school culture. Discovering better ways of enhancing reading and math skills are important and so is the development of policy and programmatic changes that improve school cultures. The two go hand in hand.

This discussion has focused as much on paying attention to ways of overcoming negative and pathological experiences in school culture and other impediments to learning as on ways of achieving excellence in selected skills. Former Johns Hopkins University professor Ernest Gruenberg, a brilliant psychiatrist, epidemiologist, and specialist in public health, said many years ago when he was director of the New York State Mental Health Commission that we probably know more about how to prevent mental illness than we know about how to promote mental health. Further, he said, our prevention programs for disease at this stage in our knowledge probably will be more effective than programs for the promotion of well-being. Believing, as we do, that there is a close association between care giving in education and health, we assert that educational practices designed to reduce pathology in school settings and overcome impediments to learning probably will be more effective at this stage in our knowledge than our efforts to promote excellence in the performance of selected skills. Obviously, we should attempt to do both—reduce negative influences and promote positive influences. However, if we are limited in what we can do, we should devote our energy first to eliminating negative influences.

This frame of reference requires new paradigms for educational reform, paradigms that focus as much attention on upgrading the worst as on promoting the best, paradigms that give guidance in how to overcome failure as well as how to achieve success, paradigms that embrace both equity and excellence, in summary, paradigms that are based on the theory of complementarity (Willie, 1994: 65–74).

## THE PROBLEM OF TRACKING

We conclude this analysis with a discussion of tracking. However, this analysis will examine tracking by schools rather than by grades or sections within grades. Jeannie Oakes's fine book, *Keeping Track: How Schools Structure Inequality*, published by the Yale University Press in 1985, immediately made a major contribution to educational practice by documenting what many believed but had not proven: that tracking arrangements are harmful ways of organizing learning environments and that they harm the least among us more than they harm the greatest among us.

By adopting Controlled Choice as a student assignment plan that fully desegregates the entering grades of all schools, Boston rejected racial tracking by schools, especially in elementary and middle schools. Consequently, the thirty-three overchosen and most attractive schools have distributions of students by race that are similar to the racial makeup of the total public school system's student body. Boston's Controlled Choice plan proves that integration can be an attractive educational experience and that whites do not have to be the prevailing population in schools that are preferred. When the thirty-three overchosen schools and the remaining schools in Boston (excluding the examination schools) are combined, none of the city's five largest racial and ethnic groups is a majority of enrolled students.

If students in Boston were assigned to elementary schools by reading ability, Whites and Asians would be grouped in one set of schools where children's reading achievement scores would be above the national norm, and African Americans, Hispanics, and Native Americans would be housed in another set of schools where children's reading scores are below the national norm, according to data presented in Table 8.6. The average reading score for Native Americans is above the national norm in overchosen elementary schools but below the national norm in other elementary schools; because the number of students in other schools is three times greater than the number in overchosen schools, the average reading achievement score for all Native Americans is less than the national norm. Boston does not assign students to elementary schools by achievement level and, therefore, has fully integrated elementary schools by race in overchosen and other schools.

If students were assigned to middle schools by reading achievement scores, clearly there would be racial segregation also, according to data presented in Table 8.7. There would be White schools in which children had scores above the national norms and schools for people of color with children scoring below the national norm. The same pattern of school assignment by race would exist for high schools, as seen in Table 8.8, if students were grouped or tracked by reading achievement scores. Boston does not assign students to middle schools by achievement level and, therefore, has fully integrated middle schools by race in overchosen and other schools. However, there is something troubling about the pattern of student assignments in high schools.

Asian and White students in overchosen high schools are proportionately fewer than Asian and White students in overchosen elementary schools, as seen in Tables 8.8 and 8.6. We take note of this fact because these are the same two popula-

**Table 8.6** Characteristics of the Student Body and Teaching Staff in Overchosen and Other Public Elementary Schools, Boston, 1993–94

*Elementary Schools:*

Average Indicators in Overchosen Schools

|  | Students | Teachers | Reading (0-99) | Math (0-99) | Absence | Suspension | Dropout | Bus ride | Walk | Promotion |
|---|---|---|---|---|---|---|---|---|---|---|
| Asian | 13.1% | 6% | 60.3 | 78.6 | 11 | 0 | 0.0% | 46% | 54% | 99% |
| Black | 45.8% | 22% | 50.7 | 54.4 | 17 | 2 | 3.8% | 87% | 13% | 97% |
| Hispanic | 18.3% | 7% | 45.5 | 58.5 | 20 | 2 | 3.8% | 68% | 32% | 98% |
| Native Am. | 0.3% | 0.3% | 78.1 | 67.6 | 11 | 3 | 0.7% | 97% | 3% | 97% |
| White | 22.6% | 64% | 67.6 | 73.3 | 17 | 2 | 4.9% | 49% | 51% | 98% |
| Averages |  |  | 54.9 | 61.9 | 17 | 1.8 | 4.1% | 70% | 30% | 98% |

*Total students: 1,903*
*Grades:        1 and 5 (elementary)*

Average Indicators in Non-Overchosen Schools

|  | Students | Teachers | Reading (0-99) | Math (0-99) | Absence | Suspension | Dropout | Bus ride | Walk | Promotio |
|---|---|---|---|---|---|---|---|---|---|---|
| Asian | 7% | 3.2% | 50.0 | 74.0 | 16 | 6 | 0.0% | 61% | 39% | 98% |
| Black | 48% | 29% | 46.4 | 50.7 | 21 | 12 | 1.4% | 59% | 41% | 95% |
| Hispanic | 25% | 8.6% | 41.3 | 54.0 | 22 | 9 | 0.8% | 56% | 44% | 94% |
| Native Am. | 0.6% | 0.2% | 44.6 | 43.3 | 31 | 7 | 0.0% | 45% | 55% | 98% |
| White | 20% | 59% | 62.0 | 67.1 | 23 | 7 | 0.6% | 45% | 55% | 98% |
| Averages |  |  | 48.6 | 56.2 | 21 | 10 | 1.0% | 56% | 44% | 97% |

*Total students: 7,093*
*Grades:        1 and 5 (elementary)*

**Table 8.7** Characteristics of the Student Body and Teaching Staff in Overchosen and Other Public Middle Schools, Boston, 1993–94

### Middle Schools:
Average Indicators in Overchosen Schools

|  | Students | Teachers | Reading (0-99) | Math (0-99) | Absence | Suspension | Dropout | Bus ride | Walk | Promotion |
|---|---|---|---|---|---|---|---|---|---|---|
| Asian | 10.0% | 2% | 43.3 | 72.5 | 9 | 42 | 1.8% | 64% | 32% | 97% |
| Black | 41.7% | 23% | 45.8 | 46.4 | 15 | 36 | 1.2% | 72% | 28% | 92% |
| Hispanic | 27.8% | 10% | 34.5 | 42.3 | 16 | 35 | 1.5% | 60% | 40% | 93% |
| Native Am. | 0.3% | 0.4% | 41.5 | 45.7 | 13 | 41 | 1.1% | 64% | 36% | 96% |
| White | 20.2% | 67% | 58.3 | 61.5 | 16 | 35 | 1.5 % | 52% | 48% | 96% |
| Averages |  |  | 45.1 | 50.9 | 15 | 36 | 1.4% | 64% | 36% | 94% |

*Total students: 3,563*
*Grades:      6 and 8* (middle)

Average Indicators in Non-Overchosen Schools

|  | Students | Teachers | Reading (0-99) | Math (0-99) | Absence | Suspension | Dropout | Bus ride | Walk | Promotion |
|---|---|---|---|---|---|---|---|---|---|---|
| Asian | 6.6% | 3% | 38.9 | 74.9 | 10 | 47 | 1.1% | 74% | 26% | 97% |
| Black | 56.3% | 37% | 41.7 | 41.7 | 16 | 58 | 1.7% | 47% | 53% | 92% |
| Hispanic | 24.8% | 8% | 31.6 | 37.4 | 16 | 70 | 1.3% | 48% | 52% | 95% |
| Native Am. | 0.4% | 0.5% | 53.5 | 44.9 | 13 | 59 | 1.0% | 31% | 69% | 91% |
| White | 11.9% | 52% | 54.6 | 53.9 | 18 | 60 | 1.2% | 47% | 53% | 95% |
| Averages |  |  | 40.5 | 44.5 | 16 | 61 | 1.5% | 49% | 51% | 93% |

*Total students: 3,189*
*Grades:      6 and 8* (middle)

**Table 8.8** Characteristics of the Student Body and Teaching Staff in Overchosen and Other Public High Schools, Boston, 1993–94

### High Schools:
Average Indicators in Overchosen Schools

|  | Students | Teachers | Reading (0-99) | Math (0-99) | Absence | Suspension | Dropout | Bus ride | Walk | Promotion |
|---|---|---|---|---|---|---|---|---|---|---|
| Asian | 9.9% | 5% | 16.4 | 48.5 | 15 | 81 | 8.6% | 79% | 38% | 96.8% |
| Black | 53.1% | 16% | 37.0 | 36.1 | 20 | 56 | 6.3% | 92% | 18% | 91.6% |
| Hispanic | 23.8% | 4% | 31.6 | 32.7 | 26 | 68 | 7.4% | 79% | 33% | 92.3% |
| Native Am. | 0.2% | 0.5% | 40.5 | 68.0 | 8 | 62 | 7.7% | 97% | 19% | 95.2% |
| White | 12.9% | 75% | 54.6 | 56.9 | 22 | 53 | 6.1% | 76% | 44% | 95.4% |
| Averages |  |  | 35.7 | 38.9 | 22 | 61 | 6.8% | 85% | 29% | 87.0% |

*Total students: 2,095*
*Grades:      9 and 12 (High)*

Average Indicators in Non-Overchosen Schools

|  | Students | Teachers | Reading (0-99) | Math (0-99) | Absence | Suspension | Dropout | Bus ride | Walk | Promotion |
|---|---|---|---|---|---|---|---|---|---|---|
| Asian | 8.4% | 4% | 18.6 | 62.4 | 20 | 79 | 10.8% | 78% | 31% | 96.6% |
| Black | 49.8% | 24% | 33.8 | 32.1 | 27 | 133 | 11.1% | 65% | 42% | 92.3% |
| Hispanic | 24.3% | 6% | 26.4 | 32.6 | 27 | 139 | 12.1% | 56% | 46% | 92.4% |
| Native Am. | 0.3% | 0.8% | 30.4 | 14.5 | 48 | 117 | 11.0% | 69% | 53% | 91.2% |
| White | 17.2% | 66% | 50.4 | 46.7 | 26 | 116 | 11.1% | 32% | 58% | 94.7% |
| Averages |  |  | 33.1 | 37.5 | 26 | 127 | 11.3% | 58% | 45% | 85.2% |

*Total students: 3,842*
*Grades:      9 and 12 (High)*

tions that would be grouped together if there were tracking in Boston elementary schools based on reading achievement levels. The White student population decreased from 22.6 percent of the students in overchosen elementary schools to 12.9 percent of the students in overchosen high schools; and the Asian student population decreased from 13.1 percent of the students in overchosen elementary schools to 9.9 percent of the students in overchosen high schools, despite the fact that the city-wide proportion of White high school students is 18.5 percent and that for Asian high school students is 11.5. Clearly, the proportions for these two groups in overchosen high schools are less than their proportions in the total public high school system.

This trend for these two racial groups causes one to wonder whether tracking is present in Boston secondary schools that disproportionately selects able Asian and White students into some high schools and away from others. This query is appropriate, because the proportion of White students in overchosen schools always exceeds their proportion in other schools at the elementary and middle school levels but not at the high school level.

Thus, we ask: What happened to the Whites of high school age who were enrolled in overchosen elementary and middle schools? Why do they not continue to enroll in overchosen high schools in proportions that are similar to their city-wide proportion, as seen in earlier grades? Apparently, White students are underrepresented in secondary overchosen schools because they have been tracked into the Boston Latin School and the Boston Latin Academy, two schools that admit students by examination (the Secondary Student Aptitude Test). While the proportion of White students in all Boston high schools is 18.5 percent, the proportion of Whites in the combined student bodies of the Boston Latin School and the Boston Latin Academy is 37.9 percent, twice their city-wide proportion. In the Boston Latin School alone Whites are 50.9 percent of its student body. Whites and Asians are substantially overrepresented in the student bodies of these two schools and, together, constitute a two-thirds majority of their students. All other population groups are disproportionately underrepresented in the combined student bodies of the Boston Latin School and the Boston Latin Academy. The White and Asian populations in these two high schools are more than twice as great as they would be if Whites and Asians were distributed among all high schools in a random way.

There are 2,856 White students enrolled in fifteen high schools throughout the city. However, 1,082 of these White students are enrolled in Boston Latin and Boston Latin Academy. Thus, 38 percent of all White public school students in Boston are enrolled in only two of its fifteen high schools. Based on this evidence, we conclude that tracking in Boston schools at the high school level has racial fairness implications, since African Americans, Hispanics, and Native Americans are disproportionately underrepresented in substantial numbers in these two public schools but are not disproportionately underrepresented in substantial numbers in overchosen schools.

In addition to draining off White students who normally would enroll in overchosen and other high schools, Boston Latin and Boston Latin Academy also track White students with the highest reading achievement scores into their student bodies. While Whites have an average reading achievement score 5 percentile points above the national norm in overchosen high schools and at the national norm in other high schools, Whites have a reading achievement score 46 percentile points above the national norm in the Boston Latin School and 39 percentile points above the national norm in the Boston Latin Academy.

The Asian high school population is disproportionately concentrated in three high schools—the Boston Latin School, the Boston Latin Academy, and the John O'Bryant School of Mathematics and Science. The 1,781 Asian students in Boston public high schools represent 11.5 percent of the system's secondary school student population. In these three schools, however, Asian students are 29.3 percent of their combined student bodies. The proportion of Asian students in these schools is more than twice what it would be if Asians were distributed randomly among all high schools. These three high schools enroll 955 Asian students, which represent 54 percent of the 1,781 Asian high school students in the Boston public schools.

The schools that track into their student bodies a disproportionate number of White students and Asian students and a disproportionate number of high-achieving students in reading get more attention than other high schools. Scholars of school tracking have discovered that weaker schools and weaker students are harmed more than the stronger schools and stronger students are helped. The overchosen high schools have an average reading score of 36 for students in all racial groups and the other high schools have an average reading score of 33 for students in all racial groups. These scores in overchosen and other high schools are not only well below the national norm compared with Boston's Latin School and Latin Academy scores, which are well above the national norm, these scores for high school students in overchosen and other high schools (excluding the examination schools) are the smallest difference between these two kinds of schools seen at any of the grade levels according to data in Tables 8.6, 8.7, and 8.8.

Of Boston's twelve non-examination high schools, one has lost its accreditation and three are on probation, according to the *Boston Globe* (November 16, 1995: 29), and a few others have been notified that they may be placed on probation. There is clear and present evidence that the school system has not paid due attention to high schools in Boston. We claim that the inattention given to some high schools is because of the excessive attention given to the three examination schools.

We call attention to the excluding effects of tracking in Boston at the secondary level because they are unfair and seem to be unnecessary in achieving effective and attractive learning environments. The thirty-three overchosen elementary, middle, and high schools in Boston with fully desegregated student bodies demonstrate that these schools with students that manifest a range of reading skills can be very attractive learning environments.

In view of the precipitous drop below the national norm in reading achievement scores in overchosen as well as other high schools compared to reading achievement scores nearer the national norms in Boston's elementary schools, it would appear that the high school tracking facilitated by the three examination schools has had a negative effect on all high schools, an effect that is not seen among elementary schools where there is no tracking. This study confirms findings reported in the social science literature that tracking seems to have a negative effect. In our study, the negative effect seems to be found among secondary schools that are not counted among the elite.

## A FAIR ADMISSIONS POLICY

Even if the examination schools have been assigned the responsibility of educating the brightest and best of Boston students, the examination schools must carry out this responsibility in a way that is fair. It is unfair to use an ethnocentric standard of admission derived from one group that is projected on all groups. It is well documented in the social science literature that the practice of ethnocentrism is always harmful to the group or groups that are made to conform to standards that are not their own. If the examination schools have been set aside to educate the most promising students, they are obligated as public schools to educate the most promising students in all population groups. These facts indicate that admitting the brightest and best students in each racial group by group-specific standards in the long run will not be harmful to the mission of the examination schools but will be a fairer way of making the opportunities available in these schools available to all students in an equitable way.

When the Controlled Choice plan was prepared for Boston in 1988 by Charles V. Willie and Michael Alves, the planners reported that "some high schools are not attracting sufficient numbers of students and there is excess capacity at the high school levels. [Thus], some high schools could be consolidated to provide sufficient resources for a more enriched curriculum." The planners stated that "the high school situation in Boston is in a crisis and needs immediate and careful attention" (Willie and Alves, 1988: 23).

The planners felt that their "truncated planning period" did not permit sufficient time to do a thorough study and they, therefore, recommended that a "panel of experts on high school education ... [should] be commissioned to make a ... study of the high school situation and report findings and recommendations to the Superintendent and to the School Committee in the summer of 1989" (Willie and Alves, 1988: 23–24).

This recommendation was never implemented. Thus, the high schools in Boston have continued with the Latin and technical high schools tracking into their student bodies a disproportionate number of students with high reading scores and a disproportionate number of White and Asian students.

Before 1988, the Boston community was warned of the segregative tracking effects of the examination schools. Back in 1975, a panel of four court-appointed masters (Jacob Spiegel; Edward McCormack, Jr.; Francis Keppel; and Charles Willie assisted Judge W. Arthur Garrity, Jr., of the U.S. District Court in fashioning a school desegregation plan for the Boston public schools) called for "desegregating the three examination schools by requiring that their student populations be in line with city-wide racial-ethnic composition, as in all other magnet schools" (Dentler and Scott, 1981: 128). Robert Dentler, a court-appointed expert who also assisted the Judge, said that "no other feature of [the master's] report was more hotly debated than that [having to do with criteria for selecting examination school students]" (Dentler and Scott, 1981: 128).

Providing further evidence that tracking arrangements harm the least preferred schools within a system Dentler said that "the ... selection process allowed parents to think of [the examination] high schools as elite and to denigrate other offerings of the system" (Dentler and Scott, 1981: 128). All parties to the case, including the attorneys for the plaintiffs, were so accepting of tracking arrangements that the proposal of the panel of masters was not adopted. The final court order incorporated a compromise consensus solution supported by all parties to the school desegregation case that "at least 35 percent of each of the entering classes at Boston Latin School, Boston Latin Academy and Boston Technical High [School] ... [should] be composed of Black and Hispanic students" (Dentler and Scott, 1981: 129).

The Boston school committee so supported the tracking arrangement facilitated by the examination schools that it appealed the compromise and consensus stipulation, "as well as other features of the plan adopted by the court." The U.S. Court of Appeals upheld the order of the U.S. District Court but advised the lower court "to safeguard the elite character of the examination schools" in the future (Dentler and Scott, 1981: 129).

The record shows that over the years, high schools in Boston (other than the examination schools) have been permitted to drift with little attention given to finding ways to help them provide a quality education. By the 1993–94 school year, none of the twelve regular high schools had an average reading score at or above the national norm. However, the three examination schools had average reading scores well above the national norm. In fact, they are the only high schools with average reading scores above the national norm. Of the six schools with the lowest average reading scores for all 117 schools, five are non-examination high schools, as seen in Tables 8.3 and 8.4.

Despite these warning signs, and despite the requirements of the Controlled Choice student assignment plan that "schools ... having difficulty ... attracting and retaining students as indicated by low parental and student applications ... should be targeted for ... special school improvement initiatives" (Willie and Alves, 1988: 56), the Boston community took little, if any, positive action to enhance the non-examination high schools until accreditation was withdrawn from one of the high schools during the 1994–95 school year. This embarrassing event was the final outcome of sanctioning a tracking arrangement among high schools.

In their book *The Good Society*, Robert Bellah, Richard Madsen, William Sullivan, Ann Swidler, and Steven Tipton include a chapter titled "Democracy Means Paying Attention" that speaks to negative consequences of the tracking issue in Boston high schools. These authors state that "allowing ... enormous disparities to go on indefinitely runs the risk of a renewal of ... conflict that will endanger all our hopes" (Bellah et al., 1992: 274). To prevent this from happening, they admonish us to pay attention! This means paying attention to the least among us as well as to the greatest among us. Thus far, Boston has not paid sufficient attention to all of its high schools and now is suffering the consequences of inattention.

## SUMMARY AND CONCLUSIONS

This study has revealed that multiracial, attractive city schools of achievement are possible and can be attained when sufficient attention is given to both instrumental and affective goals in education. Instrumental goals are concerned with student achievement. Affective goals have to do with school culture, which is sometimes labeled school climate. To fulfill these goals, strong school leadership is necessary. The Controlled Choice method of student assignment indicates that multiple school goals—school desegregation, school improvement, and student choice of school of enrollment—are important, but they must be fulfilled simultaneously to achieve maximum effect.

This study also revealed that fully desegregated schools in which neither Whites nor any of the other racial or ethnic groups is a majority can be very attractive schools. About 30 percent of the 117 schools in Boston met this criterion of attractiveness.

Although the average reading score was consistently higher in overchosen schools as a collectivity compared to all other schools combined (except the three examination schools), it was not substantially higher. The correlation coefficient for reading achievement scores and the proportion of students in first-choice schools is only .39; this fact means that some students pick schools as their first choice for a variety of reasons, including but not limited to the reading achievement of their peers. The main differences between overchosen and other schools were substantially lower suspension and dropout rates in overchosen schools. We believe these lower rates are a consequence of positive school cultures in these buildings.

While attractive elementary and middle schools were fully desegregated, overchosen high schools had a disproportionate lower number of White and Asian students and students with high reading scores. Further examination of this phenomenon revealed that these population groups were disproportionately tracked into the three elite examination schools. Moreover, the community seemed not to pay sufficient attention to the remainder of Boston's high schools as they lavished attention on the examination high schools. Consequently, the non-examination high schools by and large have drifted as mediocre institutions, with none having a student body in which students' average reading score is at or above the national reading norm. This study confirms the findings of other studies that tracking tends to harm the weak among us.

Our first conclusion is that attractive inner-city schools exist and that they are a function of strong leadership, a positive school culture, and a community that pays attention to them and helps them fulfill multiple goals of desegregation, choice, and school improvement simultaneously. Our second conclusion is that tracking by schools is harmful to a school system because it enhances some schools at the expense of others and permits the non-elite schools to settle into mediocrity. Our third conclusion is that we probably will be more successful by expending increasing efforts on overcoming impediments to education than on attempting to achieve excellence, especially in a system that encourages universal education.

We obviously need to learn more about desegregated, overchosen schools as social organizations that have unique and positive school cultures. We also need to examine the leadership styles of principals in these schools, including what they and others do to create and maintain a safe learning environment and a supportive educational community. Qualitative data are needed for these studies.

## NOTE

This chapter was written with Dr. George Hagerty, president of Franklin Pierce College, Rindge, New Hampshire. Acknowledged with appreciation are the NYNEX Foundation and the Boston Globe Foundation for grants that supported the study reported in this chapter, which was first published in the September 1996 edition of *Equity and Excellence in Education*. Reproduced with permission of the Greenwood Publishing Group, Inc., Westport, CT. Dr. Haiyan Hua assisted with the statistical analysis.

## REFERENCES

Bellah, R., et al. 1992. *The Good Society*. New York: Vintage Books.

Dentler, R. A., and M. Scott. 1981. *Schools on Trial*. Cambridge, MA: Abt Books.

National Education Goals Panel. 1993. *The National Education Goals Report* (Summary Guide). Washington, DC: U.S. Government Printing Office.

National Education Goals Panel. 1994. *Data Volume for the National Education Goals Report*. Washington, DC: U.S. Government Printing Office, pp. 8–11.

Oakes, J. 1985. *Keeping Track*. New Haven: Yale University Press.

Office of Planning, Research and Development. 1994. *School Profiles*. 11th ed. Boston: Boston Public Schools.

*Phi Delta Kappan*. 1980, 4. Why Do Some Urban Schools Succeed? Bloomington, IN: Phi Delta Kappa.

Willie, C. 1994. *Theories of Human Social Action*. Dix Hills, NY: General Hall.

Willie, C., and M. Alves. 1988. *Proposed Student Assignment Plan, Boston Public Schools*. Boston: Boston School Committee (December).

# 9

# RACE, SOCIOECONOMIC STATUS, AND ACADEMIC ACHIEVEMENT: AN ANALYSIS OF THEIR INTERACTIVE EFFECTS

Because of the extraordinary interest in race and social class in the United States and in developed countries throughout the world, we decided to determine if there is an association between achievement as indicated by standardized test scores and the racial and socioeconomic characteristics of public school students.

Back in 1978, more than two decades ago, William J. Wilson published a book titled *The Declining Significance of Race*. In it, he declared that social class has become more important than race in determining access to power and privilege for blacks in the United States. The Association of Black Sociologists passed a resolution that year rejecting the Wilson findings and declaring that "[his] book omits significant data regarding the continuing discrimination against Blacks at all class levels" (reported in Willie, 1979: 177–78).

Education is one power resource in this nation. It would be interesting to determine whether U.S. citizens have differential access to it because of their race. Such an analysis is more definitive if it holds the level of education constant for both minority and majority racial populations.

To test the Wilson hypothesis that income discrimination against Blacks is caused by inferior education and not by racial prejudice, we compared the median earnings of poorly educated Whites and poorly educated Blacks. Adult family members were classified as poorly educated if they had received only an elementary school education or less. Controlling for education and using 1982 data collected during the height of the debate about whether or not race was declining as a significant factor, we discovered that in the United States poorly educated Blacks earned 23 percent less than poorly educated Whites and that college-educated Blacks received 22 percent less income than college-educated Whites (U.S. Bureau of the Census, 1985: 447). The obvious conclusion is that well-educated Blacks did not fair any better than poorly educated Blacks in attaining parity in income with Whites of similar education (Willie, 1988: 76; 1989: 151).

The debate of yesteryear about race, social class, income, and ability or achievement has continued into the new millennium with increasing concern about achievement, a variable on which school reformers who are preoccupied with standards tend to fixate. Social and behavioral scientists like Richard Herrnstein and Charles Murray tend to attribute much of the achievement gap between Blacks and Whites to race or family heritage (Herrnstein and Murray, 1994: 143–154). Specifically, they state, "to raise the chances of getting a college degree, it helps to be in the upper half of the distribution for either IQ or socioeconomic status. *But the advantage of a high IQ outweighs that of high status*" (Herrnstein and Murray, 1994: 143, emphasis added). And social and behavioral scientists like Christopher Jencks and Meredith Phillips believe "the claim that test scores are only a proxy for family background is ... false" (Jencks and Phillips, 1998: 7). The findings, opinions, and beliefs of the social and behavioral scientists mentioned above demonstrate the absence of unanimity.

## DATA AND METHOD

To shed more light on these issues, we decided to examine the association, if any, between achievement as indicated by reading or math test scores and the racial and social class characteristics of public school students in sixty-seven county school districts in Florida. One of the variables selected to indicate achievement was the proportion of fourth-grade children in each school district who scored at Level 3 and above on the reading portion of the Florida Comprehensive Assessment Test (FCAT). Level 3 students have partial success with the challenging content of the test but perform inconsistently. Level 4 students answer most of the test questions correctly, except the most challenging. Level 5 students have success with the most challenging content of the test and answer most of the questions correctly. Approximately 54 percent of all fourth-grade students in Florida performed at Level 3 and above during the 1999–2000 school year. The remaining number—46 percent—performed below these levels. The other achievement indicator used was the school district average achievement score in math on the FCAT for fourth-grade students.

The variable selected to indicate social class or socioeconomic status was the proportion of children eligible to participate in the federal free and reduced-cost lunch program in Florida public schools. Fifty-six percent of the students met this criterion and, therefore, were classified as children affiliated with low-income families.

The variable selected to indicate race was the proportion of minority students attending public school in Florida school districts. Forty-six percent of the students

**Table 9.1** Correlation Coefficients Describing the Relationship between PCTFRE (percentage of free/reduced lunch students), PCTMIN (percentage of ethnic minority and multiracial students), and RD4ACH2 (percentage of fourth-grade students scoring at Level 3, 4, or 5 on the FCAT reading test) in Sixty-seven Florida Districts

|         | RD4ACH2 | PCTFRE | PCTMIN |
|---------|---------|--------|--------|
| RD4ACH2 | 1.00    |        |        |
| PCTFRE  | -.70*** | 1.00   |        |
| PCTMIN  | -.57*** | .44*** | 1.00   |

~p<10; *p<05; **p<01; ***p<001.

**Table 9.2** Partial Correlation Coefficients Describing the Relationship between RD4ACH2 and PCTFRE, Controlling for PCTMIN (n=67)

|         | RD4ACH2 | PCTFRE |
|---------|---------|--------|
| RD4ACH2 | 1.00    |        |
| PCTFRE  | -.61*** | 1.00   |

~p<10; *p<05; **p<01; ***p<0001.

were minorities—mostly African Americans, Hispanics, Asian Americans, and Native Americans. The remainder (54 percent) were White. One should be reminded that in this study the school district is the basic unit of analysis. There are sixty-seven county school districts in Florida.

Correlation coefficients presented in Tables 9.1, 9.2, and 9.3 have to do with the percent of fourth-grade public school students scoring at Levels 3, 4, and 5 on the reading section of the Florida Comprehensive Assessment Test (RD4ACH2), the percent of minority students in each of the Florida public school districts (PCTMIN), and the percent of students eligible to participate in the federal free and reduced-cost lunch program in each Florida public school district (PCTFRE).

## FINDINGS

As seen in Table 9.1, the distribution for Florida students by reading achievement test scores is most strongly associated with the distribution of such students eligible for free and reduced-cost lunch. The correlation coefficient for these two variables of $-.70$ is very significant and indicates that about half of the variance (49 percent) for one factor may be attributed to the distribution pattern of the other factor. The distribution of students by race, also, is significantly related to the distribution of students by reading achievement test scores. But the correlation coefficient of $-.57$ is substantially less than the level of association revealed for

**Table 9.3** Partial Correlation Coefficients Describing the Relationship between RD4ACH2 and PCTMIN, Controlling for PCTFRE (n=67)

|  | RD4ACH2 | PCTMIN |
|---|---|---|
| RD4ACH2 | 1.00 |  |
| PCTMIN | -.41*** | 1.00 |

~p<10; *p<05; **p<01; ***p<0001.

achievement and socioeconomic status (which is −.70). The correlation coefficient for race and achievement indicates that only about one-third of the variance (32 percent) in the distribution of one factor may be attributed to the distribution pattern of the other factor.

Analysis of these correlation coefficients indicates that socioeconomic status has a stronger association with academic achievement among public school students than does race, as mentioned earlier. Nevertheless, it should be noted that the association between both achievement and socioeconomic status and achievement and race are significant. And the association between achievement and each of these two variables is negative—that is to say, when the proportion of low-income children increases in a school district the proportion of high-achieving children tends to decrease, and when the proportion of minority children increases the proportion of high-achieving children tends to decrease.

Clearly, both socioeconomic and racial factors are associated with academic achievement. But because of differences in their magnitude or strength of association, it is probably fair to conclude that they have independent as well as joint effects on the distribution of children by level of achievement.

The partial correlation coefficients in Tables 9.2 and 9.3 describing the association between reading achievement and socioeconomic status while holding race constant, and reading achievement and race while holding socioeconomic status constant, reveal some interesting things about race and social class. Holding race constant, the association between student achievement and socioeconomic status is reduced from −.70 to −.61. In other words, controlling for the effect of race, socioeconomic status accounts for slightly more than one-third (37 percent) of variance in the distribution of student achievement scores versus about half (49 percent) of the variance when race is not controlled. However, when holding the effect of socioeconomic status constant, the correlation coefficient between race and achievement is reduced from −.57 to −.41; this fact means that only about one-sixth (17 percent) of variance in the distribution of achievement may be attributed to race-related characteristics of children when the effect of social class is controlled.

The partial correlation coefficients reveal that both race and socioeconomic status are significantly related to the distribution pattern of student achievement scores. However, the association between achievement and race is weakened more when the effect of socioeconomic status is cancelled than is the association between achievement and socioeconomic status when the effect of race is cancelled.

Another important finding of this study is that race and socioeconomic status are not duplications of each other. One factor is not a stand-in for the other. The correlation coefficient between these two variables, as revealed in Table 9.1, is .44. An increase of minority students in a school district tends to be associated with an increase in students of low socioeconomic status. Please note, however, that the association between race and social class is positive and significant but weak. Beta weights obtained for these distributions indicate that only one-fifth of variance in the distribution of children by socioeconomic status may be attributed to their racial characteristics. Eighty percent of variance in the co-variation of these two factors may be attributed to other influences.

So, while the controversy about race and social class waxes and wanes, our findings suggest that social and behavioral scientists should continue to search for other factors that influence achievement, since neither race nor social class alone accounts for more than half of the variance in the distribution of student achievement scores.

Our guess is that studies of the combined effects of race and social class might be more useful in understanding student achievement than focusing on one or the other of these variables. Also studies may be most informative that examine contextual influences such as communities and learning environments that are well balanced with minority and majority racial populations of children or that are imbalanced in favor of one group, and communities and learning environments that are well balanced socioeconomically with children of all income levels or that are imbalanced in favor of one group. Our research in Charleston County, South Carolina, during the 1990s revealed that differences in achievement scores between White and Black children were lower in racially mixed or socioeconomically mixed schools than in schools that were racially or socioeconomically homogeneous (Willie et al., 1998). Louis Kriesberg tells us about other benefits of balance: "when power differences are not extreme, the outcome is more likely to be a compromise than an imposition" and concessions are most likely when there is parity between different population groups (Kriesberg, 1982: 240).

This discussion on achievement as it relates to race and social class points us away from preoccupation with personal characteristics and toward school as a learning community. A pilot study in Tampa, Florida, during the 1999–2000 school year, mentioned in chapter 7, revealed that in one relatively large student attendance region, a majority of schools that received an "A" rating by the state had racially mixed student bodies and that a majority of "D" schools were racially homogeneous in favor of minorities and/or socioeconomically homogeneous in favor of low-income students.

An analysis of Florida school districts with the lowest achievement scores in mathematics on the FCAT, as seen in Table 9.4, reveals a high correlation between low achievement and racial and socioeconomic imbalance in favor of minority students and low-income students as was mentioned earlier. The eleven school dis-

**Table 9.4** Math Mean Score in Lowest Achieving School Districts, Percent of Students Eligible for Free/Reduced-Cost Lunch, Percent of Minority Students and District Public School Population, Florida, 2000

| District | Math Mean Scale Score Year 2000 | % of Students Eligible for Free/ Reduced-Cost Lunch Year 2000 | % of Minorities Year 2000 | Student Population |
|---|---|---|---|---|
| Gadsden | 600 | 82 | 94 | 8,020 |
| Desoto | 609 | 60 | 42 | 4,666 |
| Madison | 612 | 60 | 58 | 3,507 |
| Jefferson | 612 | 69 | 68 | 1,938 |
| Hamilton | 614 | 65 | 55 | 2,228 |
| Dade | 614 | 60 | 88 | 360,112 |
| Putnam | 615 | 60 | 33 | 12,647 |
| Glades | 615 | 64 | 54 | 1,172 |
| Sumter | 617 | 61 | 32 | 5,868 |
| Taylor | 619 | 45 | 26 | 3,805 |
| Hendry | 619 | 63 | 60 | 7,539 |
| STATE AVERAGE | 626 | 56 | 46 | |

Note: Minorities include African American, Hispanic, Asian, Native American, and multiracial students.

tricts with the lowest math achievement scores are in the bottom one-sixth of the sixty-seven school districts. Ten of these eleven districts exceed the statewide average of low-income students and seven of the eleven districts exceed the statewide average of minority public school students.

We call attention to the fact that these low-achieving school districts are either very small or very large. Dade County has over 300,000 students and the small districts range from 1,172 to 12,647 students, averaging out at 5,139 students. Both the very large and the very small school districts are likely to experience racial and socioeconomic imbalance or isolation in favor of minority students and low-income students. A conclusion derived from this analysis, therefore, is that neither small nor large is always better than its opposite.

A confirmation of this idea is seen in Table 9.5, which includes twelve Florida school districts in the top one-sixth of the distribution of mathematics achievement test mean scores. These school districts tend to be between large and small; they range from 1,210 to 59,491 students, averaging out at 21,632 students per district.

**Table 9.5** Math Mean Score in Highest Achieving School Districts, Percent of Students Eligible for Free/Reduced-Cost Lunch, Percent of Minority Students and District Public School Population, Florida, 2000

| District | Math Mean Scale Score Year 2000 | % of Students Eligible for Free/ Reduced Cost Lunch Year 2000 | % of Minorities Year 2000 | Student Population Year 2000 |
|---|---|---|---|---|
| Liberty | 646 | 47 | 17 | 1,210 |
| Santa Rosa | 642 | 31 | 9 | 22,226 |
| St. Johns | 641 | 23 | 15 | 19,046 |
| Sarasota | 639 | 35 | 19 | 34,682 |
| Clay | 637 | 23 | 16 | 27,607 |
| Okaloosa | 637 | 28 | 21 | 30,248 |
| Seminole | 637 | 26 | 31 | 59,491 |
| Leon | 636 | 31 | 43 | 31,542 |
| Martin | 636 | 31 | 25 | 16,236 |
| Calhoun | 635 | 49 | 18 | 2,213 |
| Flagler | 635 | 40 | 22 | 6,287 |
| Jackson | 635 | 54 | 36 | 7,580 |
| State average | 626 | 56 | 46 | |

Note: Minorities include African American, Hispanic, Asian, Native American, and multiracial students.

We have serious doubts that a remedy focusing only on individuals will be effective. We believe that change is needed that modifies the community, including school districts and their learning environments. Small districts need to be linked together into service delivery areas and very large districts need to be decentralized into smaller service delivery areas.

Thus, we recommend that Florida and any state with school districts that are small and homogeneous should implement a program of school regionalization that links these small counties and school districts with adjacent school districts. Through regional schools, especially at high school and middle school levels, more resources may be made available to enhance the quality of education that these regional schools could offer. Moreover, education in the regional schools would be improved because student bodies in the cooperating districts would be larger and school student bodies would be more diversified, a characteristic mentioned earlier that seems to be related to some schools that were awarded an "A" rating by the state.

Large city school districts like Dade County and large urban school districts elsewhere in the nation could benefit very much from the implementation of Controlled Choice student assignment plans that overcome the harmful effects of racial, ethnic, and socioeconomic student populations concentrated in segregated neighborhoods. Controlled Choice overcomes the harmful effects of segregation by elimination of neighborhood schools and making a large number of schools available to all students residing in a service delivery area that also functions as a student attendance zone that is near the average size of school districts with high achievement scores. The freedom to choose schools outside one's neighborhood according to enrollment fairness guidelines in big cities has the same effect that regional programs have for small rural or small suburban school districts. They make available more and sometimes better educational opportunities to all students. Always, this student assignment method, if properly implemented, increases student body diversity.

For reasons mentioned above, therefore, we recommend regionalization for small, low-achieving school districts that are imbalanced or isolated in favor minority and low-income students as a way of increasing their resources and achieving more diversity. Also, we recommend Controlled Choice student assignment plans for larger urban school districts with many neighborhoods of low-achieving students that are imbalanced or isolated in favor of minority and low-income students. This plan guarantees diversity by creating decentralized service delivery areas of about 25,000 students that also function as a student attendance zone for several different racial and socioeconomic populations and several schools that provide a variety of attractive educational opportunities.

We recommend these remedies because both race and socioeconomic status continue to be significantly related to academic achievement and concentrations of minority and low-income students are significantly related to academic achievement in a negative way, and finally overcoming the negative effects of these associations is probably best achieved by modifying communities, particularly learning communities, so that they are more diversified and have many educational offerings that may be more compatible with the needs of a variety of students.

## REFERENCES

Herrnstein, Richard, and Charles Murray. 1994. *The Bell Curve*. New York: The Free Press.
Jencks, Christopher, and Meredith Phillips. 1998. "The Black-White Test Score Gap: An Introduction." In Christopher Jencks and Meredith Phillips (eds.), *The Black-White Test Score Gap*. Washington, DC: Brookings Institution Press, pp. 1–15.
Kriesberg, Louis. 1982. *Social Conflict*. 2d ed. Englewood Cliff, NJ: Prentice Hall.

Oliver, Melvin, et al. 1995. *Black Wealth, White Wealth*. New York: Routledge.

U.S. Bureau of the Census. 1985. *Statistical Abstract of the United States*. Washington, DC: U.S. Government Printing Office.

Willie, Charles V. 1979. *Caste and Class Controversy*. Dix Hills, NY: General Hall.

———. 1988. "The Black Family: Striving toward Freedom." In J. Dewart (ed.), *The State of Black America 1988*. New York: National Urban League.

———. 1979. *The Caste and Class Controversy on Race and Poverty*. Dix Hills, NY: General Hall.

Willie, Charles, et al. 1998. *Equity and Excellence: A Plan for Educational Improvement of the Charleston County Public Schools*. Charleston, SC: The Charleston Planning Project for Public Education.

Wilson, William J. 1978. *The Declining Significance of Race*. Chicago, IL: University of Chicago Press.

# PART III

## CONCLUSIONS
## AND RECOMMENDATIONS

# 10

# CONCLUSIONS

Based on information presented in this book, we conclude that the delineation of a school district into service delivery units or student attendance zones that vary from 15,000 to 30,000 students in size is the most efficient and effective way to organize a public school system with multiple school facilities and a pluralistic population. We further conclude that the students who reside within a school district's service delivery units or student attendance zones should be allowed to choose the public schools they attend by their own rank-order of preference.

Controlled Choice is the name we give to this method of delivering educational services in relatively large student attendance zones. We briefly summarize the components of an effective Controlled Choice plan and indicate actions that are contraindicated:

- All schools in a district should be schools of choice available to all students in ways that are fair.
- The practice of organizing school districts by individual school boundaries and mandatorily assigning students to public schools nearest their homes should be eliminated in favor of creating relatively large geographic attendance zones that have a range of schools from which students may choose.
- Students who have filed their rank-order of school choices with a school system may reject schools to which they are assigned, but schools cannot reject students unless their presence would violate enrollment fairness guidelines.
- Attractive schools whose applications exceed the number of available seats according to enrollment fairness guidelines must admit students by lottery.
- Enrollment fairness guidelines that are used to assign students to their schools of choice may consider student characteristics such as socioeconomic status, race, or ethnicity; siblings already enrolled in the school; and the proximity of a student's residence to a nearby school. Student assignments may consider some or all of these characteristics. However, the total student body should not be filled exclusively with students representing only one characteristic unless all other students have rejected that school. By considering a number of student characteristics during the school choice application and assignment process, Controlled Choice guarantees diversity in a school's student body.

- Controlled Choice guarantees school improvement by creating competition between schools for the enrollment of students and by indicating which schools are most attractive and which schools are least attractive based on the number of students who selected a school as first or second choice. Attractive schools should be candidates for replication and the least-chosen schools should be targeted for school improvement measures that may include reproducing the features of the attractive schools.

- By creating Parent Information Centers in each service delivery area or student attendance zone, Controlled Choice encourages parents to participate actively in the school selection process and make informed decisions about the schools they want their children to attend.

- Controlled Choice provides an opportunity for parent and community participation in zone school improvement councils that have the responsibility of serving as advocates for the schools and students in their zones and for ensuring that the educational services available in their zones are equal to those being provided elsewhere in the school district.

- Controlled Choice is a comprehensive school reform method that is least disruptive to implement since it largely affects only those students who need to be assigned to a public school, including students enrolling at the entering grade of the district's elementary, middle, and high schools and other students who newly enroll in the district during the school year.

- Controlled Choice also promotes stability and educational continuity by allowing students currently enrolled in a school when the plan is first implemented to remain in that school until they complete the school's highest grade, and by allowing newly enrolled students who are assigned to a school under Controlled Choice to remain in that school until they complete the school's highest grade.

- Controlled Choice overcomes the pain and disruption of annually redistricting individual school attendance boundaries when some schools become overcrowded or demographically imbalanced.

- By making all public schools available to all students who reside within relatively large student attendance zones, Controlled Choice serves the public interest in an equitable way. It disassociates school selection and attendance, which is a public interest phenomenon, from home buying or home rental behavior, which is a private interest phenomenon.

Among contraindicated practices for fair Controlled Choice student assignment procedures are these:

- *Selected geographic neighborhoods in a school district should not be exempted from participating in a Controlled Choice student assignment plan.*

Elimination of exemptions should apply to all neighborhoods, including neighborhoods that are so-called "naturally integrated." The fairness principle requires equal treatment for all individuals, groups, and neighborhoods within a school district. School district student assignment plans that exempt some neighborhoods tend to generate hostility and bitterness among students and their families in other neighborhoods who are required to participate. Also, students and families exempted from participation in a district-wide student assignment plan may look upon their exemption as entitlement. This attitude may contribute to further estrangement in the community, especially among school patrons not exempted.

• *Relatively large and heterogeneous student attendance zones should never accommodate the coexistence of single school-specific attendance areas or smaller student attendance areas with the larger zone.*

Embedding a school-specific or smaller attendance area within a relatively large student attendance zone is confusing and unfair. All schools in a Controlled Choice student attendance zone should belong to all students, regardless of where they happen to reside within the zone. Any appearance of favoritism should be avoided.

• *Contiguous residential neighborhoods should be linked together to create a Controlled Choice student attendance zone, thereby avoiding suspicion of gerrymandering.*

To the extent practicable, each student attendance zone in a Controlled Choice student assignment plan should have a resident student population that reflects the demographic characteristics of the district's total student population. However, such large student attendance zones may include students whose characteristics vary from the demographic characteristics of the students in the whole school district. In deciding on the size of the variation that should be permitted, the delineators of zone boundaries should be careful not to create zones that marginalize a particular group of students who represent 20 percent or more of the district's total student population. Exceptions are possible given the varying residential housing patterns of people of color and income level, but such exceptions should be used sparingly in a Controlled Choice plan.

• *Magnet schools, pilot schools, and charter schools should not have application and enrollment periods that differ from the other schools of choice in a Controlled Choice student assignment plan.*

To offer separate application and enrollment time periods for certain schools of choice is to differentiate the school system into more-important and less-important schools. Symbolically, the schools that are chosen first are believed to be better than other schools. If a district allows parents and students to apply for some schools at a certain time and then allows choice of the remaining schools at a later date, the district may well create the impression that it includes first- and second-class schools. Also, in a Controlled Choice plan, existing magnet schools may remain district-wide schools of enrollment, but consideration should be given to locating new magnet schools within zones as a way of enriching educational offerings in each zone and as a way of reducing transportation costs connected with district-wide schools.

• *Controlled Choice should not be introduced to and implemented in a school system without enrollment fairness guidelines for student assignments.*

As indicated in the professional literature, so-called "freedom-of-choice" plans have not been successful in attaining diversity, equity, and fairness in the distribution of educational resources by schools among students with a variety of group affiliations. Enrollment fairness guidelines guarantee all students equal access to all educational opportunities available in a school system. Since race, social class, and gender have served as barriers that prevent equal participation in the educational system, it is right to provide racial, socioeconomic, or gender fairness guidelines (any or all of these) for student assignments. The guidelines will ensure that dominant people of power, whomever they may be in these aggregations, do not get in line first and take all of the "goodies" before subdominant people of power have a chance to obtain their fair share.

Since our studies show that socioeconomic status has a correlation coefficient with achievement scores that is higher than the coefficient for race and achievement, we recommend the use of socioeconomic status as one variable that can be used in creating enrollment fairness guidelines. Despite their overlap, it should be stated that race and socioeconomic status do not duplicate each other. Thus a more comprehensive approach to enrollment fairness guidelines would use socioeconomic status, race, and gender so that all groups are guaranteed their proportional access to all educational offerings in a school district.

We note that racially and socioeconomically balanced schools tend to have higher student achievement scores than schools that are both racially and socioeconomically imbalanced. Thus, we conclude that in the United States the presence of diversity in a school's student body is an achievement asset; and the absence of diversity, especially in schools that are racially and socioeconomically isolated with low-income children and students of color as prevailing populations, is an achievement liability. In other words, high-achieving schools tend to have a more pluralistic and complex student body than low-achieving schools.

Our analysis indicates that diversity is something of value, that in addition to being a legal goal sanctioned by the U.S. Supreme Court in *Brown v. Board of Education*, it also contributes to beneficial educational outcomes. Therefore, the trend toward resegregation of schools by race and socioeconomic status in some school districts is inconsistent with the lofty goals of educational excellence being promoted in current school reforms. Indeed, our studies reveal that some of the most eminent schools in the United States are schools with diversified student bodies.

Our finding about eminence and diversity confirms our assertion that excellence and equity complement each other and that one without the other is incomplete. The implication of this finding is that we should be aware of focusing on single variables only in school reform. There is no magical elixir that will cultivate good education and banish ignorance. Beyond diversity already mentioned, we have discovered that "whole school change" is more effective than betting on a single variable to bring enlightenment to a school and its student body. "Whole school change" recognizes the variety of learning styles found among students in a single school and tailors its approach to meet these multiple needs. Ironically, "whole school change" is better able to accomplish its mission by using a single instructional model such as literacy as a common focus. A more focused approach is a way of achieving unity in a diverse educational setting.

In Cambridge, we discovered that schools in which students had the highest average achievement scores were those with a focused approach and not those that included several magnetic attractors programs that served some but not all of their students.

Thus, it seems that effective schools are those with a common focus which, nevertheless, cultivate several elements that support good education such as strong instructional leadership by the principal, active teacher recruitment and retention practices, research-based approaches to teaching and learning, and multiple approaches to school improvement. This discussion leads to the conclusion that the most effective school reform is derived from a focused approach flexibly implemented.

Our study also has revealed that teaching and learning occur within a context, and that it is inappropriate to focus on students without considering the educational settings that do or do not support and sustain them. School culture and student capacities are linked in the learning enterprise. Regardless of ease or difficulty with which students learn, all deserve the full support of the systems with which they are affiliated. Thus, our school reform model provides "whole school improvement" and "system-wide support."

We introduced in this book detailed information about Parent Information Centers, new players on the educational stage. They are outreach units for school systems, which meet parents where they are in their communities and provide them with sufficient information and assistance to obtain appropriate educational services for their children.

Parent Information Centers are designed to "level the playing field" for all sorts and conditions of families, helping them find congruence between the needs of children and the offerings of schools. Parent Information Centers, by way of their fairness procedures for enrolling students in schools of choice, prevent dominant people of power from taking all of the seats and educational goodies in the best schools and leaving only educational crumbs for less fortunate others. Parent Information Centers are innovations that came into being with Controlled Choice. They probably will be useful for years to come.

Despite the resegregation of schools throughout the United States, we are mindful of the fact that some school districts are reluctant to use racial fairness guidelines for the purpose of assigning students to schools in a way that is fair to students of all racial groups. Administrators and policy makers for some school districts are fearful that courts of law will disallow the use of racial fairness guidelines. The legal memorandum in the Appendix prepared by attorney Janet Pulliam of Little Rock, Arkansas, should be consulted for information on how courts of law have dealt with the use of racial fairness recently.

There is no evidence that racial fairness guidelines as used in Controlled Choice will prohibit a school district from gaining unitary status. Some districts in Florida, Massachusetts, Illinois, California, and elsewhere have been declared unitary by federal courts because of the Controlled Choice student assignment plan they implemented. But for administrators and policy makers who remained concerned about the efficacy of racial fairness guidelines, we offer socioeconomic status guidelines as an equitable alternative. We propose that socioeconomic fairness guidelines should be used along with racial fairness guidelines or, instead of these, to guarantee access of all sorts of students to all educational offerings of a school district. Socioeconomic status and race are not duplicative variables, as mentioned earlier, although there is some overlap in their distributions.

Socioeconomic status is used as an enrollment fairness guideline to guarantee that students belonging to low-income families have the same opportunity to participate in educational programs of study as students belonging to non-poor and affluent families. Our experience as educational planners suggests that the indicator of socioeconomic status most readily available to school districts is the proportion of students eligible or ineligible for free lunches. We recommend that the proportion of children eligible or ineligible to participate in this federal program should be used to determine the number of seats that are made available to low-income and non-poor and affluent children in each school. One may use the proportion of students eligible or ineligible for free lunches for the total school district when allocating seats in schools that enroll students on a district-wide basis; and one should allocate seats in schools that enroll students within a student attendance zone on the basis of the proportion of students eligible or ineligible for free lunches who reside in that zone. Appendix C indicates in a detailed way how to develop effective controlled choice plans.

Since these guidelines are used as a way to achieve fairness and inclusiveness, and since this book has demonstrated that a high concentration of students with low socioeconomic status in a single school seems to be associated with low average achievement scores, there is every reason to believe that courts of law will not look with disfavor on the use of socioeconomic fairness guidelines, since they are used to fulfill an important educational goal.

Finally, we share our observations about school district size. Some policy makers assert that small school districts are more effective than large school districts. Small and large, of course, are relative terms. We do know, however, that when a population group is below a certain critical mass in some settings its impact upon social organization may be negligible. And we also know that social organization can be so large that it loses communication with its component parts.

For example, in a state like Florida, nine of the eleven county school districts in which students have the lowest average scores on the statewide math test have student populations below 10,000. However, another county among those with lowest average achievement scores in mathematics has a student population of over

360,000. Thus, school districts with low average achievement scores can be either large or small. Based on this information, we conclude that large is not always worse and that small is not always better.

Florida data also reveal that Santa Rosa County with a student population of approximately 22,000, is at or near the top of most achievement score distributions. Eleven of the twelve county school districts with the highest average mathematics achievement scores had student populations below 35,000.

Those findings suggest that educational service delivery areas or student attendance zones that vary from 20,000 to 35,000 may be the appropriate sizes for achieving a number of useful educational outcomes. Thus, we recommend that school districts with less than 20,000 students should consider the development of regional relationships with other school districts to achieve the critical mass of students necessary for an enriched educational program. We recommend that school districts with more than 40,000 students should seriously consider organizing into multiple heterogeneous student attendance zones for the purpose of decentralizing the development, delivery, and assessment of educational services. This is precisely the way that student attendance zones in Controlled Choice plans are expected to function.

The benefit of decentralized student attendance zones is increased if staff connected with central administration is deployed to provide leadership by giving direction to the development of educational programs of enhancement, implementing remediation for inadequately performing schools, and facilitating decision-making processes in zone school improvement councils and in school-based and community-based initiatives.

To summarize, we recommend Controlled Choice as an effective student assignment plan because it (1) provides the opportunity for all school-age children to choose the public schools they attend; (2) empowers all parents to make informed decisions about the public schools they believe are best suited for their children; (3) grants all student groups fair access to all educational opportunities, services, and facilities; (4) promotes school improvement by holding each school site accountable for the educational achievement of the students it serves; (5) encourages public schools to compete for students by developing attractive and effective educational experiences for all students; and (6) guarantees student body diversity and the educational benefits derived from such enhanced learning communities.

# Appendix A

# LEGAL MEMORANDUM[1]

## *Janet Pulliam*

TO:        Charles V. Willie, Ph.D.
           Harvard School of Education

FROM:      Janet L. Pulliam

DATE:      October 17, 2000

SUBJECT:   Legal Memorandum to Charles V. Willie, Ph.D.

## I.  ISSUES PRESENTED:

This legal memorandum is intended to respond to the following issues:

A. Does the Controlled Open Enrollment Law of the state of Florida have language which would prohibit a school district from becoming unitary?

B. Does the Florida Controlled Open Enrollment Law have language which would facilitate a district's becoming unitary?

C. Can the Florida Controlled Open Enrollment Law be used for voluntary desegregation in school district's that are not under court order?

## II.  RESEARCH CONDUCTED:

To analyze the issues presented, we have reviewed the Florida education statutes, relevant Florida case law, and significant opinions in the United States Supreme Court, the U.S. Court of Appeals, and the U.S. District Courts dealing with the issue of voluntary desegregation. In addition, regulations promulgated by the U.S. Department of Education and amicus briefs filed by the U.S. Department of Justice were reviewed. The issue of voluntary desegregation is one of some recent litigation and one in which there is conflicting authority.

### III. ANALYSIS:

The statute analyzed is provided here as Exhibit One. Thus far there are no reported cases in which a court has analyzed the statute with respect to school desegregation, and we found no challenge to it at this time.

**A.** *"Does the statute have language which on its face would prohibit a school district from becoming unitary?"*

Answer: NO. There is no language on the face of the statute, which would prevent a school district from becoming unitary. In fact there is language in Paragraph (4) stating specifically that required school boards shall adhere to federal desegregation requirements and that no Controlled Open enrollment plan shall be implemented that conflicts with federal desegregation orders. This language seems to place a burden on the proposing district to make certain that the proposal does not conflict with the existing federal court orders and places a burden on the state to make certain that the proposing district has so done. While it is not a statutory requirement, if I were advising a Florida School Board under Court order that was proposing a plan under the Controlled Open Enrollment Law, I would certainly seek input and agreement with the plaintiff class and in all likelihood would seek the Court's approval. If advising the State, I would recommend that the State ascertain from the proposing Board whether input and agreement of Plaintiff class had been accomplished and if not, an effort should be made to do so.

**B.** *Does the controlled open enrollment law have language in it that would facilitate a district in becoming unitary?*

Answer: YES. To analyze this question we have relied not only on U.S. Supreme Court precedent in the unitary status cases but have looked specifically at case law where Florida school districts have been either declared unitary or have been denied unitary status. Most instructive are *U.S. v. Bd. of Public Instruction of St. Lucie County*, 977 F. Supp. 1202 (S.D. Fla. 1997) (*St. Lucie*) and *Manning v. School Bd. of Hillsborough County, Fla.*, 24 F. Supp 2d 1277 (M.D. Fla. 1998) (*Tampa*), Clarification Order 28 F.Supp 2d 1353 (Dec. 4, 1998).

While the *St. Lucie* Court was approving a consent decree submitted by the parties, the Court's findings to some degree track with this statute. In discussing the District's Controlled Choice assignment methodologies implemented with the help of Dr. Charles Willie and Dr. Michael Alves, the *St. Lucie* Court found that the District was carrying out an exemplary "parental choice plan desegregation plan in which no schools are racially identifiable and in which stability of assignment, racial fairness and improvement in education are the primary notions." The Court points out that the Southeastern Desegregation Assistance Center is privileged to use the District as a model of how it can be done.

Most importantly, the Court makes findings about what the St. Lucie School District has done voluntarily that it was not required to do by Court order. Specifically, the District voluntarily established an external monitoring body to review the Controlled Choice Plan, the student transfer guidelines, and facilities planning.

The decision further points out that the district voluntarily monitors demographic projections in order to plan effectively for racially and ethnically diverse school enrollments in the future. This perhaps explains the word "demographic" in Paragraph (f) of the statute here, and clearly, the rapid population growth of Florida would require demographic planning to prevent racial or ethnic isolation. In any event, the opinion is clear that the voluntary efforts on the part of the District were considered significant in the Court's willingness to find that the District had complied in good faith and showed no evidence of returning to its former desegregationist ways.

In *Tampa*, while finding much well done in the District, the Court refused to grant the district unitary status. The denial was based on the Court's finding that the Board had failed to demonstrate a good faith commitment to the Court's Orders. In doing so the Court noted that "the relevance of good faith is that it conveys the notion that unitariness is less of a quantifiable moment in history of a desegregation plan than it is the general state of successful desegregation." Surely, a district seeking to obtain a unitary status order would benefit by voluntary action to achieve desegregation to the greatest extent practicable taken without order of the Court.

The *Tampa* case is also instructive because the Court instructs the district to evaluate desegregation tools that have been successful in other districts to determine whether they can be successful in *Tampa*. The Court could not have been unmindful of St. Lucie's Controlled Choice Plan. It appears the Florida Open Enrollment Statute is an opportunity for Districts to propose Controlled Choice plans to operate together with other student assignment methods.

Finally, the Court's clarification order in *Tampa* reminds the Defendants that they cannot unilaterally determine that they have not caused the current segregation in the school. That is precisely why they must continue to take affirmative action to desegregate the schools until they seek unitary status and the Court finds that the school system is unitary. Moreover, the Court instructs the Defendants that they cannot assume that demographic shifts are necessarily independent of prior unconstitutional practices. "The school district bears the burden of showing that no causal link exists [between the racial imbalances and the prior unconstitutional practices and unconstitutional inaction], and absent such a showing, the district must continue to make affirmative efforts to remedy racial imbalances while subject to court order." *Lockett v. Board of Educ. of Moscogee Co. Sch. Dist.*, 92 F.3d 1092, 1099 (11th Cir. 1996).

The lottery provisions should be carefully constructed to comply with the necessity of narrowed tailoring. Any plan approved by the State should have a Parent Information Center whose purpose is to carry out Paragraphs (i) and (h). The plan should clearly set forth the process of hardship student assignments. Finally, the statute is silent on the necessity of the integrity of the office of student assignment and the data. Much can be accomplished and many problems of potential litigation can be avoided if the State will require approval of all plans to include these rudimentary elements of successful controlled choice plans.

## C.   Can local school districts use the Florida Statute for voluntary race con-scious assignments?

Answer: YES, but with certain caveats best explained by a look at existing case law. In *Brown* and its progeny, U.S. Supreme Court has discussed the discretion and authority of local school districts to take affirmative actions to remedy the effect of *de jure* segregation.

### 1. Supreme Court Case Law

Significantly, in *Swann v. Charlotte-Mecklenburg*, the Court wrote:

> School authorities are traditionally charged with broad power to formulate and implement educational policy and might well conclude, for example, that in order to prepare students to live in a pluralistic society each school should have a pre-scribed ratio of Negro to white students reflecting the proportion for the district as a whole. To do this as an educational policy is within the broad discretionary powers of school authorities: absent a finding of a constitutional violation, how-ever, that would not be within the authority of a federal court.

The Court has used the same language or similar language in other cases that reflect its position in *Swann* that local school officials have the inherent authority to make race-conscious voluntary measures that integrate schools. *North Carolina St. Bd. of Education v. Swann*, 402 U.S. 43, 45 (1971); *McDaniel v. Barresi*, 402 U.S. 39 (1971).

Significantly, the Supreme Court in 1982 reaffirmed its position that school districts have inherent authority to make race-conscious assignments. In *Washington v. Seattle School District No. 1*, 458 U.S. 457 (1982), the Court struck a state statute that limited the ability of school officials to make race-conscious student assignments in order to reduce *de facto* racial segregation as violative of the Fourteenth Amendment. In *Seattle*, the District articulated its compelling state interest as one to promote diversity, even in the absence of unlawful segregation. This holding has as its underpinning that school officials are permitted in some circumstances to make voluntary race-conscious student assignments to create more diverse student bodies. The *Seattle* Court specifically reaffirmed *Swann*'s recognition of the value of diverse student enrollments. "Attending an ethnically diverse school may help ... prepar[e] minority children for citizenship in our pluralistic society, while we may hope, teaching members of the racial majority to live in harmony and mu-tual respect with children of minority heritage." 458 U.S. at 473.

### 2. Executive Branch Support for Voluntary Race-Conscious Efforts

The current administration of the Department of Education and the Department of Justice has reaffirmed as federal public policy that local school districts not under court orders may have a compelling governmental interest in reducing racial iso-lation and promoting diverse student bodies.

Further, congressional support is found in the passage of the Magnet School's Assistance Program administered by the Department of Education. This program was created by Congress with its purpose defined as "the elimination, reduction, or prevention of minority group isolation in elementary and secondary schools." 20 U.S.C. §7202; 28 C.F.R. §2801. And, magnet funds are made available not only to Districts under court order, but also to Districts implementing voluntary plans to promote diverse student enrollments. 20 U.S.C. §7205; 34 C.F.R. §2802.

The U.S. Department of Education, however, has acknowledged school districts' using race conscious admissions policies must demonstrate that the race-conscious policy is "narrowly tailored to achieve the compelling state interest in reducing, eliminating or preventing minority group isolation." 63 Fed. Reg. 8021, 8022 (1998).

Finally, the U.S. Department of Justice has strongly supported a school district's authority and the state's compelling interest in reducing racial isolation and encouraging diverse student enrollments. The U.S. Department of Justice in its amicus briefs has relied on the Supreme Court precedent cited above, the Magnet Schools Assistance Program, legislative history, and educational research for its support of voluntary race-conscious assignments.

It appears that the State of Florida has legislated public policy to promote race-conscious assignment and choice. The demographic criteria tied with race seem to be an intention to avoid racial isolation which has a stronger compelling state interest than mere diversity alone.

### 3. Race Conscious Challenges
Recently, there have been a number of Court challenges to race conscious voluntary remedies but none in the Eleventh Circuit, which is Florida's Circuit. I do believe a careful analysis of each of those could assist you in developing educational models but have not been requested to do that. An analysis of what courts have found to be "narrowly tailored" or "not narrowly tailored" should be of assistance in developing plans that can withstand a Constitutional challenge should one be filed.

While not as helpful as a case by case analysis, the U.S. Department of Education has set forth factors to be considered in "narrow tailoring" in its "Notice to School Districts for Magnet Assistance." The Notice further provides that among the factors to be considered in determining narrow tailoring are: (1) whether the district tried or considered race-neutral alternatives and determined that those alternatives were not or would [not] have been effective; (2) the scope and flexibility of the use of race, including whether it is subject to a waiver; (3) whether race determines eligibility for a program or whether race is just one factor in the decision-making process; (4) the duration of the use of race and whether it is subject to periodic review; and (5) the degree and type of burden imposed on students of other races. 63 Fed. Reg. at 8022.23.

While I do not here review the cases challenging race-conscious remedies, in the Fourth and Ninth Circuits, which go in opposite directions, I do include here an analysis of the Second Circuit's decision in the Rochester School District. I select the Rochester opinion as instructive because it is voluntary, *de facto*, not under court order and does an excellent job analyzing the required elements of "compelling state interest" and "narrowly tailored." *Brewer v. West Irondequiot Central School District*, 212 F 3d 738 (2nd Circuit 2000) (Rochester).

In Rochester, the Urban District and the adjacent suburban school district of Monroe County entered into a voluntary interdistrict transfer program to reduce racial isolation within their Districts due to *de facto* segregation. Under the program only minority students were allowed to transfer from the Urban District to a suburban school. The student's application was initially approved, but later revoked based on her race. The student filed suit under § 1983, alleging that the transfer program constituted race discrimination in violation of her Fourteenth Amendment rights. The District Court held that the denial of the student's transfer based on her status as a nonminority violated her equal protection rights because the school district had failed to demonstrate that the transfer program was narrowly tailored to serve the compelling state interest of promoting diversity.

The Second Circuit reversed and remanded. Using strict scrutiny, the panel first addressed the compelling state interest prong. While the District Court had concluded that the defendants had not raised *de facto* segregation as a reason supporting its interest in avoiding racial isolation, the panel found that the existence of *de facto* segregation was central to the school district's argument but that they had failed to sufficiently articulate it in the District Court. Based on its review of the record, the panel found clear evidence that racial segregation in the school districts in question had increased over the years sufficiently to establish a substantial question regarding the existence of *de facto* segregation. As a result, the panel concluded that the issue of whether the program's goal of reducing racial isolation in order to alleviate the effects of *de facto* segregation serves a compelling state interest justifying the use of racial classification requires a full trial. The panel rejected the District Court's reliance on *Hopwood* and the proposition that the use of racial classification is permissible only when there is past identifiable government discrimination. Citing several other Circuit Court and Supreme Court decisions, the panel stated that "the Fifth Circuit is the only circuit since *Bakke* to hold that a non-remedial state interest, such as diversity, may never justify race-based programs in the educational context." On the contrary, it found binding precedent in *Parent Association of Andrew Jackson High School v. Ambach*, 598 F.2d 705 (2nd Cir. 1979) (Andrew Jackson I), and *Andrew Jackson High School v. Ambach*, 738 F.2d 574 (2nd Cir. 2984) (Andrew Jackson II), both of which held that reducing *de facto* segregation serves a compelling state interest. The Court in *Andrew Jackson II* declared that "to promote a more lasting integration is a sufficiently compelling purpose to justify as a matter of law excluding some minority students from schools of their choice under the obviously race-conscious Rate of Change Plan." The *Brewer* panel observed that it was a well-established principle, supported by both state and Supreme Court case law, that local school districts have the power to voluntarily remedy *de facto* segregation existing in schools because it involves educational policy over which they have broad discretionary powers. Reviewing *Bakke, Wygant,* and *Croson,* the panel distinguished the cases on the grounds that none of the cases addressed the issue of racial isolation in public schools.

Turning to the narrowly tailored prong, the panel concluded that the District Court's narrow-tailoring analysis had incorrectly focused on the question of whether the program was narrowly tailored to achieve the goal of "true diversity." Instead, it focused its analysis on whether the program was narrowly tailored to achieve its primary goal of reducing the racial isolation caused by *de facto* segregation. The panel concluded that if reducing racial isolation is a constitutionally permissible goal under the holdings in the *Andrew Jackson* cases, then there is no more effective means of achieving that goal than to base decisions on race.

## IV.  SUMMARY:

There is nothing on the face of the statute that would keep a District under court order from becoming unitary. Secondly, the statute's language provides Districts an opportunity for voluntary race-conscious assignments, which could be used in unitary status hearings to support the District's good faith burden. Significantly, the demographic criteria allow Districts, whether under court order or voluntarily, to have a compelling state interest in avoiding racial isolation.

All plans should set out clearly the compelling state interest that justifies the use of race as a factor in the plan and intervention should demonstrate that it is narrowly tailored.

No opinion was requested on the issue of socioeconomic status and that has not been researched nor presented in this memorandum.

The statute gives the State of Florida, working with the local school boards, the opportunity to prevent racial isolation and to allow parental choice.

## THE 2000 FLORIDA STATUTES

Title XVI—Education

Chapter 228—Public Education: General Provisions

### *228.057 Public school parental choice.—*
(1) As used in this section, "controlled open enrollment" means a public education delivery system that allows school districts to make student school assignments using parents' indicated preferential school choice as a significant factor.

(2) Beginning with the 1997–1998 school year, each district school board may offer controlled open enrollment within the public schools. The controlled open enrollment program shall be offered in addition to the existing choice programs such as magnet schools, alternative schools, special programs, advanced placement, and dual enrollment.

(3) Each district school board shall develop a controlled open enrollment plan which describes the implementation of subsection (2).

(4) School districts shall adhere to federal desegregation requirements. No controlled open enrollment plan that conflicts with federal desegregation orders shall be implemented.

(5) Each school district shall develop a system of priorities for its plan that includes consideration of the following:

(a) An application process required to participate in the controlled open enrollment program.

(b) A process that allows parents to declare school preferences.

(c) A process that encourages placement of siblings within the same school.

(d) A lottery procedure used by the school district to determine student assignment.

(e) An appeals process for hardship cases.

(f) The procedures to maintain socioeconomic, demographic, and racial balance.

(g) The availability of transportation.

(h) A process that promotes strong parental involvement, including the designation of a parent liaison.

(i) A strategy that establishes a clearinghouse of information designed to assist parents in making informed choices.

(6) Plans shall be submitted to the Commissioner of Education by June 30, 1997. The Commissioner of Education shall develop an annual report on the status of school choice and deliver the report to the Governor, the President of the Senate, and the Speaker of the House of Representatives at least 90 days prior to the convening of the regular session of the Legislature.

(7) Notwithstanding any provision of this section, a school district with schools operating on both multiple session schedules and single session schedules shall afford parents of students in multiple session schools preferred access to the controlled open enrollment program of the school district.

(8) Each school district shall annually report the number of students applying for and attending the various types of public schools of choice in the district, including schools such as magnet schools and public charter schools, according to rules adopted by the State Board of Education.

### 228.2001 Discrimination against students and employees in state system of public education; prohibitions; equality of access; strategies to overcome underrepresentation; remedies.—

(1) This section may be cited as the "Florida Educational Equity Act."

(2)(a) Discrimination on the basis of race, national origin, sex, handicap, or marital status against a student or an employee in the state system of public education is prohibited. No person in this state shall, on the basis of race, national origin, sex, handicap, or marital status, be excluded from participation in, be denied the benefits of, or be subjected to discrimination under any education program or activity, or in any employment conditions or practices, conducted by a public educational institution which receives or benefits from federal or state financial assistance.

(b) The criteria for admission to a program or course shall not have the effect of restricting access by persons of a particular race, national origin, sex, handicap, or marital status.

(c) All public education classes shall be available to all students without regard to race, national origin, sex, handicap, or marital status; however, this is not intended to eliminate the provision of programs designed to meet the needs of students with limited proficiency in English or exceptional education students.

(d) Students may be separated by sex for any portion of a class which deals with human reproduction or during participation in bodily contact sports. For the purpose of this section, bodily contact sports include wrestling, boxing, rugby, ice hockey, football, basketball, and other sports in which the purpose or major activity involves bodily contact.

(e) Guidance services, counseling services, and financial assistance services in the state system of public education shall be available to students equally. Guidance and counseling services, materials, and promotional events shall stress access to academic, career, and vocational opportunities for students without regard to race, national origin, sex, handicap, or marital status.

(3)(a) No person shall, on the basis of sex, be excluded from participating in, be denied the benefits of, or be treated differently from another person or otherwise be discriminated against in any interscholastic, intercollegiate, club, or intramural athletics offered by an educational institution; and no educational institution shall provide athletics separately on such basis.

(b) Notwithstanding the requirements of paragraph (a), an educational institution may operate or sponsor separate teams for members of each sex if the selection for such teams is based upon competitive skill or the activity involved is a bodily contact sport. However, when an educational institution operates or sponsors a team in a particular sport for members of one sex but does not operate or sponsor such a team for members of the other sex, and athletic opportunities for that sex have previously been limited, members of the excluded sex must be allowed to try out for the team offered unless the sport involved is a bodily contact sport.

(c) This subsection does not prohibit the grouping of students in physical education classes and activities by ability as assessed by objective standards of individual performance developed and applied without regard to sex. However, when use of a single standard of measuring skill or progress in a physical education class has an adverse effect on members of one sex, the educational institution shall use appropriate standards which do not have such effect.

(d) An educational institution which operates or sponsors interscholastic, intercollegiate, club, or intramural athletics shall provide equal athletic opportunity for members of both sexes. In determining whether equal opportunities are available, the Commissioner of Education shall consider, among other factors:

1. Whether the selection of sports and levels of competition effectively accommodate the interests and abilities of members of both sexes.

2. The provision of equipment and supplies.

3. Scheduling of games and practice times.

4. Travel and per diem allowances.

5. Opportunities to receive coaching and academic tutoring.

6. Assignment and compensation of coaches and tutors.

7. Provision of locker room, practice, and competitive facilities.

8. Provision of medical and training facilities and services.

9. Provision of housing and dining facilities and services.

10. Publicity.

Unequal aggregate expenditures for members of each sex or unequal expenditures for male and female teams if an educational institution operates or sponsors separate teams do not constitute nonimplementation of this subsection, but the Commissioner of Education shall consider the failure to provide necessary funds for teams for one sex in assessing equality of opportunity for members of each sex.

(e) An educational institution may provide separate toilet, locker room, and shower facilities on the basis of sex, but such facilities shall be comparable to such facilities provided for students of the other sex.

(4) Educational institutions within the state system of public education shall develop and implement methods and strategies to increase the participation of students of a particular race, national origin, sex, handicap, or marital status in programs and courses in which students of that particular race, national origin, sex, handicap, or marital status have been traditionally underrepresented, including, but not limited to, mathematics, science, computer technology, electronics, communications technology, engineering, and career education.

(5) The State Board of Education shall adopt rules to implement this section.

## NOTE

1. Memorandum reprinted courtesy of Janet L. Pulliam.

# Appendix B

## MEMORANDUM ON TRANSPORTATION[1]

### STUDENT ASSIGNMENT AND PUPIL TRANSPORTATION UNDER A SYSTEM OF PUBLIC SCHOOL CHOICE

*Michael Turza, Director of Business Services, Milwaukee Public Schools*

From the early days of desegregation to school choice, the cost and scope of transportation services provided for students has been a major issue for school districts. This report will attempt to detail the issues involving transportation, the types and levels of service offered, and establish a framework for discussing transportation within a public school choice assignment plan.

### STATE OF FLORIDA STATUTES AND COMMISSIONER OF EDUCATION RULES

Florida statutes 6A-3.001 through 6A-3.037 govern the transportation of students to and from school. In general, the statutes do not pose limitations on transportation, and in some respects provide enabling legislation to foster school choice. Section 6A-3.001, *Basic Principles for Transportation of Students*, enables students to cross district attendance areas provided both districts agree.

Other statutes appear reasonable and reflect transportation statutes in many other states. Do the Florida student transportation rules help or hinder the adoption and implementation of county-wide public school choice plans? My initial response is that they do not hinder, and may assist in, the adoption of county-wide school choice plans.

### PUPIL TRANSPORTATION UNDER A SYSTEM OF PUBLIC SCHOOL CHOICE

While it is important to minimize transportation costs under a school choice plan, one must not forget that the purpose of choice plans is to give parents educational options. Transportation must enable parents the opportunity to exercise these choices. Parents must also have a high likelihood that their choices will be granted.

If the demand for programs exceeds the number of seats available, a random selection process will result in a widely dispersed student population, and a costly transportation program. Successful programs should be replicated in various parts of the district, with seats closely matching demand.

Expanding seats in popular programs will enable the district to "regionalize" program offerings. By establishing transportation or assignment regions, the average time and mileage per bus route and the number of bus routes required can be significantly reduced. School districts should examine school selection data to ensure popular programs are available in multiple areas of the county.

Parent Information Centers are effective resources to minimize transportation costs. School placements can be matched to transportation availability, reducing the amount of transportation for isolated students. Parents can be informed of school choices where transportation service exists, providing one-stop service to parents. The use of computerized routing software gives staff the tools necessary to coordinate school assignments with transportation.

## OPTIONS TO REDUCE TRANSPORTATION COSTS

An effective way to reduce transportation costs is changing the starting/ending times for schools. A third tier allows a bus to service three instead of two schools each day. By changing starting/ending times, greater vehicle utilization can be achieved, thus eliminating the need for additional buses. Since fixed costs of a vehicle average 65–70 percent, increasing the bus's time and mileage only adds variable costs.

Modifications to the school day should be aggressively explored in every district. Alternate school calendars also offer opportunities to reduce transportation costs. As transportation costs are spread over a longer period of time, per pupil cost will decline.

State statute 6-3.017(6)(c) states that no student should be on the bus longer than fifty minutes for an elementary school and one hour for a secondary school. If this regulation is adhered to, considerable transportation costs will be incurred. School districts should explore if this regulation can be modified to give districts greater flexibility in scheduling bus routes. There is little difference to a child from having a sixty–seventy minute bus trip, as opposed to a fifty-minute bus trip. My experience suggests few parents voice a concern over the time their child spends on a school bus.

## NEXT STEPS

The observations and suggestions outlined here are based on a review of state statutes, Web pages, and correspondence. Certain general ideas and methods can be applied statewide. However, each school district has unique conditions that offer opportunities to both improve transportation services and reduce costs. As school districts are implementing school choice solutions, a review of the transportation system should be conducted concurrently.

## NOTE

1. Memorandum reprinted courtesy of Michael Turza.

# Appendix C

# MEMORANDUM BY THE AUTHORS REGARDING WAYS OF CREATING AN EFFECTIVE CONTROLLED CHOICE PLAN

A major limitation of contemporary approaches to educational reform is the tendency to share with the public bad news about the academic achievement of students but not the good news. Moreover, we tend to tell professional educators what changes are necessary to enhance student achievement but are silent on how to implement these changes. The *Brown I* decision of the Supreme Court in 1954 declared that racially segregated education is inherently unequal but gave only limited suggestions on how to achieve integrated schools in the *Brown II* decision of 1955.

The contents of this memorandum describe how to design student assignment plans that guarantee student body diversity, choice, and school improvement. As stated elsewhere in this book, these three goals contribute to an effective education when implemented simultaneously. Controlled Choice is designed to grant more options to students regarding school of enrollment, to guarantee diversity in the student population of all schools, and to promote school improvement.

Our first assumption is that all schools in a district should be available to all sorts and conditions of students in an equitable way. This assumption is based on the notion that equity and excellence are complementary and should coexist.

To facilitate equitable access by all students to all schools, we discourage the traditional practice of mandating the assigning students to neighborhood schools, largely because residential segregation is real in most urban areas. Neighborhoods tend to embrace concentrations of people with similar socioeconomic, racial, ethnic, and other cultural characteristics. When students are required to attend schools in the neighborhood where they live, such schools tend to have segregated student bodies that, according to the Supreme Court, are inherently unequal.

Thus, we advise smaller school districts to make all schools available to all students by creating a student attendance zone coterminous with boundaries of a school district. Transportation should be provided by the school system for all students who do not live within walking distance of a school.

Large school districts may eliminate long bus rides by organizing two, three, four, or five student assignment zones consisting of contiguous neighborhoods that, together, constitute a diversified student population more or less similar to the composition of the student population in the total school district. Each student attendance zone should accommodate ten to twenty elementary schools. And, each student attendance zone should have a similar number of schools that offer a similar range and quality of education. Thus, in a relatively large school district with several student attendance zones, each zone should be more or less equivalent to all other zones.

To guarantee diversity in all schools, enrollment fairness guidelines are essential. Freedom-of-choice student assignment plans without enrollment fairness guidelines tend to result in segregated student bodies. Controlled Choice prohibits such student bodies because they tend to be associated with low average achievement scores in mathematics and language arts for schools with large concentrations of students of color and students affiliated with low-income families.

Enrollment fairness guidelines for each school may be based on the proportions of racial groups or the proportion of socioeconomic groups within the student attendance zone or the whole school district. Both race and socioeconomic status are salient characteristics in the United States. A school district may choose to create enrollment fairness guidelines based on both race and socioeconomic status or only one of these characteristics. Race and socioeconomic status are not duplicative variables; they have both independent and joint effects on the distribution of average achievement scores by school.

While the proportion of students assigned to each school should be similar to the proportion of students in each racial or socioeconomic group in the total school district or the total student attendance zone, variations from these proportions by 5 to 10 percentage points usually will not imbalance a student body or contribute to racial or socioeconomic isolation in a school, especially if each of the complementary population groups is greater than 20 percent of the total school district or student attendance zone total population.

In determining the population groups to identify for the purpose of achieving diversity in a school's student body, we advise using a dichotomous racial variable of white students and students of color as complementary components, a dichotomous socioeconomic variable of students eligible for free and reduced price lunch versus students not eligible to participate in this Federal program. These are data that are regularly recorded in the Information Management System of most school districts and do not require extra effort for their collection.

To achieve diversity in the racial or socioeconomic status composition of a student body, we recommend that attention be focused on the entering grade for each level of schooling such as kindergarten or first grade for elementary schools, sixth grade for middle schools, and ninth grade for high schools. This approach achieves diversity, as students in the entering grades are promoted during succeeding years. Any student assigned to a school may remain there until the top grade has been completed. And, no student enrolled in a school before the diversity program was initiated is forced to leave before graduating.

We do not recommend a rolling admissions program for entry grades. Such a program allows some people who better understand the assignment system to enroll first, take the best choices available, and leave fewer alternatives for others. It is best for students and their parents to visit schools during the first semester and file an application form of rank-ordered choices of schools at a certain time—January or February—so that assignments can be made by March or April for the next school year.

Applications for schools of choice should be filed with central administration in a designated place like a Parent Information Center and not in the office of the preferred school. A central place reduces the likelihood of tampering.

If insufficient seats for a particular population group are available, a lottery is a fair way of randomly selecting the large number of students who wish to attend that school. The lottery is group-specific, because seats reserved for students are by race, socioeconomic status, or both characteristics. We should also note that the proportion of seats reserved for any racial or socioeconomic group may change from year to year as the number of people in the community representing these groups increases or decreases.

If students affiliated with a particular racial or socioeconomic group do not choose a school in numbers that correspond to the number of seats reserved, then unclaimed seats may be made available to any students who wish to matriculate in that school. This arrangement is followed after two or three enrollment rounds have been completed during the spring season. Until these rounds have been completed, variation from the reserved proportions in any school should be limited to not more than 5 or 10 percentage points. This variation may be implemented immediately during the first round of assignments, if reserved seats for any group are not fully used.

A diversified student body similar to the proportion of racial or socioeconomic groups in the school district or the student attendance zone is the goal to be achieved so that all students have equal access to all educational opportunities in the community. By assigning seats for each group in terms of the proportions in the district or zone, preference is not shown to any group. The number of seats reserved for students affiliated with a group is the same number of seats they could occupy in a school if students were randomly assigned.

A few additional factors that we have found to be of value in assigning students through controlled choice are proximity preferences and sibling preferences. To prevent families who selected domiciles near a particular school from complaining that the traditional neighborhood school assignment practice changed after they had chosen a residence under different rules of admissions to schools, we recommend up to 50 percent of the seats within a school be made available to students who live near enough to walk to school. This proportion may increase as long as occupancy of these seats conforms with the enrollment fairness guidelines mentioned earlier. Our experience has revealed that because all students have access to all schools in a Controlled Choice plan, many students in the proximity zone of one school prefer to attend another school that is perceived to be more compatible with their needs even though it is in a distant area. Thus, the proximity preference is seldom taken by all students who are eligible to receive it. If, however, the proximity preference is oversubscribed, a lottery is held for all students who wish to enroll in the neighborhood school. We also believe that a family-friendly policy of granting sibling preference is in order. If one sibling is already enrolled in a particular school, other siblings receive priority assignment to that school if the family wants all of its children to attend the same school. Sibling priorities are not legacies. One sibling's presence triggers priority for other siblings in the same family only if the older sibling is still enrolled in a particular school.

Maintaining stability in a school's student body is something of value. We encourage the use of waiting lists up to the first marking period of the first semester. Openings that do occur in a school of preference may be filled from the list at any time before the first marking period; after this period, a student must remain in one's school of assignment until the next school year. Such a student may fill out an application to transfer to another school that, if granted, will take effect at the beginning of the next school year. And, a student who received an assignment to a school of choice may likewise transfer, if one wishes to do so, to another school during the next school year.

Our experience with Controlled Choice reveals that 90 percent of all students in entering grades for elementary, middle, and high schools receive their first-choice or second-choice school; that less than 10 percent of all students in entering grades for elementary, middle, and high schools are administratively assigned; and that less than 5 percent of all assigned students wish to transfer to another school after they have been assigned to a school of choice.

The school improvement component of Controlled Choice is based on an analysis of the annual choice data. Because students no longer have to attend schools in their neighborhood, all schools are obligated to make themselves attractive. Least chosen schools should be targeted for improvement and overchosen schools should be replicated. We recommend the establishment of a School Improvement and Visiting Committee in each student attendance zone to examine all schools that are under chosen and to make recommendations to the superintendent of schools regarding what should be done to upgrade a school. By using the choice data as an indicator of the reputation of each school, a school district may use its limited resources to upgrade least chosen schools each year. If this is done regularly, eventually there will not be any unattractive schools.

# INDEX

# ABOUT THE AUTHORS

CHARLES V. WILLIE is The Charles Wiliam Eliot Professor of Education Emeritus, Harvard Graduate School of Education.

RALPH EDWARDS is Visiting Associate Professor and Senior Research Associate, Northeastern University.

MICHAEL J. ALVES is Senior Equity Specialist, Education Alliance, Brown University.